DON'T MISS OUT

The Ambitious Student's Guide to Financial Aid

23RD EDITION

ANNA AND ROBERT LEIDER

Book Design by Bremmer & Goris Communications, Inc.

Care and diligence have been taken in organizing and presenting the data contained in *Don't Miss Out,* however, Octameron does not guarantee its accuracy. This edition contains information relevant to the 1999/2000 academic year. The next edition will be available in September, 1999.

Address editorial correspondence to:
Octameron Associates
PO Box 2748
Alexandria, VA 22301

703/836-5480 (voice)
703/836-5650 (fax)
info@octameron.com (e-mail)
www.octameron.com

Address bookstore inquiries to:
Dearborn Trade
155 North Wacker Drive
Chicago, IL 60606
Outside Illinois, 800/245-BOOK
In Illinois, 312/836-4400 x270

ISBN 1-57509-032-5

PRINTED IN THE UNITED STATES OF AMERICA

TABLE OF CONTENTS

IV The Major Money Sources

Part V: The Big Alternatives

Part VI: Special Opportunities

CHAPTER 1

USING THIS GUIDE

College Planning is a Family Affair

College planning is a family affair. Students can't say, "Let my parents worry about it." Parents shouldn't say, "It's my student's problem." Everyone must understand the process and start the search early, otherwise two things will happen. At best, you will end up paying more for college than you should, or can afford. At worst, you will make a frantic last-minute college choice that is not in your best interest.

The sequence of topics in this guide parallels the steps you should take in your quest to finance college. First, you must define your monetary need and second, you must learn how to finance that need. Please don't skip straight to the scholarship resource chapters. For most people, equating the financial aid process with an isolated search for scholarships is an unproductive way to spend time, and the time of the kind organizations offering assistance. Instead, start at the beginning.

Organization of Guide

In Part I of this guide you'll explore the larger trends in higher education finance, and learn to separate fact from fiction.

In Part II you'll learn the special vocabulary of financial aid. You'll meet the players in the financial aid game, and you'll learn how to calculate your family contribution—the amount of money your family will be judged capable of contributing to college costs. We'll guide you through the entire aid application process and show you how to take charge of each step along the way. Why is taking charge important? First, it will help you increase your eligibility for aid, and improve the composition of your award—more grants and fewer loans. And second, it will give you a major advantage in the competition for scarce tuition dollars over those who drift through the process passively or who don't enter the maze at all.

In Part III, you move from fundamentals to more advanced topics. You become a master of the financial aid game—college selection, personal finance and tax strategies. You learn the best moves for two different situations: when college entrance is approaching fast and when college is still years away.

In Part IV, you meet the major money sources—the colleges, Uncle Sam, and the states. They dispense billions of dollars. By getting to know their programs well, you will not overlook a single penny that is due you.

Part V introduces you to two major alternatives for financing college costs—your boss, and the US military. You might not like the suggestions, but you should know about them, and consider or reject them at this point in the process.

Part VI groups special opportunities. You've already had the meat and potatoes course. Now you are looking for the cake or maybe just the frosting. You'll find sections here for the bright, the career-oriented, the athlete, the graduate student, and for minorities and women. The tips at the end of Part VI bring together the ideas developed earlier at greater length. Use these tips as a review.

There is no Part VII. But if there was, it would be an award ceremony where we present you with the title of "Financial Aid Guru."

Yes! Send me a summary of the Higher Education Act of 1998.

At press time, Congress had not yet finished reauthorizing the Higher Education Act (HEA) for the 1999/2000 school year. We have noted possible policy changes throughout the book, however, if you would like our HEA summary, please contact us with your request (or send a copy of this page), and we will mail it to you as soon as it is available (most likely in late October, 1998).

Name ____________________

Address ____________________

City, State, Zip ____________________

E-mail ____________________

Octameron Associates
1900 Mount Vernon Avenue
Alexandria, VA 22301
703. 836. 5650 (fax)
reauthorization@octameron.com

CHAPTER 2

PAYING FOR COLLEGE IN THE YEAR 2000

It Takes Special Knowledge

For some families, a college education can be the largest expenditure they will ever make—more costly than a new home and with fewer years to make the payments. Even though this may not be what you want to hear, don't throw up your hands and walk away. Financial help is available—plenty of it. But there is more to getting aid than matching a list of scholarship leads to a pile of stationary. It takes special knowledge. For instance:

Knowing the Written (and Unwritten) Rules. Thanks to tax code changes, and new infusions of financial aid dollars at the federal, state and college level, students should now have an easier time paying their college bills; the process of getting all this money, however, is more complicated than ever, and families who don't know the rules, will pay more for college than their savvier peers.

Knowing How to Apply. In theory, student aid should go to those who need it most. In practice, it goes to those who know how, when and where to apply. By taking charge of the application process, you have an advantage over those who just do as they're told. That advantage translates into larger awards, and more desirable awards (i.e., awards you don't have to repay).

Knowing About the Buyer's Market. At most schools, competition for good students is intense. This competition creates opportunities—opportunities you can maximize.

Knowing Basic Personal Finance Techniques. Investments, gifts, low-interest loans, education bonds, lines of credit... When properly used, these techniques can help your cash flow and reinforce the availability of student aid. When improperly used, they cancel your eligibility for aid. You want to achieve the former and prevent the latter.

Knowing How to Tell Good Advice From Bad Advice. Advice on college planning is plentiful. But not all of it is good. Some is dated. Some is wrong. And some is tainted by the self-interest of those who offer it.

Special knowledge is what this guide is all about. **Don't Miss Out** will teach you and your family how to formulate your own financial aid strategy—one that will lead you to a good, affordable higher education.

The Big Picture

The good news is that 1999/2000 will bring nearly $80 billion in student aid (and tax relief). Another bit of good news is that even more money is out there to be had. One of Uncle Sam's biggest student aid efforts, the Stafford Loan, is an entitlement program. That means everyone who is eligible for a loan can get a loan. But it takes an application. As the great Confucius would have said: "Apply forget—no loan you get."

The good news is balanced, as always, with bad news. In 1999/2000, student expenses (tuition, room, board, books, fees, and transportation) will total $134.98 billion. So even with new tax breaks and larger Pell grants, families must still be prepared to pick up over 40% of the tuition tab, about $55.12 billion.

Take a good look at the following pie chart. Note that Uncle Sam, Colleges, States, and Employer-Paid plans are the main sources of student aid. Not private scholarships. Our advice: When you look for financial aid, head for the tables with the biggest plates. Don't make the search for crumbs—that small percent of the Student Aid Pie which represents private scholarships—your number one priority. NOT SMART!

The Aid Pie*

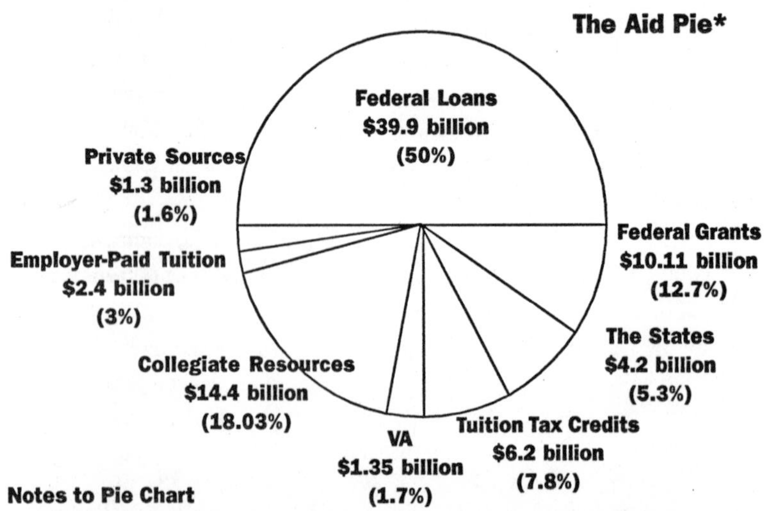

Notes to Pie Chart

Federal Loans include amounts awarded under the Stafford and PLUS programs, Perkins revolving fund, and health professions loans.

Tuition Tax Credits include the Hope scholarship and lifetime learning incentives estimated to be worth $31 billion over 5 years beginning in 1998.

Employer-paid Tuition includes company-based scholarships, tuition reimbursement, and experiential education programs.

Federal Grants include Pell, SEOG, SSIG, Work Study, AmeriCorps, ROTC, military educational bonuses, military academies, health profession programs, various graduate programs, and numerous smaller programs.

Veteran's Administration includes the GI Bill and various educational benefits to dependents of veterans.

College Resources include scholarships, the collegiate share of Work Study, non-subsidized student employment programs, loans from the colleges' own resources, and tuition remissions.

The States include the state share of federal programs, state grant programs, state work-study programs and special loan programs that supplement Stafford and PLUS.

Other categories are self-explanatory.

*Figures are all estimated for the 99/00 academic year based on FY99 Budget requests or data from prior years.

Looking to the Future

Paying for college isn't a one-shot deal. You must think in terms of this year's costs, next year's costs, and the following year's costs. If tuition strains you now, how desperate will you be by the time you are a Senior, and graduating? You must have a sense of all the external factors that can come into play, those that assist your effort to meet educational expenses, as well as those that impede you. A lot will happen during the next few years. You should be conscious of these trends and make them part of your long-range plan. What follows are the most important ones.

Trend A: College Costs to Increase Faster Than Inflation

Beginning this fall, and continuing over the next 10 years, the number of people going to college will increase from 14.6 million to 16.1 million. This surge means schools will be able to spread their fixed costs—physical plant, maintenance, staff and faculty salaries—among more paying customers. Combine this with concerted efforts by colleges to cut costs, and the result should be smaller annual tuition increases; we predict a rate just slightly ahead of inflation. Why not a rate equal to inflation? There are many reasons why rising tuition can't be likened to increases in the cost of bread. For example:

Higher Education is Labor Intensive

For this reason, technological gain does not have as great an impact on "productivity" in the academic world as it does in the industrial world. College students cannot be turned out like Model Ts. Great teaching, as Socrates and Plato knew, comes from conversation between two inquiring minds. Furthermore, in fields such as engineering and computer science, industry provides much higher salary scales than college departments. In consequence, graduate students are turning to industry rather than teaching, and professors keep moving from campus to corporate suites. To fight this trend, colleges must offer more attractive salary packages.

State Support is Lagging Behind Costs

The nation's public schools depend on state appropriations for 60% or more of their support. When state appropriations don't keep pace with rising costs, these schools must compensate by raising in-state tuitions and skyrocketing their out-of-state charges (it's okay to slip it to out-of-staters: they pay taxes and vote somewhere else).

Red Tape

The specially-formed Commission on the Cost of Higher Education recently compiled a list of federal regulations affecting higher education—it was three pages long, single-spaced and included everything from occupational safety to care of humans and animals in research to gender equity to campus crime to historic preservation. In fact, up to 12.5% of every tuition dollar goes toward complying with myriad state and federal regulations.

Computermania and Technology

College after college is grabbing headlines by announcing that every student will be equipped with a personal computer. These now-essential computers must be linked by networks and supported by mainframes. They need wiring, cooling, maintenance, and a training staff. And since they become obsolete faster than you can click a mouse, they must be upgraded or replaced at a dizzying pace. All this costs money. Furthermore, if colleges are to be on the leading edge of technology, they must have the latest in laboratories, research equipment, and machinery. Most of them don't have it now. Getting it (and maintaining it) will cost billions. Even a school lucky enough to be "given" a new $40 million lab will need three times that much of its own money to maintain it—unless the wealthy benefactor whose name now adorns the new science center thought to include extra money for custodial services and test tubes.

Fuel Costs and Deferred Maintenance

These are, proportionally, a far greater burden on colleges than on families. Old buildings, drafty halls, and students who overload the circuits with gadgets ranging from hair dryers to VCRs to multimedia computers keep the meters spinning. Also, colleges are plagued with leaky roofs, crumbling foundations, cracking asphalt and inaccessible pipes. Ivy won't hold up the walls forever. Our campuses need over $26 billion in repairs.

The Robin Hood Syndrome

Financial aid budgets, with few exceptions, can no longer meet the financial need of all students. The common solution is to raise tuition through the roof; those who can pay, in effect, subsidize those who can not. Slowly, however, as families come to realize how few students actually pay "sticker price," colleges are feeling pressure to rethink their pricing strategies. Instead of discounting tuition for as many as 90% of their students, some schools are actually lowering tuition for everyone!

Why don't more schools follow this lead? Simple, they'd lose their ability to use price as a tool in influencing the composition of the student body. Unfortunately, they soon may not have a choice. An increasing number of wealthy students are opting for public schools, where they receive the same state subsidies as their less affluent classmates. This will hurt the ability of more expensive colleges to use "full pays" to subsidize other students' tuitions.

Graduate Student Subsidies

Along these same lines, undergraduate tuition often subsidizes the education of graduate students, especially in the social sciences and humanities where grant money is increasingly scarce.

Price vs. Quality

While many families feel uneasy over rising tuitions, an abundance of students (and parents) still judge quality by price; the greater the price, the higher the perceived quality, and the greater the applicant pool.

Price Fixing

For 35 years, many of our most prestigious schools met to agree on the amount of aid they would offer their common (overlapping) applicants so students could select a college based on academic preferences rather than economics. It also prevented bidding wars for the top students, which in turn, preserved aid funds for truly needy students. Families, however, saw it differently. In their eyes, this process denied them all the aid to which they were entitled. More importantly, it assumed they were unable to make decisions about what was important to them in selecting a college. If price was a factor, then it was their right to have a choice of aid packages. For two years, the Justice Department investigated these "Overlap Schools" on possible antitrust violations, dropping charges after schools agreed not to collaborate on financial aid awards or discuss prospective tuition rates. As predicted, the bidding wars began (Trend C).

Recruiting Costs

Visiting high schools. Providing toll-free phone numbers. Designing and maintaining ever-hipper web sites. Printing and mailing glossy color viewbooks. Hosting campus visits for students as well as counselors. Recruiting costs at private four-year institutions average over $1,500 per student enrolled. At four-year public colleges, that cost is a mere $700.

Club (M)ed

As students and parents become more sophisticated shoppers, they expect more for their money, for example, ample sports and recreational facilities, adequate levels of campus security, health care facilities (complete with resident psychologists, psychiatrists and drug/alcohol abuse counselors), and extensive career placement offices. Rooms must be wired for computers, hair driers and stereos. And dining halls must accommodate a variety of dietary requirements. All of this costs money. The irony is, the very people who complain about rising college costs are in part responsible for urging tuitions upward.

College is Less Expensive than People Think

Not all colleges cost $30,000 a year. In fact, 45% of all undergraduate students go to community colleges, where annual tuition averages about $1,500; another 38% attend state universities, where annual tuition averages $3,000. Even most private colleges charge less than $13,000. Add $7,000 for room, board and miscellaneous, and for what amounts to $35 per day at a public school or $70 per day at a private one, you get a room (including heat, water and electricity), three meals a day, professional health care, recreational facilities, a wide range of social and cultural activities, counseling services, career assistance, and an education.

Unfortunately, most families are widely misinformed about these costs. In a recent survey, they overestimated the annual price of public four-year colleges by nearly $9,000 and private four-year colleges by over $8,000.

Trend B: Tuition Price Wall

Families can manage only so many loans, while state and federal governments can fund only so many grants. The only other way to keep higher education affordable is for colleges to lower their prices. Fortunately many schools recognize they can't keep fiddling around with pricing strategies, but must do more to control their operating costs. In fact, about 80% of our nation's colleges are taking lessons from corporate America (or is it Dilbert?) for help in improving their operations. Business buzzwords like downsizing, rightsizing, repositioning, benchmarking, outsourcing, and reengineering have become campus mantras as schools find ways to live within their means. With personnel costs making up nearly 70% of some collegiate budgets, what this really means is lots of layoffs, buyouts and early retirements. (Or, as they say in the business world, the "release of resources" or an increase in "career-change opportunities.") Is this a sign that with top colleges now costing over $30,000 per year we've finally hit a price wall? Let's hope so! Otherwise, no matter how wise a financial aid consumer you become, private colleges may soon become unaffordable for most middle income families.

Trend C: Let's Make a Deal

Do you enjoy the car buying process? Do you feel confident that you've beaten the salesperson at his or her own game? Or do you feel like every one else gets a better price? Some of us will do just about anything to avoid haggling over a price, and feel very badly that some financial aid administrators have been put in a position where even the wealthiest parents and students feel as though it's their right to negotiate for more aid. Unfortunately, as more and more schools use tuition discounts (or "merit scholarships") to meet recruiting goals, the process of awarding financial aid based entirely on "need" is now more of an ideal than an actuality. Even schools that say "no deals" are sometimes willing to consider "additional information" about "special circumstances." As The *Washington Post* editorialized, those who are more sophisticated or better advised will haggle while the less connected or less confident will not. This cleavage between the "information haves" and "information have-nots" is doubly dangerous when located at the very gateway to education-based upward mobility.

Trend D: Your Fickle Uncle Sam

Uncle Sam is the main dispenser of student aid. But Uncle changes his programs every year; sometimes, twice a year. His programs expand and shrink in dollar volume. Money that is authorized may never be appropriated. Money that is appropriated can be rescinded. Eligibility for the programs is as variable as the dollars. In Year One you may be eligible. In Year Two you are out. In Year Three you are in again—but for a different amount of aid. Uncle needs close watching. To watch him intelligently, you must develop a working acquaintance with "authorizations," "appropriations," "budget reconciliations," and "rescissions." Better still, read the new edition of this book which comes out every fall. We'll do the Uncle-watching for you.

Trend E: Impact of Tax Reform

To complicate matters, Uncle is using the tax code to encourage "desirable" behavior, like getting students to go to college. Last year's package of tax credits and deductions amounts to a $31 billion windfall for the college-bound, provided they're willing to cope with both IRS and Department of Education regulations as they make their college plans. In addition, new rules for IRAs and capital gains means many families will have to re-evaluate all their investment strategies if they want to take advantage of new tax breaks. Of course, understanding the 834 new tax provisions may require families to spend more in consultant and accountant fees than any resulting tax break is worth. Finally, after all the hullabaloo over achieving our first balanced-budget in decades, the slightest economic downturn is going to send politicians from both parties scuttling to rescind all their prior generosity.

Trend F: Colleges Want You

Colleges want you. For all but about 100 schools, selectivity is out the window. Today, 91% of all students are accepted by one of their top two college choices. This widens your opportunity to shop wisely and well. And the more marketable you are—good grades, leadership, musical talent, athletic ability—the more financial aid opportunities you will find.

One caution: Under pressure to recruit students, college materials keep getting slicker. Some use direct mail and phone solicitation. Many have turned to the Internet for a more direct sales pitch via the Web. Some even develop glitzy marketing campaigns to co-ordinate "message" and produce 30-second prime time TV ads worthy of Madison Avenue. Don't be too critical of schools for these practices. Their survival may be at stake. But do raise your consumer guards and evaluate collegiate mass-marketing techniques with the same objectivity and skepticism you reserve for other product promotions.

Trend G: Fascination with Excellence

Major studies have focussed on the decline of excellence in elementary and secondary schools. Nearly every proposed solution requires tons of money. Lengthen the school day. Lengthen the school year. Pay some teachers more than others. Pay all teachers more. Make everyone wear uniforms. Build single sex schools. Plug a computer into every socket. Put a computer in every home. All these solutions cost money, and while a nation of literate, math whizzes sounds wonderful, in a finite economy, that money must come from somewhere. Most likely, it will come from money that otherwise might have gone to financing your higher education.

But again, there is an upside. The enshrining of excellence legitimizes the states' and colleges' use of academic scholarships to attract high-performance students. Expect continued growth in such awards.

Trend H: Cash Flow Problems—Cash Flow Help

When tuitions rise faster than available student aid, families must make up the difference. But this is not a "vive la difference" to be cheered. It's a nasty cash flow problem which, in case you don't understand, is when you have money, but it's not "liquid." It is tied up in assets like your house, and you certainly don't want to sell your house just to pay the college bills.

But take heart. Problems create solutions. Financial innovators have developed plans to ease your cash flow without requiring you to place a "For Sale" sign in front of the family castle. A lot is going on. And, we'll cover it just about the time you throw up your hands and say, "We can't do it. No way." Research shows this happens around Chapter 7.

Trend I: Mighty Mouse

More and more college information is but a mouse click away; especially admission and financial aid advice. Thousands of colleges maintain home pages containing everything from virtual campus tours to virtual course catalogues to virtual alumni news. You may also find links to student home pages, letting you "meet" potential classmates. And you can sometimes follow a school's athletic teams, read its student newspaper, or visit the campus art museum. To find a school's address, use a search engine like Yahoo! (http://www.yahoo.com) and look up the category, Education: Colleges and Universities.

For an overview of financial aid sites in cyberspace, start with Mark Kantrowitz's Financial Aid Information Page (http://www.finaid.org). You'll find links to student aid publications, student aid organizations, loan sources, scholarship databases and college financial aid offices.

To become a cyberspace activist, try the Alliance to Save Student Aid (http://student-aid.nche.edu), the United States Student Association (http://essential.org/ussa), College Parents of America (http://www.collegeparents.org) or the National Association of Graduate and Professional Students (http://www.nagps.org/NAGPS/). This last site is updated most frequently, and is useful for undergrads as well.

Throughout this book we've included Web addresses where appropriate, but like snail mail addresses, they change frequently (and unlike snail mail, they are not reachable if so much as a "~" or a "/" is out of place). Your best bet is to learn to use one of the many search engines to pinpoint the company or type of information you need.

Trend J: How the Rich Get Richer

Children from wealthier families are more likely to go to college. Those with a college education earn more money. Their children are even more likely to go to college. Their children will earn even more money. And so it goes. Today, about eighty percent of all children from families with incomes in the upper quartile graduate from college; around eight percent of all children from families with incomes in the bottom quartile graduate from college.

A college education indeed prepares you for a fulfilling life—through broader cultural awareness, deeper knowledge, greater self-confidence, sounder health, keener citizenship and vastly expanded resources for personal happiness. But if philosophical reasons aren't enough, a college education will also help you stay employed and earn more money. Here are some recent figures from the Census Bureau. Note: These are averages; women should subtract about 12%, and men should add about 12% to get a more realistic idea of what you can expect to earn!

Highest Education Completed	*Annual Income*	*Unemployment Rate*	*Family Income*
< High School	$12,809	13.5%	$32,199
High School	$18,737	7.7%	$45,146
College	$32,629	2.9%	$75,311
Master's	$40,368	n/a	$90,956
Doctorate	$54,904	n/a	$115,415
Professional	$74,560	n/a	$138,118

CHAPTER 3

COMMON MYTHS & MISCONCEPTIONS

Practically everyone we know equates the search for financial aid with a search for scholarships. Get rid of that belief quickly! And repeat after us three times: To obtain financial aid, sophisticated families:

- Understand how their financial situation affects their aid eligibility.
- Apply to all the major assistance programs for which they are eligible.
- Apply early, accurately and honestly.
- Select colleges most likely to present them with a good aid package.
- Discuss (if appropriate) the possibility of an improved aid package with the financial aid administrator.
- Become knowledgeable about favorable options—commercial or otherwise—for financing expenses not covered by aid awards.

These steps can be worth thousands of dollars. Any other approach will make you the unknowing looking for the unfindable. To avoid wasting time and money, read this chapter on the myths that envelop the financial aid field. And remember: You don't profit from these beliefs; only the people who sustain them do.

Won't a Scholarship Replace My Money?

Most people believe scholarships put money in their pocket. Example: You have been assessed a $5,000 per year contribution to High-Priced U. One lucky day, you win a $1,000 scholarship. You now say your contribution will be $4,000. Right? Wrong. Your contribution is still $5,000. Colleges take the $1,000, add it to your available resources, and take away $1,000 of the loan or grant it had planned to give you. In other words, scholarships help pay your college bill, but they do not necessarily reduce your share of the bill.

Question: If that's so, why do clubs and organizations work so hard to raise scholarship money? **Answer**: They are not familiar with financial aid packaging. If they were, all the money raised through candy bar sales and church suppers would go to a different purpose.

Question: Why do colleges urge students to find scholarships? **Answer**: Your scholarship frees collegiate aid the school can now use to help another student. In other words, Student A's scholarship actually benefits Student B. This may not have been the donor's intent, but it is a generous act and should not go unthanked. Remember: Only the money goes to the other student. You retain the honor of having won the scholarship.

Question: Is it ever worthwhile to look for scholarships? **Answer.** Yes. If the school will use the money to replace a loan component of your aid package, that's money you won't have to repay. Also, if you aren't eligible for need-based aid, then the scholarship helps pay your share.

Is There a Special Scholarship for Me?

Every day we get letters from people who tell us their life stories and then ask "is there a special scholarship for me?" These letters sadden us, because we know the writers haven't followed the smart route for getting financial aid. Most financial aid comes from Uncle Sam, your state, or your college and is based on need. If college costs more than your assessed contribution, you are eligible for aid. Your age, sex, race and career ambitions have nothing to do with it.

Even if you do find a "special scholarship," remember, there's a big difference between being eligible and winning. For example, your odds of winning a 4-H award (250 awards, 500,000 seniors as 4-H members), are only 2000:1. To increase your chances, you could purchase a one-week old piglet, feed it 20 times a day until it weighs 1700 pounds. Then rent a forklift and a truck, take it to the state fair, and hope it wins a blue ribbon in the heavy hog competition. This might improve your odds to 20 or 30 to 1. But what about the costs of raising a 1700 pound porker?

Think we're kidding? Coca-Cola gets 122,000 applications for its 150 awards; odds of winning, 813:1. ESPN gets 20,000 applications for its 8 awards; odds of winning, 2,500:1. **Our advice:** Go the traditional route first. Then, if you have nothing to do, and you need practice writing essays and filling out applications, and you want to help the Postal Service stay in the black, start looking for a "special scholarship." You may even find one.

What About Unclaimed Scholarships?

Every year you hear reports of millions (or billions) in unclaimed scholarships. These reports usually come from computerized scholarship search companies who hope you will send them $25-$200 to find those millions. We're sure a few scholarships do go unused every year, but for once, we'd like to see companies citing these vast untapped resources provide some concrete examples. According to financial aid professionals, the money you hear about represents unused employee tuition benefits.

Money From Foundations & Corporations

The College Board estimates that private foundations and corporations give out nearly $8.1 billion in aid, but it's not money you apply for directly. Foundation money mainly goes directly to universities where it's used to help students at the doctoral or post-doctoral level. There is some foundation money for undergraduates, but that money usually has narrow local restrictions, e.g., for students in Teenytiny County. Such grants are well publicized in the local paper.

Corporate money usually goes to employees or children of employees, either in the form of tuition reimbursement or company scholarships. Some corporations do give money to students whose parents aren't on the payroll, but this is usually done via grants to colleges; the colleges in turn select the recipients—you can't apply for them directly.

Computerized Scholarship Searches

If you need information on federal or state student aid, don't pay a computer service. Uncle Sam and your home state publish free pamphlets detailing all their programs.

If you need information on collegiate student aid, don't pay a computer service. The college will tell you what you need to know.

If you need information on scholarships offered by your employer or church, don't pay a computer service. Ask your boss or minister.

If you need information on local scholarships, don't pay a computer service. Check the HS bulletin board.

Most experts agree, computerized search services seldom help you find private aid. At their very best, they provide you with a few leads, as opposed to actual dollars; but we've heard too many horror stories of families being duped out of processing fees to recommend this route to anyone. Federal investigations shut down many shady dealers every year, but anxious parents make an easy target, so a new crop of mail fraud perpetrators springs up every year.

Don't Get Ripped Off

The Federal Trade Commission (FTC) recently cracked down on five companies that by its estimate milked $10 million from middle-income families desperately searching for financial aid. In "Six Signs That Your Scholarship is Sunk" (http://www.ftc.gov/bcp/conline/edcams/scholarship/sixsigns.htm), the FTC warns against unsolicited sales pitches like, "The scholarship is guaranteed or your money back," or "We'll do all the work," or "You're a finalist." No one can guarantee you a scholarship. No one can apply for scholarships on your behalf. And no one can make you a winner in a contest you've never entered. Mark Kantrowitz's FinAid page also offers tips on spotting questionable offers and lists of suspicious companies (http://www.finaid.org/finaid/scams.html).

Free Scholarship Searches on the Web

Are there any exceptions? Yes, if your state, or college, or high school has a service you can use for free or a small fee (you should NEVER pay more than $25). Also, if you have Internet access, you can do a free search thanks to several on-line databases. Most make their money via site advertising and peddling your name to other companies, which means you have to register before you can use the service—but that's a small price to pay for loads of useful leads.

- CASHE (http://www.scholarships.salliemae.com)
- CollegeEdge Scholarship Search (http://www.collegedge.com/FA)
- ExPAN Scholarship Search (http://www.collegeboard.org/fundfinder/bin/fundfind01.pl)
- FastWEB (http://www.fastweb.com)
- FreSch: The Free Scholarship Search Service (http://www.freschinfo.com/index.phtml)
- MACH25 (http://www.collegenet.com)
- Minority On-Line Information System (http://www.fie.com/molis/scholar.htm)
- SRN Express (http://www.rams.com/srn)
- RSP Funding Focus (for America Online users, Keyword "RSP")

Before you get carried away, however, re-read the paragraphs explaining how scholarships don't necessarily replace your money, then take another look at the pie chart in Chapter Two. *Tracking down private scholarships should be your last priority in your search for financial aid, not your first.*

Besides, even if you find a possible "match," you still have to complete the scholarship applications, write the scholarship essays, and gather the scholarship recommendations—all this on top of your regular admission applications and financial aid forms.

Income Shifting Doesn't Always Pay

Many people can't accept the fact that they are in a higher tax bracket than their children. They will shift assets from themselves to their offspring, thinking the income from these assets will then be taxed at a much lower rate. Sometimes they even construct elaborate trusts with the help of lawyers and accountants whose fees can run upwards of $1,000.

But oftentimes, all this maneuvering is for naught. Investment income in excess of $1,400 for children under 14 is taxed at the parent's rate. Tax rates for trusts can be higher than tax rates for most families. And student assets are currently assessed at a higher rate than parent assets in determining family contribution to college costs.

The Lesson? Make sensible, sound plans. And worry less about "beating the system." You'll understand better after you read Chapters 7 and 8.

Know Your Sources

Everybody knows the Consumer Reports' Income Tax Guide takes a somewhat different slant to its subject than publications from the IRS. Consumer Reports' objective is to show you ways to save on taxes while the IRS seeks to extract the last drop of blood. You may value the IRS guide for its mechanical instructions, but not for its substantive advice on holding on to more of your money.

So it is with paying-for-college guides. Before you use one, make sure you know its origin. Is it like this one, and written from the viewpoint of those who pay the money (parents or students)? Or does it come from those who get the money (colleges or collegiate organizations)? Or those who give the money (Uncle Sam and the states)? The guides may address the same subject, but their treatment could be many dollars (your dollars) apart.

"Reading" On-Line References

While some of the best "InfoBahn" resources are education-oriented, remember, there is no virtual editor checking facts and biases, so if at all possible, identify the information source and heed the warnings above. What often passes for "information" is really an advertisement that offers information—bankers trying to lure you into borrowing more than you really need, stockbrokers trying to scare you into investing more than you can afford, and publishers trying to tease you into buying their books and magazines. (Guilty. You'll find us at www.octameron.com) Also, on a recent browse, many of the sites which boasted helpful names turned out to be scholarship search firms. Avoid them (except for the free ones listed earlier).

Finally, most site sponsors play to our dwindling attention spans, and fill their pages with attractive, fun graphics and superficial program summaries. In the time you spend clicking from site to site to site, reading the same thing, over and over and over, you can learn far more by curling up with a good book, for example, *Don't Miss Out.*

Reading Old References

When it comes to student aid, any reference older than one year is out of date. If you use an older reference, you will be badly misled with regard to loan sources, subsidies, interest rates, eligibility, grants size, tax laws, saving techniques, government regulations, and college costs. Even web sites, which should be easy to keep current, frequently have dated material. Look for the tag line showing when the page was last updated. This wisdom is especially true for students starting school in the 1999/2000 year—they will be affected by 1998's reauthorization of the Higher Education Act.

Confused? Strangled by Loopholes and Red Tape?

If you run into snags or get confused by all the techniques we cover in this book, request our free brochure *We Can Help* (Octameron, PO Box 2748, Alexandria, VA 22301). It describes our college admission and financial aid services. Neither cost very much and both can save you a bundle—both in money and in time.

Our Tuesday Special. We keep an experienced counselor by the phone nearly every Tuesday from 10 a.m. until 4 p.m. EST, to answer questions you may have about college financing (or selection or admission). The conversation will cost you $30 which you may charge against your VISA or MasterCard. Call (703) 836-5480.

CHAPTER 4

DEFINITIONS & PLAYERS

Short Definitions

Grants and Scholarships are aid awards you do not have to repay. They are gifts, however some require you to perform a service. The recipient of a band scholarship, for instance, may have to dress up in a costume complete with spats, march around a football field, and blow into a tuba whenever the college so directs.

Loans are sums of money you must repay. To qualify as financial aid, loans must carry a lower interest charge than prevailing commercial rates. They must also offer favorable repayment provisions. For example, in the Stafford Loan program, borrowers do not start paying interest on the loan nor do they have to retire any of the principal until after completing their studies.

Work-Study counts as financial aid when the financial aid office arranges your employment. Earnings from work you find yourself are not included as part of financial aid. Such earnings are added to the sum you are judged capable of contributing to college costs.

Enrollment Status impacts on aid eligibility. To qualify for most federal aid, you must be at least a half-time student. Half-time is generously defined. It consists of six semester or quarter hours per academic term for schools on the semester, quarter, or trimester system; or 12 semester hours or 18 quarter hours per school year for schools that use a credit hour system. Also under this system, the amount of your award changes with your status. A $1,000 award for a full-time student becomes a $750 award for a three-quarter-time student (one majoring in the waltz?) and $500 for a half-time student. **A tip:** If you are a part-time student and wish to qualify for more aid, take an additional course each semester.

Accreditation is a process that ensures the school's programs meet at least a minimum level of quality. Make sure your school has been accredited by a nationally-recognized association. You don't want to waste your tuition dollars getting a worthless education, and if you attend a nonaccredited school, you will not qualify for federal or state student aid.

Eligible Program is one that leads to a degree or certificate and meets other "integrity" rules established by Uncle Sam. To get federal aid, you must be enrolled in an "eligible program." Students working toward associate, bachelor, professional or graduate degrees need not worry about what constitutes an "eligible program." Students looking at proprietary schools (for a two month study, for example, of computer repair) should take heed. Most student aid fraud takes place in vocational programs of less than two years, and Uncle Sam is trying his best to separate the wheat from the shaft.

The 1st Player—The Student

Financial aid programs define students by dependency status. They are either dependent students or independent students.

A dependent student is one who is at least partially dependent on his or her parents for support. The income and assets of both student and parent are used to calculate the family's contribution to college costs.

An independent student is not dependent on parental support. Only the student's financial resources (and those of any spouse) are evaluated to determine contribution to college costs. An independent student may also be classified as a dislocated worker as defined below ("The 2nd Player—The Parents"). To be considered independent, under federal regulations, a student must meet one of the following conditions:

1. Be 24 years of age by December 31 of the award year (December 31, 1999 for the 1999/2000 award year).
2. Be an orphan or ward of the court.
3. Be a veteran of the Armed Services.
4. Be married or have legal dependents other than a spouse.
5. Be a professional student, or a graduate student.
6. Be judged independent by the financial aid administrator based on documented unusual circumstances.

Establishing independence can give you an advantage: By not having to include parental income and assets on your financial aid application forms, your college contribution will most likely be lower and that will result in more student aid.

To preserve scarce aid funds, most states and almost all colleges have gone beyond the federal test to impose additional restrictions on your declaration of independence. These include written proof that your parents (or even grandparents) cannot provide any support whatsoever. This is especially true for students who are "independent" according to Uncle Sam's definition, but who have moved back home with mom and dad to save some money.

If you're a single undergraduate under the age of 24 who truly is "independent," see Chapter 9 for advice on appealing your dependency status.

The 2nd Player—The Parents

Parents may be loving, caring, supportive role models. The financial aid process doesn't care. Its main interest: Are they married, separated, divorced? Is there a stepparent who can foot the bill? Here is the impact of marital status on financial aid:

Both Parents Are Alive and Married to Each Other. The income and assets of both parents are fair game for the financial aid computer.

Parents Are Divorced or Separated. The federal financial aid form is only interested in the income and assets of the parent with whom the student lived for the majority of the twelve months preceding the date of the application.

A Parent Remarries. If the parent with whom the student lived for the majority of the twelve months preceding the date of the application remarries, the stepparent's income and assets are evaluated just as though he or she were a natural parent.

These rules apply to federal aid and, generally, to state aid. Colleges, when deciding how to dispense their own money, are not bound by these rules. They can probe deeply into the resources of the divorced or absent parent who got off scot-free under federal regs.

The financial aid process also cares about the parent's employment status—aid administrators give special consideration to "dislocated workers." For example, they may recalculate family contribution using expected income, rather than prior year income. If you fall into this category, let the financial aid administrator know. In general "dislocated worker" refers to an individual who has been:

1. Fired or laid off (or has received notice of termination), or
2. Unemployed for a long period with little chance for reemployment in the same or similar occupation in the area where he or she resides, or
3. Self-employed (including farmers) but now unemployed because of a natural disaster or poor economic conditions within the community.

The 3rd Player—The Colleges

Colleges are classified as either private or public.

Private colleges can be more innovative in developing attractive aid packages and tuition assistance programs. They are not as circumscribed by red tape as tax-supported schools. Private colleges also have more latitude in how to spend their money. Again, it's their money, not the taxpayer's (this also means they're apt to pry more deeply into your family's finances to decide if you are deserving of their limited funds).

Public colleges, being tax-supported, are usually less expensive. As a general rule, students seldom pay more than 30% of the actual cost of education. The state pays the balance. Also, public colleges have two sets of fee structures: a lower one for state residents and a higher one for out-of-staters. At one time, it was easy to establish state residency to qualify for the lower rate. Today, it's more difficult. Most states have created elaborate bureaucracies, the efficiency of which appears to be judged in direct proportion to the number of residency denials issued.

One more thing. Private and public colleges have no great love for each other. The lack of affection is rooted in money. The privates resent the subsidies that permit public schools to offer lower tuitions. They would love to end this "unfair competition" by qualifying for subsidies of their own. Moreover, they see their own turf invaded when public schools, not fully sated by subsidies, seek funds from corporations and philanthropies. The public schools, for their part, resent the infusion of state money into private college coffers, especially if the state's commitment to its public schools has diminished. Furthermore, they're learning their new corporate friends don't give out money without expecting something in return—and corporate priorities can run counter to the school's public mission.

Most of this hostility ends when the two must present a united front to fend off repeated efforts to slash the federal education budget.

The 4th Player—Need Analysis Processors

Before a college can consider you for aid, it must know how much you can pay. Families that can pay $10,000 won't be eligible for as much as families that can spare only $1,000. Determining how much you can pay without becoming a burden to your neighbors is called *Need Analysis.* Public and private schools now use what amounts to two varying systems.

The process for determining eligibility for federal aid begins with a longish form called the Free Application for Federal Student Aid (FAFSA). Uncle Sam prints thirty-five million FAFSAs each year, and contracts with several regional processing systems to send data from your completed FAFSA to a central processing system. More will be said about FAFSAs in Chapters 6, 7 and 10.

Because the formula used to calculate your EFC is mandated by Uncle Sam, it is known as the Federal Methodology. And since all EFCs are calculated by the same computer, you gain nothing by submitting your FAFSA to one application processor over another.

The 5th Player—The College Board

The process of determining eligibility for collegiate aid is another story. Why? There is no uniformity. Many colleges (especially wealthy, expensive, private colleges) insist on additional knowledge about your family's finances to determine eligibility for their own programs. For a not-so-small fee, The College Board/College Scholarship Service is happy to collect (and evaluate) this information for them using Financial Aid PROFILE. The core of PROFILE is similar to the FAFSA, but the College Board customizes each form with additional questions as requested by the colleges to which the student is applying for aid. A glance at the 1999/2000 PROFILE registration form lists only about 300 participating colleges (as well as 120 private scholarship programs), which means many students will be stuck completing separate institutional aid forms as well. You'll learn more about PROFILE in Chapter 6. For now, just remember, it's important to find out which schools require what forms to make sure you're considered for every aid source possible.

The 6th Player—The Financial Aid Administrator

For college students, the financial aid administrator can be the most important person on campus. The FAA can take the family contribution and—ouch—increase it or—hooray—reduce it. The FAA can draw from money under the college's direct control or certify the student's eligibility for money not under the college's control. The FAA can decide on the contents of the student's aid package. Is it to be grants the student will not have to repay? Or will it all be loans? In short, the FAA is the final arbiter of how much the family must contribute to college costs and how much outside help, and of what kind, the family will receive.

Unfortunately, FAAs are working under increasingly stressful conditions. At most schools, they have no real say in setting tuition rates, developing operating budgets, or establishing enrollment goals (in terms of numbers or diversity), yet their offices are under constant pressure to make certain enough of the "right" students can afford tuition so the school meets its enrollment goals and balances its budget. The admission office wants to know why musical Johnny didn't enroll (would an extra $2,000 have done the trick?) while the budget director wants to know why needy Dee Dee got $3,000 when splitting that money might have lured no-need Joey and low-need Marky thus bringing in twice the tuition. To add to this stress, FAAs must keep their aid decisions ethical and consistent and make certain their schools don't run afoul of one of the 7000 sections of Uncle Sam's Higher Education Act.

So why do people become financial aid administrators? A quick look at some top ten lists on the FinAid Web site revealed the following:

Ten... No salary cap like in the NBA and NFL.

Nine... Get to develop lots of forms, then cut them up for scratch paper.

Eight... More nifty acronyms than the military.

Seven... Love meeting irate people.

Six... Can order all the FAFSAs I want.

Five... Get all the respect of a Little League umpire.

Four... Enjoy watching students cry.

Three... Staff meetings. Staff meetings. Staff meetings.

Two... Get to answer every question with "it depends."

AND THE NUMBER ONE REASON GIVEN
FOR BECOMING A FINANCIAL AID ADMINISTRATOR...

I Need Analysis!

Seriously, get to know your school's financial aid administrator. He or she can make the difference between winning and losing (and besides, is truly one of the nicest, most helpful people you'll meet on campus).

CHAPTER 5

THE CONCEPT OF "NEED"

Ubi Est Mea? (Old Latin Proverb. Translation: Where is Mine?)

Many high school students believe they cannot receive financial aid for an expensive private school if their parents can afford to send them to a state school. Others think almost all financial aid is set aside for minority students. Of course, neither of these assumptions is true.

The Official Definition of Need

Most financial aid is based on the concept of "need." Need is a number—nothing more, nothing less. It should never be confused with "needy." This is how financial aid administrators determine the need number:

Visualize three bars, Bar A, Bar B and Bar C.

Bar A is the cost of attendance at the college of your choice.

Bar B represents your family's expected contribution to college costs, as determined by need analysis (see previous chapter).

And **Bar C** is the amount of "outside" student aid you receive (e.g., private scholarships and veteran's benefits).

Bar A—the cost of attendance—is a variable. It varies from college to college. It can even vary within one school, depending on your student status, the courses you take, how far away you live, etc. Bar B and Bar C are constant (unless there is a drastic change in your family's situation). It doesn't matter where you plan to buy your education. The amount you must contribute from your own resources should be the same.

If Bar A is larger than Bar B and Bar C combined, you have need.

Bar A—Cost of Attendance		
Bar B—Family Contribution	Bar C—Outside Aid	Need

The Student Definition of Need

While schools define need as "cost of college minus expected family contribution," students seem to define it as "cost of college minus financial aid." This kind of thinking won't get you far!

A Numerical Example

Let's illustrate "need" for a family judged capable of contributing $5,000 per year to each of three colleges: College X which costs $20,000; College Y which costs $10,000; and College Z which costs $7,000. Assuming the student finds a $2,000 scholarship, that family's need is $13,000 at College X ($20,000 - $5,000 - $2,000); $3,000 at College Y ($10,000 - $5,000 - $2,000); and $0 at College Z ($7,000 - $5,000 - $2,000).

A Whole New Can of Worms

Colleges that rely primarily on federal and state resources to make up financial aid packages seem satisfied with the FAFSA system.

Unfortunately, colleges with lots of institutional aid to distribute feel the FAFSA does not gather enough information to judge a family's true ability to pay. Accordingly, many no longer use the word "need" to describe FAFSA results. Instead, they refer to the results as a "family's eligibility for federal student aid." These schools then use an application of their own (or the College Board's PROFILE) to gather additional information and determine a student's "need" for institutional funds.

More will be said about how this affects the aid package in Chapter 6. For now, just be warned that at most schools, awarding aid based entirely on "need" (as determined by a uniform method of need analysis) is an ideal rather than a practice.

Finally...

Neither "family contribution" nor "cost of college" is carved in stone. They can be stretched and squeezed to increase your eligibility for need-based financial aid. This is not the time to show you how to turn rock into play-doh. But it is time to let you know it can be done. In Chapter 7 you will find a plethora of ideas for stretching and squeezing.

CHAPTER 6

THE MECHANICS OF APPLICATION

Taking Charge of the Link-Up Process

The admission and financial aid cycles operate on different schedules. You select colleges in the fall, apply during the winter, and get acceptance decisions in early spring. The financial aid cycle, however, can't be formally initiated until after January first (so computers can be fed data on how much your family earned the previous year). You submit your federal student aid application as soon after 1 January as possible. Then you are kept in the dark for several months before you learn (1) how much you will have to contribute, (2) whether you have need, (3) whether you qualify for need-based, aid (4) and what your actual financial aid package will look like. Some years, students are asked to make their decision about what college to attend before they even receive their financial aid award letter.

The Good Soldier vs. The Take-Charge Applicant

If you want to assume your family contribution will not cause you a cash-flow problem, and that your need will be met at whatever college you attend, then you can trust the system and submit all your applications in the dark. You would be like the good soldier who carries out orders even though he does not understand them.

But if you assume, realistically, that (1) your family contribution will impose a cash-flow burden, (2) your full need will not be met, or (3) your need will be met in a financially burdensome manner, you cannot be a good soldier. You have to take charge of the process, protect your own interests.

For example, the Good Soldier won't learn his family contribution until late spring. He will be surprised by amount. He has little time to raise the money and may be forced to change college plans. The Take-Charge Applicant knows from the start how much college will cost his family. He has almost one year to figure out how to raise money.

The Good Soldier, when selecting colleges, does not consider their ability to meet her family's need fully or their willingness to present her with an attractive aid package. The Take-Charge Applicant makes the schools' ability to meet her need and develop an attractive aid package part of her college selection and application strategy.

In other words, as a Take-Charge Applicant, you guard against shocks and surprises. You allot adequate planning time. You improve your chances of having all your need met and met in an attractive manner. You may even succeed in lowering your family contribution and qualifying for more aid.

What is Meant by Taking Charge?

Taking charge is not complex. You won't have to enroll in a muscle-building course or graduate from Officer Candidate School. All you have to do is read this chapter and act on its advice. The take-charge process has three elements:

1. **Learn the Money Numbers Ahead of Time.** Before you complete any aid applications you should know the size of your family contribution, the costs of your selected colleges, and the resulting need you will have at each of these schools.
2. **Execute the Application Process With Speed and Precision.** That's how you insure you'll be first in line for aid, before the "Sold Out" signs light up.
3. **Know About Influence Points.** College selection, preparing for need analysis, the speed and accuracy with which you apply, the evaluation of aid offers, financial aid administrators—these are all influence points. How you handle yourself as you approach these points will impact on your family contribution, aid eligibility, and size and composition of your aid award.

STEP ONE: LEARN THE MONEY NUMBERS AHEAD OF TIME

The first step is to learn the money numbers ahead of time. You do that by securing answers to three questions:

1. How much will our family be expected to contribute to college costs? For federal aid, this will be a constant. For institutional aid, it may vary.
2. What are the total costs at my chosen college(s)? This is also a variable.
3. What's our need going to be at each college of my choice?

Once you have the answer to Question #3—even if it's just an approximation—you can begin some sensible financial planning.

Question One: How Much Must We Pay?

For dependent students, family contribution is made up of four elements:

- Parents' Contribution from Income
- Parents' Contribution from Assets
- Student's Contribution from Income
- Student's Contribution from Assets

If you are an independent student, your family contribution is based on only your own income and assets (as well as those of your spouse, if you are married).

Family contribution for the purposes of federal aid is calculated by Uncle Sam's central processor. Family contribution for the purposes of institutional aid might be calculated in a slightly different fashion, either by the College Scholarship Service or by the institution itself. Both systems of need analysis operate on the same principle: They let you shelter some of your income and assets for taxes, living expenses and retirement—then they want whatever's left.

You should know that the income protection allowance—the money left to you for shelter, food, clothing, car operations, insurance and basic medical care—is based on the Department of Labor's "low budget standard." If you have gotten along on a low budget standard, the need analysis formula will fit you like a glove. But if you have become locked into a higher standard of living, with mortgage payments, fat utility bills, two cars, summer vacations, an occasional trip to the theater, and so on, the small allowance won't do you. It won't cover expenses. And your assessed family contribution will appear impossibly large.

Question. Why should I calculate family contribution myself? Lots of Internet sites will do it for me; so will the guidance office computer.

Answer. By making the calculation yourself, you will develop an appreciation of the formula, its components, and the weights assigned to each component. This knowledge will serve you well later in the cycle, if you should have to discuss your aid award, and its calculation, with a financial aid administrator.

The Federal Methodology

The Federal Methodology determines your eligibility for all federal programs, most state programs, most private donor programs and most collegiate programs. It has the biggest impact on your eligibility for student aid. Incidentally, 95% of parents and students don't understand need analysis. Can you imagine that? Plunking down $50,000 or $100,000 for an education and not knowing how your share of that cost is assessed! You, as one of our readers, will be among the 5% who know.

To calculate family contribution under the Federal Methodology, go to Appendix 1,2 or 3, depending on your student status. Your calculations won't match the need analysis computer to the penny, but the result will be close. Here are some things to know before you start filling in figures:

Dependent Students

- All income and tax data comes from the previous calendar year. If you start college in September 1999, the previous calendar year is 1998.
- All asset data is as of the date you submit the need analysis form.
- If your parents are divorced or separated, use the income and asset figures of the parent with whom you will live for the greater part of the twelve months prior to the date of the application.
- If your parent has remarried, you must include your stepparent's income and asset information.

Independent Students

- All income and tax data comes from the previous calendar year. If you start college in September 1999, the previous calendar year is 1998.
- All asset data is as of the date you submit the need analysis form.

The Simplified Need Test

This simplified version of the Federal Methodology excludes all family assets from the need calculation. It applies to families whose total parental adjusted gross incomes (or, in the case of independent students, the student and spouse's total AGIs) are under $50,000 and who are eligible to file a 1040EZ, a 1040A, or who do not file a tax return at all. Families with incomes under $50,000 who file a 1040 only because they need to claim their tuition tax credits are also eligible for the Simplified Need Test.

The Institutional Methodology

The Institutional Methodology is used by some states, some private donor programs, and a few hundred colleges, mostly higher-priced private colleges to determine eligibility for state or private or collegiate resources. The Institutional Methodology is based on the Federal Methodology, but with a few twists: To estimate what private colleges (and some public colleges) will expect you to contribute, you'll have to make some changes to your calculations.

1. Include home equity in the value of your assets. Your family contribution should increase by an amount equal to about 5.6% of this equity.
2. Add unreimbursed medical expenses that exceed 4% of your AGI to your allowances against income. Your family contribution should decrease by as much as 47% of this amount.
3. Exclude consideration of the Hope and Lifetime Learning credits. Your family contribution should increase by as much as 47% of this amount. (Note: Schools may ask the College Board to override this modification thereby letting students keep the full benefit of their tax credit).
4. Use a slightly lower rate to estimate state and local taxes paid. Your family contribution may increase by a few hundred dollars.
5. Add repayment of parental education loans to your allowances against income. Your family contribution should decrease by as much as 47% of this amount.
6. Add business and rental losses back into income. Great tax shelters won't help you get more money for college. Your family contribution should increase by as much as 47% of this amount.
7. Add tuition expenses of up to $6,000 for each student enrolled in private secondary schools to your allowances against income. Your family contribution should decrease by as much as 47% of this amount.
8. Forget about including back-to-school parents in the "number of family members enrolled" figure.
9. Assume a minimum contribution from student income of at least $900 (some schools will expect at least $1,600).
10. Independent students may have to submit parental data for evaluation.
11. Independent students may also have to include 75% of their IRA/ Keogh assets with their asset data.

Private schools can make many other adjustments as well. Examples:

1. If your concurrently enrolled siblings' cost of education is obviously less than the evenly divided parental contribution figure, expect your expensive private school to reflect that in modifying parental contribution. In other words, if parental contribution equals $20,000, and your sibling is enrolled half-time at a community college with total costs of around 5,000, your school will probably want three-quarters ($15,000) of the parental contribution, rather than just half ($10,000).
2. If your parents are divorced, you should assume the private college will ask about the income and assets of the parent whose information is not

listed on the FAFSA. If the divorce was recent, they may expect a larger contribution than if the divorce was 16 years ago.

3. If you want to prepare for the absolute worst, add in other assets. For example, private colleges may ask for the current value of your retirement accounts (IRAs, Keoghs, 401 (k)s, pensions, annuities) and question you about sibling assets (to make sure you're not hiding money in baby brother's bank account). Often, these additional questions are to assess your ability to borrow money.

In Summary

Again, the Federal Methodology determines eligibility for federal aid (and most state aid). It's a strict formula with little room for negotiation. The Institutional Methodology is used by many colleges to award need-based collegiate aid. The formula is not legislated so individual discretion can be wide and the room for negotiation sometimes great (depending on the policies of the school, and the desirability of the student).

Completely confused? One counselor from New Jersey lamented, "We now have two financial aid delivery systems, one for private colleges and one for public colleges."

Question Two: How Much Will College Cost?

OK. You've estimated your family contribution. Now you need to know how much it will cost to attend the college of your choice. College costs and tuition are not synonymous. College costs, also known as "Cost of Attendance," "Cost of Education" or "Student Expense Budget"—are an aggregate of six or seven elements.

1. *Tuition and fees* are generally the same for all students.
2. *Book and supply expenditures* depend on the courses you select. You can purchase these items in the college store, in the community, or you can save some money and buy them in a used book emporium.
3. *Housing charges* may vary depending upon where you choose to live; in a dorm, off-campus in an apartment, or at home, in your old room.
4. *Meal charges* can also vary. There is one figure if you purchase a school meal plan. There is another if you plan to cook for yourself (translation: pasta, pizza, tuna, and fast food). And there is still a third figure if you're enjoying home-cooked meals—it makes no difference how much this arrangement might add to your parents' costs.
5. *Miscellaneous expenses* represent all the money you spend at places other than the college. This includes upkeep of clothing, health

insurance, even a small allowance for CDs, pizzas, and an occasional night out. The personal expense category can be very flexible. If you are handicapped, for instance, or have child care bills to shoulder, this item can be set very high. If you qualify for a student loan, your school will add the loan's associated costs (the guarantee fee and insurance premium) to your budget.

6. *Transportation*, too, is flexible. It may be based on two or three roundtrip flights between campus and home or it may represent commuting expenses.
7. *Computer Expenses.* Many colleges require students to own computers. Rental or purchase expenses can become part of your student budget.

Financial aid administrators establish expense budgets for each category of student who attends their college. There may be separate budgets for dependent students living in a dorm, in an apartment, or at home, and subcategories for single and married independent students. For example, at one school, the cost of college for a single student, living at home is $12,270; the cost for a single student living in a dorm is $16,70; the cost for a single student living in an off-campus apartment is $16,770; and the cost for a married student with child care expenses is $22,870.

Here are some points to ponder about expense budgets:

- Some items, such as room and board when you live at home, may not represent a special outlay for your family.
- By being frugal, your expenses may be lower than the college allots.
- If your expense budget does not appear to accurately reflect some of your college-related expenses, let the aid administrator know. Any increase in the expense budget increases your eligibility for aid.

All the comprehensive college guides (see your guidance counselor) give college cost estimates—augment this information by writing directly to colleges and asking for their most current catalogue. Also remember, if the information you're using is for the 1998/99 year, and you aren't starting college until 1999/2000, you should add 5% to the total cost figure to get a better idea of the rate you'll be paying.

To help you get a quick idea of the relationship between your family contribution and the cost of college, on the following page, we've developed an average cost-of-attendance table for different types of schools, projected to the year 2003. We've optimistically assumed 5% annual increases. Note that your last year could cost thousands more than your first.

	4-Yr Private	4-Yr Public	2-Yr Private	2-Yr Public
1999/2000				
Resident	$23,620	$11,101	$15,100	$8,807
Commuter	$20,135	$8,966	$12,641	$6,831
2000/2001				
Resident	$24,800	$11,656	$15,855	$9,248
Commuter	$21,141	$9,415	$13,273	$7,172
2001/2002				
Resident	$26,041	$12,239	$16,648	$9,710
Commuter	$22,199	$9,885	$13,936	$7,531
2002/2003				
Resident	$27,343	$12,850	$17,481	$10,196
Commuter	$23,308	$10,380	$14,633	$7,907

Question Three: What's My Need?

Now you have all the materials you need to answer the third question: How much need will I have at each college of my choice? You do that by comparing your Family Contribution from Appendix 1, 2, or 3, with the Cost of Attendance (all six or seven elements) at each school that interests you. Remember: If you're applying to one of the wealthier private schools you should perform this comparison twice: once using the federal methodology to determine your eligibility for federal aid, and again using the institutional methodology to estimate your eligibility for institutional aid.

STEP TWO: EXECUTE THE APPLICATION PROCESS WITH SPEED AND PRECISION

The second element of the "Take Charge" plan is to execute the application process with speed and precision. To do this, you must submit your aid application as soon after the first of the year as possible. We say "as soon after" because many programs operate on a first-come, first-served basis.

Which Form Should We File?

That's up to the colleges and your home state. Be sure to find out before New Year's Day. Here are some general guidelines: Everyone must file the Free Application for Federal Student Aid (FAFSA) to be considered for federal student assistance. In addition, some families will have to use the College Scholarship Service's Financial Aid PROFILE and/or a supplemental form from their home state to be considered for collegiate or state resources. Finally, some families will have to complete an institutional aid form and send it directly to the college they hope to attend. In other words, you may have to file one, two, three or four forms depending on the wishes of your home state and the schools to which you apply.

Why So Many Forms?

Simple. College is expensive and there's not enough financial aid to cover everyone's tuition bills, so schools have to figure out who needs money the most. To do this, they: (1) Use FAFSA results to award federal aid to all who qualify; (2) Use PROFILE or institutional aid application results to find out more about a family's finances; (3) adjust the family contribution accordingly; (4) award collegiate resources to the still needy; and (5) suggest politely that everyone else borrow more money.

Students applying to in-state schools will frequently get by with filing just the FAFSA. Students applying to more expensive schools where federal and state aid doesn't cover the tuition bill (e.g., private schools and out-of-state public schools) will usually have to complete multiple forms, as described above.

The Table of Forms and Programs lists the most widely used applications and the programs they serve (including which are first-come, first served).

Where Do We Get Forms and What Do We Do with Them?

Paper FAFSAs

You may pick up paper FAFSAs in your guidance office or college financial aid office. You fill it out as soon after January 1 as possible and snail mail it to the regional processor listed on the form. You pay no fee.

The 1999-2000 FAFSA will have a new look. It's been shortened from 16 to 8 pages (four pages of instructions and four pages for the application). It's been completely re-ordered to better integrate the instructions with the questions (and to more closely match the Web-based form). And it no longer directs families with AGIs under $50,000 to skip the asset questions. Instead, all families must answer them, and the processor will determine whether the Simplified Needs Test formula applies.

Electronic FAFSAs

You may also file FAFSAs directly with the central processor using FAFSA on the Web (http://www.fafsa.ed.gov/) or FAFSA Express (http://

Table of Agencies, Forms and Programs

		Program	
Form	**Sponsor**	**First-Come, First-Served**	**Not Time Sensitive**
Free Application for Federal Student Aid (FAFSA) Renewal FAFSA Electronic FAFSA	Uncle Sam Uncle Sam Uncle Sam	Federal Campus-Based Programs Most State Programs Some College Programs Some Private Programs	Pell Grant Federal Family Education Loans (Stafford and PLUS) Federal Direct Loans (Stafford and PLUS)
State Application	Your Home State	Some State Programs	Some State Programs
Financial Aid PROFILE	College Scholarship Service (CSS)	Some College, Some State and Some Private Programs	Some College, Some State and Some Private Programs

www.ed.gov/offices/OPE/express.html). FAFSA on the Web requires a browser like Netscape 3.0 or higher; FAFSA Express requires you to download some software. Either way, electronic FAFSAs include on-line help and instructions; internal edits help prevent errors and reduce rejections. For 1999/2000, FAFSA on the Web will include an EFC Estimator, however, families won't see their EFC until *AFTER* they submit their form.

Paper FAFSAs take four weeks to process; electronic FAFSAs take only one. *If possible, save time and file electronically.* You'll get a jump on your equally-needy, but technophobic classmates. In your eagerness, however, don't click "SEND" until you've checked your answers carefully!

State Aid Applications

If your state requires a separate aid application, you may get one from your state's higher education agency (see Chapter 11) or your guidance office. Again, you fill it out (usually after January 1) and send it to the address listed on the form. You pay no fee.

PROFILE

Registration guides are in your high school guidance office. If you're applying to one of the 300+ PROFILE schools, call CSS (800/778-6888) and give your information to a customer service representative. You may also register via the College Board Online, http://www.collegeboard.org.

CSS then sends you a packet of forms, customized with each of your school's financial aid questions. Beginning with the 1999/2000 award year, if you register on-line, you may also complete the form on-line.

The basic PROFILE is similar to the FAFSA, with a few extra questions about income, assets, family members, and expected resources. But CSS has accumulated a batch of nearly 200 additional questions that schools may choose to ask. These questions pry into everything from the student's intended career objective, to whether the student has applied for any outside scholarships, to whether the family has recently sold any income generating assets (and the purpose for which they were sold), to the year, make and model of all the family's motor vehicles.

You pay a fee for all this fun; $6 just to register ($5 if you do it online), then $15 per school or program that is to receive your information. If you need to have your data sent to more than 10 colleges, you'll have to call CSS and give them the new school codes. You'll pay an additional $6 registration fee, and another $15 per school or program.

PROFILEs may be filed prior to January 1 enabling financial aid administrators to get a head start on estimating financial aid packages. Check your schools' filing deadlines carefully.

Renewal FAFSAs

Students who filed a FAFSA for 1998/99 will receive renewal FAFSAs beginning mid-November. Renewal FAFSAs are preprinted with much of the data you provided last year, so unless there's a change in information, you can skip over many questions. If you would like to file your Renewal FAFSA on-line, go to FAFSA on the Web and request an "electronic access code." After it arrives (snail mail), you can apply on-line. If you filed electronically in 1998/99, you won't receive a paper Renewal FAFSA. Instead, Uncle automatically mails you an electronic access code so you can complete your form on-line.

Avoid Making Mistakes

Over 1.5 million students file correction applications, listing new information or fixing errors. By filing a mistake-free form, you'll be ahead of all those people in the chow line.

Name, Rank and Serial Number

You must have a social security number to apply for financial aid. Furthermore, the Department of Education now verifies every applicant's name, social security number and date of birth with the Social Security

Administration. It also does a "Date of Death" match and a "Prisoner's File" match to make sure you're not dead, or in jail (most prisoners aren't eligible for federal student aid).

To minimize problems, avoid using nicknames. The computer doesn't know whether "Bill Reese" and "William Reese, Jr." are the same person. Married or divorced students must be especially careful as their last names may have changed, while their social security numbers have not.

January 1

You can't date or mail your FAFSA before January 1.

Date Due

Be sure you know when colleges want you to submit the forms. If you apply to six colleges and each has a different deadline, mail your forms in time to meet the earliest deadline. Both FAFSA and PROFILE, remember, go to colleges via middlemen, so you must start the process at least four weeks before your due dates.

Use the Right Forms

In trying to simplify the aid process by standardizing the application, Uncle has made things more complex for some students who must now file a FAFSA, PROFILE and a separate state or institutional aid application. Read each school's aid literature closely to make sure you know which forms to file.

Identify Your College Completely

You can use federal student aid at over 7,500 schools. If Uncle included an institutional code list with each FAFSA packet, he would have no money left to fund aid programs, so it's your responsibility to list schools correctly—this means getting the code list from your counselor, looking it up yourself on the Internet (http://www.ed.gov/offices/OPE/t4_codes.html), or at least recording the full name and address of every school that is to receive your financial aid information. Remember "U. of M." could mean Maryland or Michigan. "University of California" could mean the campus at Davis or Irvine.

Estimating Information

If the filing date falls before your parents have done their taxes, you can use income and tax estimates on the FAFSA. If you note, later on, that your estimates were incorrect, you'll have to provide corrections. Estimators are also the most likely candidates for verification (see below).

Comparison Between Need Analysis and IRS Forms

Aid administrators must verify at least 30% of all FAFSAs. That's when you get to produce copies of tax forms and other documents for a comparison check. Most FAFSAs are selected based on "preestablished criteria," which is bureaucratese for "something smells fishy." Lesson: Be accurate and honest in submitting your data. If you are outside a $400 tolerance range, the college will know and you will be asked to make corrections. Items on the FAFSA that must match your 1040 include adjusted gross income, income tax paid and number of exemptions. Note: A frightening number of families opt to underreport income on their FAFSAs, some by as much as $100,000. Some schools ask all families for copies of their W-2s and tax returns—as a matter of policy. And if your school doesn't catch you, the IRS will. Department of Education auditors can ask the IRS to compare family income as stated on the FAFSA with income reported to the IRS. It may take a few years, but they'll get you!

A Good Use of the Winter Holiday

On a quiet day, switch off the TV, sit down with your family, an income tax form and a financial aid application, and put red circles around the common items. At that time, you may wish to complete the tax return so you can get a headstart on filling out the FAFSA. Remind mom and dad that the FAFSA asks whether you've already filed your tax return. If at all possible, avoid the April 15 post-office crush, and complete your return as soon as you have all the necessary income documents. It will save you some possible headaches later.

Be Consistent

The FAFSA processor crosschecks data and flags questionable applications for verification. *Example One*: A dependent student claims a one-parent family but records income for two parents. *Example Two*: A family shows $100,000 in savings, but no unearned income. Conversely, a family shows $10,000 in unearned income, but has no assets. There should be some correlation between the value of your savings and investments and the amount of your unearned income. Otherwise, lights will flash, bells will sound, and investment advice will come pouring in (or, you'll be asked to share your investment secrets). In either case, you're a candidate for verification.

Change in Status

If your status changes after you submit your FAFSA (due, for example, to a family death, disability, prolonged unemployment, divorce or separation) notify the college immediately. Aid administrators can adjust your EFC to reflect your new situation.

Early Bird Gets the Worm

Apply for financial assistance as early as possible. Schools can run out of assistance money for late applicants.

Don't Make Mistakes

Mistakes cause the form to bounce. By the time you make corrections and resubmit it, you will find yourself at the end of the line and the money gone. Most common mistakes: Omitting social security number, recording an incorrect social security number, leaving questions blank when you mean zero, (write "0"), using "white-out," entering a range of figures such as $200-400, giving monthly instead of yearly amounts or vice versa (read each question carefully to learn what information is required), entering cents, leaving off numbers ($5,000 vs. $50,000), writing illegibly, and writing in the margins.

Don't Forget to Sign the Form

The FAFSA includes a statement in which you promise to use your student aid for XYZ College only and certify that you are not in default on any federal loans. Whether you file a paper FAFSA or an electronic version, you must sign a copy of this statement before Uncle will authorize any funds.

Don't Falsify Anything

The FAFSA clearly states, "If you purposely give false or misleading information on this form, you may be fined $10,000, sent to prison or both." And don't expect the financial planner you hired to bail you out.

Make Copies

Make copies of all financial aid forms and your responses to any information requests from Uncle Sam, the need analysis processor or the colleges. Make sure to send the original, however, and keep the copy for yourself.

Register for Selective Service

Males (between 18 and 25) will not be eligible for federal aid unless they do. If you are exempt from registering, file a statement accordingly.

If Necessary, Include the Processing Fee

The FAFSA is free, but PROFILE costs $5 or $6 to register and $15 for each school or program that is to receive a report. (This cost is a big reason to make sure you don't waste your time on PROFILE unless your college requires it).

What Happens Now?

Processing the FAFSA

1. You send your completed FAFSA to your regional processor (the address will be on the envelope that comes with your FAFSA). This regional processor scans your data and transmits it to the central processor.
2. The central processor matches your application information against several national databases to verify your eligibility for aid. For example, it checks your Selective Service status, your Social Security number, and your citizenship status.
3. The central processor checks your data for inconsistencies.
4. The central processor evaluates your finances and calculates your "Expected Family Contribution" (EFC).
5. The central processor incorporates your EFC into a multi-part eligibility document called a Student Aid Report (SAR).
6. The central processor sends you a copy of your SAR. Review it carefully to make certain your EFC was calculated using the accurate information. If there's an "*" next to your EFC, you've been selected as a candidate for verification. If there's a "C" next to it, you're a big winner—the central processor has identified an eligibility problem which must be resolved before you can receive any student aid.
7. The processor sends a more detailed analysis (an Institutional Student Information Record, or ISIR) to all the colleges named on your FAFSA.
8. The processor transmits your data to your state's education agency.

If you file your FAFSA electronically, your data goes straight to the central processor. The rest of the cycle is the same.

Processing PROFILE

PROFILE goes back to the College Scholarship Service (CSS) for processing. When CSS is finished, it sends you an acknowledgment. The Data Confirmation section of this acknowledgment shows what information CSS entered from your application. As with the SAR, review the data carefully. If you see a mistake, correct it using this part of the acknowledgment. Also, if you need to send your information to additional schools or programs, here's your chance.

Building the Financial Aid Package

The financial aid administrator (FAA) now rolls up his or her sleeves and goes to work. First, the FAA determines your cost of attendance (or student expense budget). Second, the FAA reviews your expected family contribution, compares it to your cost of attendance, and establishes your need (and eligibility) for most state and federal programs. Third, the FAA takes another look at your EFC to determine your eligibility for collegiate awards—about 35% of all FAAs adjust the contribution based on policies of their office. And finally, the FAA builds your Financial Aid Package.

Before they build any aid packages, however, the financial aid staff sits down and establishes a packaging philosophy—a set of guidelines to ensure consistency and equity in their treatment of all aid applicants. Unfortunately (and ironically), each school has its own ideas about consistency and equity which means your need will probably be met differently at each school to which you apply. For example, some schools award every student the maximum Stafford possible. Others award grant aid first, then self-help (loans and work). Some have rules prescribing the ratio of grants to loans, a ratio that can vary with the income of the aid applicant (lower income students receiving more grants than loans, upper income students receiving mostly loans). Most colleges freely admit to packaging need-based gift aid based on "academic desirability."

In general, when awarding money from programs they administer but do not fund (i.e., federal programs), colleges give priority to the neediest of the able. When awarding money from their own funds, colleges give priority to the ablest of the needy.

Layer One—Pell and State Grants

The Pell Grant is the foundation of every aid package (see Chapter 10). Only students with EFCs under about $2,900 are eligible for Pells. State grants make up the other part of Layer One. Most states require students to attend an in-state college to qualify for a state award.

Layer Two—Outside Scholarships

Next, the aid administrator gleefully incorporates any outside scholarships you may have found (that's money the school need not worry about providing you). This includes the $500 awarded you by your church or temple, as well as the $5,000 from your parent's boss.

Layer Three—Federal Programs

Third, if you still have need (i.e., if the cost of college exceeds your EFC plus your Pell Grant plus your state grant plus your outside scholarships), the FAA draws on four other federal programs: Stafford Loans, Perkins Loans, Supplemental Educational Opportunity Grants, and Work-Study (see Chapter 10). The way FAAs use these programs varies from school to school according to their packaging philosophy and the size of their student aid budget. Most award Stafford loans (which are limitless) first, preserving (scarcer) federal resources for students who then still have need.

Layer Four—Collegiate Resources

If the cost of college is still greater than all of your resources (your EFC plus money from all the aid programs just mentioned), the FAA can do one of three things:

1. Give you a huge award from the college's own resources. These resources include low interest loans and collegiate scholarships. The richer the college, the more resources it will have for this layer.
2. Use the Institutional Methodology (based on information you provided via PROFILE or the school's own aid application) to adjust your family contribution, and if you still have need, give you funds from the college's own resources.
3. Apologize for not being able to meet your financial need fully and suggest your parents borrow money under Uncle Sam's PLUS program (or use a commercial loan source) to help ease any cash flow problems.

Layer Five—PLUS Loans

Finally, the aid administrator will approve you for a PLUS loan. The size of your loan is limited to the total program cost less any financial aid you may have received. In other words, if school costs $10,000 and you receive $5,000 in financial aid, you may receive a PLUS loan of $5,000. The size of your family contribution does not matter so long as your parents are credit worthy. For more on PLUS loans, see Chapter 10.

Families Without Financial Need

If the family has no financial need and the school really wants the student, the FAA may offer the student a non-need based award such as an academic scholarship.

The Award Letter

The FAA will present your aid package in the form of an award letter. These letters vary in format, but most contain the following items:

1. A statement of the expense budget developed for you. Again, this varies based on factors like whether you plan to live on- or off-campus.
2. Your expected family contribution, as calculated under the federal methodology and the institutional methodology.
3. The amount of your need.

4. A description of how all or part of that need is to be met, listing each aid source and dollar amount.
5. A suspense date by when you must return the award letter.
6. Information on available procedures for "appealing" any information in the award letter with which you disagree.

If there is something you don't understand about the offer, or if you notice your EFC is different than what was sent to you by the processor on your Student Aid Report, ask the school for clarification.

Comparing Your Award Letters

While it's seldom wise to make the agonizing, final decision concerning which college to attend based on money issues alone, it's no longer realistic to exclude money as a factor. That said, it's important to make sure you're not just looking at the schools' sticker prices (that would be like comparing apples and oranges). Instead, you have to evaluate how much each school is going to cost your family in out-of-pocket money. And to make certain you're not then comparing Granny Smiths to Red Delicious, be sure to factor in the amount of loan money you'll eventually have to repay. You might find it helpful to create a worksheet (either on paper or a spreadsheet) with a side-by-side comparison of each school's package.

Compare the award letters from all the colleges to which you applied. But don't delay responding to a letter because you're still waiting to hear from other colleges. If you don't reply by the required date, the school can cancel your award and free the money up for some other deserving student. Responding to the award letter does not commit you to attendance. It just safeguards your award, should you elect to go to that college.

In responding to the award letter, your have four choices: You can accept the award in its entirety; accept some components of the award and reject others; reject the award entirely; or request a revision in the composition of awards (more grants, less loans).

Appealing Your Award

Few people still ask us if they can challenge admission decisions. Instead, everyone wants to know if they can negotiate their aid package. Our answer? An unqualified "Maybe." But before you bully your way into a financial aid office demanding a recount, it's important to know what actions will help (or hurt) your cause. Your success in appealing an award depends on a great number of factors:

1. *The availability of discretionary funds.* Private colleges usually put more money toward scholarships than public universities. They also

have greater flexibility in how they distribute their money. In any case, make your request as early as possible, because money runs out fast even at our wealthiest schools!

2. *The skill (and tact) with which you present your case.* If your family has had a recent change in situation, document the change carefully and contact the FAA. He or she can adjust the EFC calculation to allow for special conditions—mostly unpleasant things like job loss, death, disability, divorce, or unexpected or unusually high medical expenses. In these cases, the FAA will probably lower the family's income figure and recalculate. You might also ask the FAA to reduce the value of reportable assets. For example, you can easily argue a recent job loss will not only affect a family's earnings, but also eat into its savings.
3. *The caliber of the student.* If the school really wants you to enroll, the FAA can sometimes be of more help, usually by adjusting the composition of your aid package. Remember: Grants are infinitely more desirable than loans. Here's also where the line between "financial aid" and "enrollment management" can begin to blur: Informal studies show it takes about $10,000 (spread out over four years) to nab a student who might otherwise not consider a particular school. Are you the kind of student on the college's shopping list?

Will the Need-Based Route Satisfy My Need?

Maybe. Maybe not. It could be a dream package. Or it could leave you a thousand dollars short or mired deeply in debt. Remember: Few colleges have enough resources to help all applicants. Also, different colleges assess need differently. If you apply to three schools, each of which costs $8,000 more than your family's EFC, you may be offered three very different packages, ranging from the attractive to the unacceptable.

STEP THREE: KNOW ABOUT INFLUENCE POINTS

Now that you've mastered the mechanics of need analysis, it's time for the last step of the take-charge process: Know about influence points.

Influence Point: Wise College Selection

What You Can Gain: Improved financial aid package; no-need scholarships.

More Information: Chapter 9

Influence Point: Careful Preparation for Need-analysis

What You Can Gain: A lowered family contribution and increased eligibility for aid; Longer planning time for help with cash-flow requirements.

More Information: This chapter, Chapter 7, Appendices 1, 2 and 3

Influence Point: Speed and Accuracy in Applying

What You Can Gain: Increased chance of tapping into limited aid sources; Improved financial aid package.

More Information: This chapter.

Influence Point: Working with Aid Administrators

What You Can Gain: Improved financial aid package.

More Information: This chapter, Chapter 7, Chapter 9

CHAPTER 7

SHORT-RANGE PLANNING: TILTING THINGS YOUR WAY

There are six basic strategies for tilting the financial aid process in your favor. Only two are mutually exclusive—the Napoleon of aid seekers would investigate all six:

- Strategy One—Reduce Your Expected Family Contribution
- Strategy Two—Increase the Cost of Attendance
- Strategy Three—Obtain an Improved Aid Package
- Strategy Four—Replace Your Money with OPM, Other People's Money
- Strategy Five—Lower the Cost of College
- Strategy Six—Improve Your Cash Flow

Strategy One— Reduce Your Expected Family Contribution

Objective: Reduce your family contribution so your need becomes larger. In other words, make yourself eligible for more student assistance. We offer this advice with the hope you'll work with the system, not cheat it. There's a fine line between getting your fair share, and abusing financial aid rules at the expense of needier students. Most financial aid, remember, is "need-based" not "want-based." Here are some ideas to ponder:

Thoroughly Understand Need Analysis

We assume that while reading Chapter 6 you took time to complete the worksheets in Appendix 1, 2, or 3 and noted the various percentages and weights assigned to your data. These items should have caught your eye.

1. **Parent Assets vs. Student Assets.** Currently, dependent students do not rate an asset protection allowance. Their assets are taxed at 35% of their value. Parents do rate an asset protection allowance. Money held by parents, as you trace it through the formula, is taxed no more than 5.6%. That's quite a difference! $35,000 in junior's bank account becomes a $12,250 contribution to college costs. The same $35,000 in the parental account becomes a mere $1,960 contribution. Lesson: Accu-

mulate money for college, yes. But don't be so quick to accumulate in the child's name. Caveat: The House version of the Reauthorization Bill changes the need analysis formula to give equal weight to student and parent assets (the Senate version of the Bill makes no such change). In the unlikely event the House version passes, this becomes a moot strategy.

2. **Business Property.** Business assets rate an adjustment factor (e.g., 40% of net worth up to $85,000). Think hard. Do you have any income source you can turn into a business? Or can you shift assets to a sub-S corporation in which your family holds a controlling 51% interest while people outside the need analysis formula (your grandmother?) hold 49%? That's a real one-two punch. You reduce your assets first by the net worth adjustment, and second by the 49% value transfer outside the immediate family. All this will complicate your tax return, but the trade-off could be a sharply reduced contribution to college costs.
3. **The True Value of a Student Aid Dollar.** If you are in a 28% tax bracket and don't get student aid, you must earn $1.39 to have one dollar available for tuition bills. Let's turn this around. If you are successful in getting one dollar of student aid, that one dollar is really worth $1.39 to you. Lesson: The higher your tax bracket, the greater the value of any student aid dollar received.
4. **The Previous-Year Rule.** Your 1998 earnings determine your aid eligibility for the 1999/2000 academic year. Your 1999 earnings impact on the 2000/2001 year. If your income fluctuates, and you have control over the fluctuations, you might defer income from the base year to the next. That would enhance your eligibility in the coming academic year. What about the next base year? Life is filled with soap opera twists. Take it one year at a time.
5. **No Credit for Consumer Debt.** Under need analysis, you get no write off for consumer debt. If you have $10,000 in credit card debt, or you owe the bank $20,000 in car payments, that's your problem. But let's say you own stocks and have a brokerage account that lets you borrow against your portfolio. If you draw $20,000 to finish paying for the car, you reduce the value of your reportable assets by that amount. You pay less for college and have a new car to drive!

"What If" Calculations

If you have spreadsheet software, you can easily program our appendices, and simplify the following kinds of "what-if" calculations. Another option is to order our software package (see inside back cover). The results can surprise you.

Reduce Your Reportable Assets

Not all assets are created equal.

1. *Home equity is not a reportable asset under the Federal Methodology.* So what happens if you use savings to pay down your home mortgage? You'll probably be in a much better position to qualify for a low-interest federal loan. Remember, however, aid administrators are free to ask questions about home equity, and may reserve the school's own funds for renters (and expect families with pricey homes and no mortgage to borrow against this great asset).
2. *Do you need to make a large purchase before you sign and date your FAFSA?* Do you need a new car to replace the one Junior wants to take to college? How about a new stereo, refrigerator or washer-dryer? Is your heat pump about to conk out? Pay cash, if you can, or borrow against a stock portfolio. That will reduce your reportable assets—and provide you with a smooth ride, good music, some cold drinks, clean clothes and a comfortable home climate.
3. *If you've been saving in your child's name,* get his or her permission to use that money to pay your entire EFC for the first year of college. (You could also use the money for something smaller, like the increasingly essential personal computer). This will improve your chances for aid during years two, three, and four. Warning: This won't work at all schools. Some expect 35% of a student's assets in Year One, 35% of the remaining balance in Year Two, etc. Tricky, tricky, tricky!
4. *Do you have a favorite charity?* How does a gift of $1,000 impact on your family contribution (and your taxes)?
5. *Can you use reportable assets to pay down your credit card debt?* Or pay off an automobile loan? It's good financial planning, as well as good college planning.
6. *Do grandparents need some extra money?* You can each give each of your student's grandparents a gift of up to $10,000, which would reduce your assets by up to $80,000. It could also reduce your taxes, as frequently, grandparents are retired and in a lower tax bracket.

Reduce Your Reportable Income

1. *Take less pay.* Is there any way to defer year-end bonuses? Remember, need analysis looks at previous year income—1998 for the 1999/2000 award year. As Uncle Sam monitors the impact of the Higher Education Act on the federal budget and on middle income families, who knows what program adjustments he'll make in 1999. With constantly changing rules, if you can increase your eligibility even for a year, do it!

2. *Accelerate income.* If your student won't start college until 2000, try to lower your 1999 income. For example, accelerate bonuses and make certain you don't receive any 1998 state or local tax refunds in 1999.
3. *Accelerate or postpone gains.* If you plan to sell stocks or property, do it two years before college, or wait until your student has graduated. Capital gains count as income which is heavily "taxed" by the need analysis system. Also, watch out for year-end dividends on mutual funds. If the fund you're eyeing is about to pay a dividend, wait until after the payout before you buy. You'll get more shares for your money, and not have any capital gain dividends to report (per-share price drops by the amount paid out).
4. *Is it time for a career change?* Should Mom or Dad take some time off work to rethink options (and increase eligibility for financial aid)? Sadly, as much as 85% of each extra dollar your parents earn go to state taxes, federal taxes or the college bursar.

Start a Family Business

Can you move some assets into a business venture? It doesn't have to be complex, but if it doesn't show a profit in at least 3 out of 5 years, the IRS calls it a hobby. For example, the Bakers started Babycakes, Inc. to sell muffins every Saturday at their local farmer's market. Rose loves going to yard sales on weekends, so, she started a second- hand furniture business with the objects she finds. Uncle Sam rewards private enterprise with a greatly reduced expected contribution to college costs. Also remember, any money you pay your children becomes a business expense, and under the Federal Methodology, students currently receive an income protection allowance of $2,200 (the House version of the Reauthorization Bill increases this amount to $3,000; the Senate version of the Bill does not).

Save for Retirement

Need analysis wants to know how much you contribute to a retirement fund the year before college (it considers this contribution a discretionary item and adds it back in to your total income). It does not, however, ask how much you've already saved. In other words, you can accumulate money tax-free (or tax-deferred) at the same time you reduce your assets for need analysis and save for your retirement. Please note, however, that some colleges will ask about the value of your retirement funds and either ask you to borrow against them, or use that information "against" you if try to negotiate your aid package. Also, you don't want all your assets tied up in funds that penalize you for early withdrawal (e.g., before age 59 1/2). You may need some money sooner.

Declare Yourself Independent

Independent students do not include their parents' income and assets in their need analysis calculation; only their own, (generally) more limited resources. Hence, their contribution will usually be smaller, and their need larger. Should you try to declare yourself independent then, to gain access to more aid? Certainly, if you are really independent and can convince the financial aid administrator accordingly. Absolutely not, if it is a ploy. Please note: Single, undergraduate students under the age of 24 are considered "dependent" in all cases, except at the discretion of the financial aid administrator.

Use a More Favorable Need Analysis Method

Can you lower your adjusted gross income to under $50,000? If so, and you are eligible to file a 1040A or 1040EZ (even if you actually file a regular 1040) you may use the Simplified Methodology to calculate family contribution. In other words, parent and student assets are excluded from need analysis. If you can keep your AGI under $50,000 (even for just one year), do so!

Increase the Number of Family Members in College

Your parental contribution figure is divided by the number of students you have in school at any one time. If Dad needs to complete his degree, is there any advantage to his returning to school at the same time one or more children are in college? If you have two children, one year apart, with one starting college and one starting the senior year in high school, would it be advantageous for the older child to "stop out" for one year and wait for son or daughter #2 to catch up?

Caveat: The House version of the Reauthorization Bill would exclude parents from the "number of family members enrolled" figure (leaving the decision up to aid administrators). The Senate version of the Reauthorization Bill contains no such provision.

Explain Your Extraordinary Expenses or Unusual Situations

The Federal Methodology leaves consideration of special conditions to the discretion of financial aid administrators. Colleges have lots of wiggle room in deciding how to allocate their own resources. Don't try to explain away high vacation expenses or defend the necessity of a newly remodeled kitchen. But do think carefully about whether you have legitimate expenses or an unusual situation that might convince an aid administrator to recalculate your family contribution (usually by lowering the value of your assets, or using expected year income, rather than prior year).

Here are some questions to ask yourself.

- Does your family have enormous medical expenses?
- Does your family pay secondary school tuitions for younger siblings?
- Are your parents repaying their own students loans, or those of an older sibling?
- Do you have consumer debt resulting from past unemployment?
- Is your contribution from student income figure inflated because you took a year off to work?
- Did you pay more in taxes than the need analysis formula allowed?
- Do you have siblings attending pricey private colleges (who received less-than-generous aid packages)?
- Is one of your parents about to retire?
- Did the school exclude consideration of your Hope or Lifetime Learning tax credits?
- Is your new business eating up assets, rather than generating income?
- Were your parents divorced or separated after you filed your aid application?
- Are you an independent student who was required to report parental income and assets on the aid application?
- Was your home affected by earthquakes? Floods?

Go Complex, Consult an Expert

College is one of the three biggest investments of your life (retirement and home ownership being the other two), yet many families fail to treat it that way! Financial planners who really understand financial aid (and such planners are not easy to find) can help you in important ways. (1) They'll help you understand the long- and short-term financial impact of different cost-saving strategies. (2) They'll give you insight into how a particular school will view your case. (3) They may even help you draft a Letter of Special Circumstance to highlight your unique situation to the financial aid office. Finally, they'll work with you on cash flow management so you can educate your children and still have enough for retirement.

Financial planners come in different flavors. You might prefer a "fee-only" planner who has no vested interest in selling you a particular investment product. Here are some cost-lowering ideas from Bonnie Hepburn, a Certified Financial Planner with MONEYSENSE Financial Planning, a fee-only practice with college funding expertise (292 Great Rd, Acton MA 01720, 508/264-4088, http://www.win.net/~moneysense/).

"Colleges claim to award financial aid consistently and objectively, but most weigh both qualitative and quantitative factors. The more the school wants a student, the more likely it is to view special circumstances favorably. Highlight those special circumstances! Special circumstances, not middle-class whining, that's the key here. If money is short because the parent took a leave of absence from work to care for an ailing relative, let the colleges know. If the parent just spent $12,000 on a wedding for an older sibling, don't mention it.

"Remember the adage, 'You have only one chance to make a first impression.' The financial aid office at Tulane, for example, receives 1,000 letters of special circumstance each financial aid season, so limit your remarks, and make your letter brief, respectful, memorable, and of course, factually and grammatically sound.

"If you don't hear back within ten days, call and make sure your letter has been read. One of my clients waited anxiously for a response for two months. A follow-up call to the school quickly yielded an additional $6,000 grant. The more persistent a parent is, *without being a nudge,* the more likely aid is. I counsel parents with endearing personalities to make personal pleas for more aid; others, I suggest send letters.

"Beware of salespeople with superficial knowledge of the aid process; they may claim your annuity purchase will solve your college funding problems, but the single most important step in qualifying for financial aid isn't even financial. It's in selecting colleges to which to apply.

"Brand name schools (which generally are the ones with cash to spare) have many more applicants than empty desk chairs; to get financial aid (or even to gain admission), your student needs an edge. Academics, sports ability, dedicated public service, geography, or unusual experience all may motivate a school to lure your student to enroll.

"Rhode Island School of Design, for example, limits institutional financial aid to the top 10% of the entering class who also demonstrate financial need. Other schools follow similar policies, but less openly. As a result, your student probably won't receive the best aid package from a reach school. When selecting schools, consider: Will your student graduate and be the type of alumnus/a the school seeks?

"As for other considerations, choose schools likely to give your student high-quality (grant) aid and schools in regular competition with each other for students. No matter that your student plays chess rather than football, if you target schools in the same athletic conference they are likely rivals off the playing field, as well.

"When the financial aid awards are made in April, be prepared to go back and negotiate, even two or three times. Since negotiating with leverage is such an important part of the strategy, steer your student away from applying Early Decision if you're going to need substantial aid.

"Tactics such as removing home equity in a refinance and investing it in annuities can work in reducing Family Contribution, but only under certain circumstances; (1) if the school has money to give, and (2) if the school really wants your student to enroll. In these specialized circumstances, consider some of the excellent no-load (no sales charge) annuity products available.

"Last of all, be aware that financial planners can save you money but they can't work miracles. They are best at helping you reduce your cost of college, if possible, then figuring out how to pay for what remains over the number of years you'll have kids in college."

Strategy Two—Increase the Cost of Attendance

Objective: Increase the cost of attendance so your need becomes larger. This will improve your chances for a Stafford Loan or collegiate aid.

Don't Rule Out More Expensive Schools

Your EFC is $11,000 and you plan to attend a $12,000 school. The maximum (subsidized) Stafford for which you qualify is $1,000. If you now select a $20,000 school, you could get a $2,500 loan, $1,500 in work-study and $5,000 from the school's own funds. Your family contribution is the same. Remember, more expensive schools often have more aid to hand out. You never know until you apply.

Does Your Student Budget Reflect All Your Expenses?

Does the aid administrator have a true picture of your transportation costs, special medical expenses, child care, or other legitimate expenses the school may have overlooked? In some instances, FAAs can include computer expenses in your cost of attendance Many colleges also now charge students separate "technology fees" to counter the exploding costs of maintaining up-to-date computer labs. While the fee may only amount to a few hundred dollars, make sure it's included in your expense budget.

Also, co-op education students may receive an allowance for reasonable costs associated with such employment. It probably won't cover a new Armani wardrobe, but you may get an extra $500 for bus fare.

Now you try one. Unbeknownst to the financial aid staff (as well as the admission committee), one incoming student is a werewolf. What will be the student's extra expenses? Bars for the windows. Dead bolt locks. Paying for roommate to stay at the Holiday Inn during every full moon. An occasional sack of Purina dog chow. Flea collars. Rabies shots. City dog tags. A monthly shampoo and pedicure. You complete the list...

Strategy Three— Obtain an Improved Aid Package

Objective: Change the composition of your package to emphasize aid you won't have to repay. Grants and work-study are much better than loans.

Careful College Application

Apply to colleges as early as possible, before the money runs out. Also, pick colleges where you are in the top 25% of the applicant pool. The most desirable applicants get the most agreeable aid packages. That's as true at the Ivies as it is at Horned Toad State.

Negotiate for More Grants

This works only if the college really wants you, and has resources to spare. What gives you bargaining strength? Good grades and SAT scores, athletic ability, artistic talent, alumni ties, ethnic background, geographic origin, even a substantial aid package from one of the school's "competitors." Colleges like to brag about the diversity of the student body and they might be missing a pole vaulter from Idaho or a soprano from Rhode Island. You might even ask a department head (if you are a genius) or a coach (if you are a jock) to be your advocate in such negotiations. Why do colleges care about this? Long term survival! First of all, a diverse student body makes for a more rewarding academic experience for all enrolled students, but also, having enthusiastic, diverse alumni spread out over the entire country is a good way for a college to ensure a continued stream of applicants in future years.

Strategy Four— Replace Your Money With OPM

Objective: Getting Other People's Money (OPM) to pay for your family contribution is the most desirable but also the most difficult strategy. *The Wall Street Journal* told of an enterprising, financially strapped economics student who staged a one-person bike-a-thon to benefit himself. Unfortunately, pledges to his scholarship fund ($725) barely covered his expenses

($510), and after biking nearly 200 miles, alone and in the dark, he offered these words of wisdom, "stupid idea, stupid idea, stupid idea." Here are some better ones.

Money from Grandma

Direct payments to the school for tuition are not subject to the $10,000 gift tax limits, so grandparents who want to help their smart grandchildren can help pay the college bill, without having that generosity affect the financial aid calculation or anyone's tax return. No fuss. No muss.

Money from Your Boss

Many employers will reimburse you for part of your tuition expenses; the first $5,250 is tax-free. See Chapter 12 for more information.

No-Need Awards

No-need awards are scholarships given with no regard to your financial need. If you win a $2,000, no-need scholarship, you are $2,000 ahead. The recipient of a no-need scholarship can fall into one of two categories with regard to college costs: They either have need or they don't. Let's examine each situation in more detail:

Situation 1—You have need and receive a no-need award

The cost of college is reduced by the amount of your award. This reduction may eliminate (1) part of your need; (2) your entire need; or (3) your entire need and part of your family contribution. Actual numbers will determine which of these it will be. Assume the cost of college is $12,000 and your family contribution is $7,000. This makes your need $5,000.

Example 1—Your no-need award is $1,000. Offered aid package: The schools reduce your need from $5,000 to $4,000; your family contribution remains at $7,000.

Example 2—Your no-need award is $5,000. Offered aid package: The school eliminates your need; your family contribution remains $7,000.

Example 3—Your no-need award is $6,000. Offered aid package: Your need is wiped out; this time the school reduces your family contribution from $7,000 to $6,000.

This packaging may seem unfair, but colleges have little choice about how they use your no-need award—if you have financial need, federal regulations prevent schools from using no-need money to replace your EFC. In Examples 1 and 2 above, you can still benefit from the no-need award by convincing the school to use the money to replace a loan element of your aid package.

Situation 2—You have no need and the award is a no-need award

In this case, the money goes directly to you. It replaces your money. You write a smaller check when you pay the college bill. Let's assign numbers to this. Your family contribution is $9,000 and the cost of college is $9,000.

Example 1—Your no-need award is $3,000. Your family contribution shrinks to $6,000. That's all you have to pay.

Example 2—Your no-need award is $10,000. Now you're $1,000 ahead which will finance your winter tour of the Yucatan. Right? Wrong. You can only receive $9,000—the amount that eliminates your family contribution. Financial aid can't exceed the cost of attendance. In other words, it cannot provide income for you.

Where can I find no-need awards?

No-need awards tend to congregate in the following three areas.

Uncle Sam. Most of Uncle's no-need awards have a military connection and carry a service obligation, e.g., service academies and ROTC scholarships.

The States. Two programs, usually for state residents. Honor scholarships for outstanding students and tuition equalization grants for students attending in-state private colleges rather than public universities. See Chapter 11 for the address of your home state's higher education agency.

The Colleges. Colleges are the main source of no-need awards. Most are academic scholarships designed to entice bright students to enroll. See *The A's and B's of Academic Scholarships* (inside back cover).

Strategy Five—
Lower the Cost of College

Objective: Lower college costs so you reduce or eliminate your need and spare yourself the hassle of applying for aid or saddling yourself with debt.

Pick a Lower-Priced School

Choose a school where the cost of living is low (Texas, Michigan) or one that receives church subsidies (Brigham Young, St. Olaf). Or consider these options:

1. **Investigate your own State U.** Not just the flagship school, but all the others, as well.
2. **Consider community colleges.** Go for two years, then transfer to a four-year school to finish your degree. You pick up the "halo" of the prestige

college's sheepskin, but at a fraction of the cost. If you opt for this route, make sure you take academic core courses so your credits will transfer. Also, don't let yourself get derailed—it's all too easy to pick up "real world" responsibilities, and never finish your degree.

3. **Look for "Best Buys."** Each September, *Money* magazine takes 1,000+ schools, and compares their "educational quality" with their "sticker price" to create its list of "Top 100" deals (as well as 50 runners-up). *Money* also lists schools that are "Costly but worth it," "Black college buys," "Top small liberal arts schools," "Top public schools" and "Best discounted tuition rates." *U.S. News and World Report* publishes its own "Best Value" and "Most Efficient" college rankings. In general, schools that score highest do so because they charge less than schools of similar quality. Of course, the outrage over reducing "quality" to a numerical rank is almost as deafening as the outrage over basing admission decisions on standardized test scores. And as if to prove critics right, the lists developed by *Money* and *U.S. News* have very little overlap. You'll find both magazines on your real or virtual newstand (http://www.moneymag.com or http://www.usnews.com/usnews/edu/home.htm)

4. **Study in Canada.** Winters are long, and classrooms can be large (especially for first-years students), but Canadian schools are excellent, and they are actively recruiting US students. Furthermore, Canadian taxpayers subsidize tuition, and a strong US dollar makes room and board quite affordable. In fact, Canadian prices rival public tuition in the United States—for example, well-known McGill charges only around $10,000 for tuition, room and board. If you choose a Canadian school, you won't be eligible for need-based federal grants, however, you can receive subsidized federal loans, and tuition tax credits. For more information, contact the Association of Universities and Colleges of Canada, 350 Albert Street #600, Ottawa, ON Canada, K1R 1B1 (http://www.aucc.ca/).

Examine Each Element of the "Cost of Attendance"

Some are firmly established (such as tuition), but you can influence others. For example, used books cost less than new ones, softcover costs less than hardcover, and many airlines offer low student fares.

Students can sometimes save money by living off-campus with roommates, or choosing a meal plan that fits their lifestyle (don't pay for breakfast at the dining hall if you know you never wake up before noon). It's also never-too-soon to start clipping coupons. Your Sunday paper is a gold mine; so is http://www.hotcoupons.com. Remember, never pay full price for pizza!

One of the best ways to control your college costs is to stay away from credit cards. It's easy to run up large debts, and credit card shopping sprees are usually not for school-related essentials. It's not too soon to learn one of life's little lessons: The only way to stay out of debt is to spend less money than you have! You'll find out all about debt when you start repaying your student loans; don't add high-interest credit card debt to the mix.

Look for Other Savings

Parents may qualify for lower car insurance when their risky teenage driver heads to college. Also, keep track of pre-college costs. Campus visits, test prep courses, application fees and private counselors can cost thousands. Be judicious.

Accelerate College

The best way to cut the cost of college, is to cut the time you spend there. Here are some ways to shorten your college career:

1. **Take college courses while in high school.** Nearly 40 states have "dual enrollment" programs that let you take real college courses and earn credit toward high school, as well.
2. **Earn credit for advanced placement exams.** Last year, nearly 600,000 students took 921,600 tests in 31 different areas. About 1200 schools give credit for good AP scores; hundreds (including Harvard) grant incoming students sophomore standing. To counter criticism that scoring well on an AP exam is not as tough as passing a college course, many schools are boosting their minimum accepted score from 3 to 4. And some will delay giving credit until students pass the next course in the sequence. In other words, you won't receive credit for that "4" on your Calculus exam, unless you take a higher level math course after you enroll. Each credit hour you pick up can be worth as much as $400 (depending on the college's tuition costs). A test costs only about $75.
3. **Look for three-year degrees.** High profile figures from Stanford and Oberlin have praised the idea. Others feel most students need the full four years to grow, intellectually, emotionally, and occupationally. They're afraid the liberal-arts will get short-changed as students won't have enough time to take the necessary spectrum of courses.
4. **Get credit for life experience.** Every school has its own rules on what counts for what credit. The American Council on Education publishes guidelines in *The National Guide to Educational Credit for Training*

Programs. Another possibility is to take the College Board's College-Level Examination Program (CLEP) Test or the ACT's Proficiency Examination Program (PEP). These are ideal options for students who already have college-level mastery of a subject, either because of their backgrounds or job experience. CLEP Tests cost about $50 and are offered at test centers around the country. For registration information as well as test descriptions and a list of schools that give CLEP credit, click http://www.collegeboard.org/ and search for "CLEP."

5. **Whatever you do, don't take more than four years to graduate!**

Consolidate Your Credits

Regents College of New York offers dozens of associate and baccalaureate degrees. Students may enroll at any time, and move through the program at their own pace. Regents College offers no classes of its own. Rather, it accepts a wide array of credit from accredited sources including distance instruction, campus-based courses at other colleges and universities, and special assessment. Regents College also provides enrolled students with access to its own database of over 7,000 distance learning options. Students work with an academic advisor by mail, phone, fax and e-mail to plan their course of study. Regents College serves nearly 20,000 resourceful, independent learners each year. For program information, write Regents College, The University of the State of New York, 7 Columbia Circle, Albany, NY, 12203, or visit their web site at http://www.regents.edu.

Get Your Degree Via TV

The Jones Education Company, in conjunction with George Washington U., Oklahoma State, Washington State (and several others), lets you earn course credit at home that you may later apply toward degree programs at participating colleges. Sample courses include: Analytical Geometry and Calculus, American Poetry Post-1900, Women Writers, Conversational French, the US Constitution, and Economics (Macro- and Micro-). Visit http://www.meu.edu for more information.

PBS (http://www.pbs.org/learn/als/) also offers an Adult Learning Service.

Become a Cyberstudent

Do you have a travel-intensive job? Or maybe young children at home? Are you short on cash? Time? Thanks to computers, modems, and phone lines, you can now get a quality education without ever setting foot in a classroom. Costs range from $60 to $400 per credit hour.

It's nearly impossible to keep up with distance learning. In only five years, the CyberLeague has increased nearly twenty-fold (to over 1,200 schools). And by the year 2000, up to ninety-percent of our four-year colleges will offer off-site courses. Last year, 1.3 million students took distance learning courses. By the year 2000, that number will increase to six million.

Currently, students have their pick of thousands of credit and non-credit classes. Even our most selective schools are looking for ways to incorporate new learning technologies into their curriculums (without, of course, diminishing the value and prestige of their degrees). How do they work? Students use electronic mail to communicate with faculty and other classmates, get reading assignments, and submit papers, even hold extensive classroom "discussions."

The best way to learn about all these new options is to spend time investigating them on-line. The following links will get you started.

America Online (AOL) For information about AOL's Online Campus, select Keyword "Online Campus."

Globewide Network Academy (http://www.gnacademy.org). A thorough list of distance learning courses and programs.

Internet University (http://www.caso.com/iu.html). Articles about on-line education and links to over 30 course providers and 700 courses.

World Lecture Hall (http://www.utexas.edu/world/lecture/). Links to online courses worldwide, in every field of study.

Yahoo! (http://www.yahoo.com/Education/Distance_Learning/). As usual, Yahoo! is a good starting point for any Internet search.

Some traditional colleges have found that on-line teaching leads to increased demands on faculty time, making it more expensive than old-fashioned face-to-face learning. In other words, you won't always save tuition money by taking this route.

Graduate from http://www.almamater.edu

If you want a more traditional college experience (instead of taking a hodge-podge of courses from computers around the world), you can pay tuition to a single virtual school. You won't get to cheer at football games, or toss water balloons out your dorm window, but you will get to enjoy pictures of smiling students and a graphically pleasing college campus every time you click on your college's home page. Sometimes you can even hang out with your new cyberfriends in a virtual student union or join an alumni association and attend virtual college reunions.

Before you enroll, find out if you can take all your courses on-line or whether there is a residency requirement. Visit a virtual classroom, to make sure your computer can handle all the graphics. And find out how many enrolled students have actually graduated (in fairness, remember, these programs are so new that many don't have any graduates yet).

Athena University (http://www.athena.edu). This virtual school aims to deliver a classical liberal arts education wholly through Internet technologies.

California Virtual University (http://www.california.edu). California's Governor opted out of the Western Governors University project (see below) so his state could achieve greater independence. With 95 participating institutions and 1,600 courses, it's on its way.

Community College Distance Learning Network. Eight community colleges from across the country have banded together to redefine "community." They expect to have nearly 500 course offerings by fall.

New School for Social Research (http://www.dialnsa.edu/). The New School has a reputation for excellence. Its course offerings are top-notch.

Thomas Edison State College (http://www.tesc.edu). Meet the faculty and staff, then decide if one of its 100 areas of study are for you.

University of Phoenix (http://www.uophx.edu/). With both real and virtual classrooms, this accredited for-profit university caters to the working student.

Washington State University (http://www.eus.wsu.edu/edp). Headquartered at the Pullman campus of WSU, the Extended Degree Program lets you earn a Bachelor of Arts in Social Sciences.

Western Governors University (http://www.wgu.edu). This collaborative effort will supplement educational opportunities in the dozen sponsoring states.

A Note on Accreditation: If your program is not accredited, you can't receive federal student aid. It's that simple. Unfortunately, Department of Education officials acknowledge that its current system is not equipped to evaluate cyberschools, which leaves thousands (millions?) of students in the lurch. The problem is two-fold: how to guard against fraud and how to ensure a quality education. Most worrisome is the possibility of virtual universities with virtual students who have real Pell Grants. The Department is trying to catch up as part of Reauthorization (of the Higher Education Act). In the meantime, choose courses carefully; for example, look for those attached to already-accredited "bricks and mortar" campuses.

Strategy Six—
Improve Your Cash Flow

Objective: To pay your family contribution without liquidating assets, hocking the family jewels, or playing Uncle Sam's paper games.

Your family contribution must be paid each semester. For those who have assembled vast quantities of worldly goods, the family contribution can represent a rather sizable sum that usually comes with a friendly note "unless this bill is paid by such and such a date your student will not be allowed to register for classes... ."

How can you pay this bill without selling the family home, jeopardizing your after-retirement financial security or taking out a high-cost commercial loan? You could turn to Uncle Sam's loan programs (the Stafford and PLUS). But Uncle's loans have some drawbacks. One, they are subject to the whims of the political process. And, two, they have the usual comet's tail of paperwork, and other rigmarole generally attached to federal programs. Here are some better options.

Choose Colleges with Innovative Payment Plans

Many colleges offer favorable loan programs, using money from their own endowment funds or from money raised by state tax-exempt bond issues. Other schools allow you to pay the family contribution in installments. See Chapter 9.

Participate in Commercial Tuition Payment Plans

Here is how most plans work: You determine your cash requirement for college—say $3,000 at the start of each semester. The commercial organization forwards that money to the school twice a year, then collects ten $600 payments from you, spread evenly over a number of months. You pay no interest, but must start making payments well before your tuition is due. Frequently, plans charge a flat $40-$50 fee and have a life insurance feature to cover bills in the event of your death. Payment plan sponsors include:

- **Academic Management Services.** 50 Vision Blvd., East Providence, RI 02914, 800/635-0120, http://www.amsweb.com.
- **America's Tuition Plan from USA Group**, 800/348-4607. http://www.usagroup.com.
- **Key Education Resources.** 735 Atlantic Avenue, Boston, MA 02111, 800/540-1855.
- **Tuition Management Systems.** 127 John Clarke Road, Newport, RI 02842, 800/722-4867, 401/849-1550, http://www.afford.com.

Borrow from a Commercial Loan Source

College costs are rising faster than family income and grant resources combined which leaves many families little choice but to borrow more money to pay tuition bills. Commercial lenders are only too happy to be of service. Families can now choose from nearly 100 alternative loan options, each with varying finance charges, interest rates, interest capitalization schedules, borrowing limits, disbursement schedules, incentives, and repayment options. It's no wonder even the savviest families are overwhelmed trying to evaluate which option is best for them. Our advice?

First, ask your college whether it has any recommendations. Many aid administrators have already evaluated the options, and may favor one or two sources. Some schools (especially those with financially-successful, debt-free graduates) even work out special deals with lenders by offering to share default risks.

Second, ask the lender for sample repayment schedules, and read the fine print. Compare Annual Percentage Rates (APRs). Make sure they were calculated using current interest rates. They change fairly often as lenders compete for your business. (Most lenders have web sites that include these repayments schedules.) As you evaluate options, remember that interest payments during your first five years of repayment might be tax deductible.

Third, consider home equity loans or Uncle's PLUS loan. You'll often find the interest rates to be substantially lower than commercial rates. If, however, you don't like the idea of borrowing against your home, or dealing with Uncle Sam, here are some of the largest commercial lenders:

Bank of America Student Maximizer lets you borrow up to the total cost of college less any financial aid. The interest rate equals the 91-day t-bill plus 3.5%, adjusted quarterly, and reduced by .25% if you use an automatic payment plan. Students pay a 5% origination fee and have 15 years to repay. Contact BankAmerica, 800/344-8382, http://www.bankamerica.com/studentunion/.

CitiBank CitiAssist allows undergraduates to borrow up to $10,000/year to a maximum of $50,000. The interest rate equals the prime plus 1%. Students pay no fees, and have up to 12 years to repay. Contact CitiAssist, 800/745-5473, http://www.citibank.com/student/

Educaid. EducaidEXTRA Premier Loan lets families borrow from $1,000 up to the total cost of college less any financial aid. The interest rate equals the 52-week t-bill plus 3.1%, adjusted quarterly. Students pay a 5% or 6% insurance premium, and have up to 15 years to repay. Contact Educaid, 800/343-1809, http://www.educaid.com.

GATE. Guaranteed Access to Education. The interest rate equals the 91-day t-bill plus 3.1%. Families pay a 3% or 5% origination fee. Contact GATE, 30 Little Harbor, Marblehead, MA 01945, 800/895-GATE, http://www.gateloan.com.

Key Education Resources offers the Achiever Loan and Key Alternative Loan. Achiever lets parents borrow from $2,000 up to the total cost of college with 20 years to repay. The interest rate equals the 13-week t-bill plus either 3.95% or 4.5% depending on the selected repayment option. Families pay a 2% - 4% loan fee. The Key Alternative Loan lets students borrow up to $7,500 during their freshman year and $10,00 thereafter to a maximum of $47,500. The interest rate equals the 52-week T-bill plus 3.1% while in school (3.25% thereafter). Families pay a 4% loan fee (9% if they don't have a co-signer). Contact Key Education Resources, 800/KEY-LEND, http://www.keybank.com/educate.htm

NELLIE MAE offers EXCEL and GradEXCEL. Families may borrow from $2,000 up to the total cost of college less any financial aid. The interest rate equals the prime rate plus .75% adjusted monthly. Families pay a 7% guarantee fee and have 20 years to repay. Contact The New England Loan Marketing Association (Nellie Mae), 50 Braintree Hill Park, #300, Braintree, MA 02184, 800/Edu-Loan, http://www.nelliemae.org.

SALLIE MAE. The Signature Student Loan lets students borrow up to the total cost of college less any financial aid. The interest rate equals the t-bill plus 3.1%. After two years of on-time repayment, this rate decreases by .5%. Families pay a 6% fee at disbursement and have 15 years to repay. Contact The Student Loan Marketing Association (SALLIE MAE), 1050 Thomas Jefferson Street, NW, Washington, DC 20007, 800/828-0290, http://www.salliemae.com.

TERI lets you borrow from $500 up to the total cost of college less any financial aid. The interest rate equals the prime. Families pay a 5% guarantee fee (or 6.5% if they choose to defer interest and principal payments until graduation) and have 25 years to repay. TERI also sponsors a Professional Education Plan for graduate students, a DUAL loan for students pursuing a second undergraduate degree, and a Continuing Education Loan for part-timers. Contact The Education Resource Institute, 330 Stuart Street, #500, Boston, MA 02116, 800/255-TERI, http://www.teri.org.

US Bank lets you borrow up to the total cost of college less any financial aid, to a maximum of $100,000. The interest rate equals the prime, reduced by .25% if you use an automatic payment plan (and an additional .25% if your automatic payments come from a US Bank account). After 48 months of on-time payments, borrowers receive a .5% reduction on the remaining balance. Students pay a 6% origination fee and have 10 years to repay. Contact USBank, 800/242-1200, http://www.usbank.com/studentloans/.

Tap Your Home Equity

Competition for your business means you can usually open a home equity account cost-free, and borrow whatever you need, whenever you need it, without having to reapply. To use the funds, you simply write a check or use a credit card. Interest rates float about one percentage point above the prime. And here's an added bonus. Any items you charge—like college tuition—become part of your home mortgage, so your interest payments on loans up to $100,000 become tax-deductible. Since you may deduct interest payments on education loans for only five years, borrowing against home equity may still be the better option.

There are two ways to access home equity: via an equity line of credit or an equity loan. A line of credit turns your home into a checking account. Interest accrues only when (and if) you use the money. Home equity loans turn your home into a pot of cash. You start repaying principal and interest whether you use the money or not. *Which is the better deal?* Home equity loans generally offer lower interest rates, but unless you plan to write a single check for four years worth of tuition, stick with the line of credit. The reason? You won't need all the money at once. In fact, in between tuition bills you should pay down as much of your debt as possible, so you never use up more of your equity than necessary.

Home equity is an extremely easy and flexible way to obtain cash flow assistance on favorable terms. In fact, they allow many families to live way beyond their means, so take care that ease of access to all this money does not result in deep financial problems and cause you to lose your home. The total monthly payments on all of your loans should not exceed 35% of your pre-tax monthly income.

When shopping for the best deal, beware of teaser rates. They're usually only good for the first six months or a year. Here are some other questions to ask: What is the rate of interest? If it's variable, how often can the rate change? On what index is it based? Does it carry a cap? Is there an annual fee? An application fee? An origination fee? Can any of the terms change without my approval? Are there any points charged? What about closing costs? Under what circumstances can the bank require repayment of the outstanding credit?

Hold a Yard Sale

Now that Junior is heading off to school, maybe it's time to start unloading his or her "stuff." Even a modest yard sale can net $1,000.

Borrow Against Your 401(k)

If you are a self-employed with a retirement plan, or, if you participate in a company pension plan like a 401(k), you may be able to borrow against it—usually half the vested amount up to $50,000, less your highest loan balance during the preceding twelve months. The interest rate hovers around the prime, you pay no fees or points, and the cash is available very quickly. To avoid tax and penalties you must repay your account within five years (longer if you use the money to buy a home). You usually make payments via payroll deductions. If you use this option, borrow enough to cover a full year's tuition, not just a semester, since employers may impose additional regulations, such as limiting loans to only one per year.

Use Your IRA

Old Rules: You were hit with a 10% penalty and a bill from the IRS. If you needed $6,000, you drew out a little extra to take care of both the bursar and Uncle Sam.

New Rules: You can withdraw money penalty-free to pay for undergraduate and graduate school expenses. *Is it really that simple?* Who knows. Rules regarding IRA distributions (IRS Publication 590) rival *Ulysses* in their complexity.

If at all possible, however, consider borrowing from other sources. Raids on your IRA and 401 (k) will cause your funds to grow much more slowly, and if you're like most parents, you really do need this money for your retirement. Also, withdrawals from old-IRAs count as income, which means you pay taxes on it. You must also report the distribution as income on your FAFSA thus really hurting your eligibility for student aid. For someone in the 28% bracket, a $10,000 withdrawal would cost $2,800 in federal taxes and add $3,384 to the EFC. Calculation: ($10,000 withdrawal - $2,800 in taxes) x 47% income assessment.

Families with new, Roth IRAs can withdraw the value of their annual contributions (but not their earnings) tax- and penalty-free. If they roll their old IRA into a Roth IRA, the converted amounts will also be available tax- and penalty-free, but not until four calendar years after the conversion.

Are You Credit-Worthy?

Many cash flow helpers are available only to credit-worthy families. If you plan to take out a commercial loan, don't wait until the last minute to apply. Banks have learned that procrastinators (in this case, families who apply in August or September) can be bad risks and reserve their better terms for better borrowers.

What does your credit report say about you? It's a good idea to review your report once a year just to make certain all the information is correct. If it isn't, let the bureau know. They are required to follow-up in a timely fashion, usually within 30 days. Here are phone numbers for the big three of credit bureaus:

- Equifax, 800/685-1111, http://www.equifax.com
- TransUnion, 800/888-4213, http://www.transunion.com
- Experian, 800/682-7654, 888/397-3742, http://www.experian.com

Credit Scoring

Increasingly, commercial lenders are relying on "credit scoring" to help them evaluate your likelihood of repaying a loan. Credit scoring is an automatic evaluation of all the information in your credit bureau report—reduced to a single number based on your general repayment patterns. For example, it assigns weights to:

- Payment history, including the frequency of any delinquencies
- Outstanding debts, including the number of debts, the average balances, and how close the balances are to the credit limits
- Credit history, and the age of the credit lines; the older the better
- New account openings, including the number of accounts opened over the past year; frequent balance shifting is considered a bad sign.
- Types of credit in use, including bank cards, department store cards and installment loans

If you are denied a loan because of your credit score, or if your lender charges you excessively high fees or interest, don't panic. Several commercial lenders offer a one-time reconsideration of your loan request. First, request a copy of your credit report and check it for accuracy. Second, appeal the lender's decision in writing, addressing the reasons you were denied a loan. Finally, consider adding a co-signer.

What People Won't Try

Students Buy Campus Property

Linda Wallace, a University of Wisconsin student, purchased a condo near the campus for $70,000. When she graduated, she sold it for a $30,000 profit—enough to pay off nearly four years of college expenses. Becky and

Louis James bought a three-bedroom house and collected rent from housemates. The James' are tickled pink with their investment. The rent covers mortgage payments. And, by owning property, they established California residency, saving each more than $1,000 a year in out-of-state tuition. Of course, Linda and the James' also saved on room and board charges.

Mom and Dad Buy Campus Rental Property

Not only do you get the benefits of deducting mortgage interest, operating expenses and depreciation, but your college student offspring can receive a steady salary while in school; a salary you may deduct as a business expense. How? By having your student live in one of the units and draw pay from you as property manager. At the same time, he or she saves on room and board. In addition, your campus visits can be written off, because, as far as the tax collector is concerned, the purpose of the trip is to inspect your property. And, if your real estate appreciates, you can sell the property and pocket the after-tax share of the capital gain. There is still one more advantage. If you purchase the property with personal assets, and you make certain the property becomes part of a formally recognized business, you have moved them into the business category which provides you with a net worth adjustment in the need analysis formula.

To take advantage of all this, be sure your property qualifies as rental (and not personal) property. In other words, Mom or Dad cannot use it for more than 14 days or 10% of the total days they rent it out. Here's why: The IRS distinguishes between personal property and rental property. The IRS limits deductible losses from personal property to the amount of rental income received. The IRS places no such limit on losses from rental property, however, these losses may no longer offset salary income. They may only offset passive income—income from limited partnerships or other rental property. Furthermore, the IRS limits the mortgage interest deduction to the amount allocated to rental use (if, however, you rent the property for 100% of the year, you may deduct 100% of the mortgage interest). There is still some good news in all this. Families with AGIs under $100,000 who actively manage their property, may use up to $25,000 of real estate losses to shelter "nonpassive " (salary) income. NOTE: The IRS has 266 pages of rules on passive/active losses. We've tried to summarize it here, but suggest you speak with an accountant or tax attorney before you undertake this kind of venture.

Get on Mom or Dad's Payroll

Can either of your parents give you a job in the family business? If so, it's a great way to shift some income! Your earnings become a tax-deductible business expense. If you're under 18, you do not have to pay social security tax on your wages. And, if you limit your annual earnings to under $4,250 ($6,250 if you contribute to an IRA), you will owe no federal income tax. Assuming you start this when you enter high school and your parents pay about 40% in federal, state and local taxes, they will receive $10,000 in deductions. Of course, under the federal methodology, schools will grab $7,975 of the $25,000 you've earned. Calculation: 35% of non-retirement assets (c. $17,000) plus 50% of prior year income ($6,250) over $2,200, but isn't that what the money was for anyway? Meanwhile, you're beginning to save for retirement. Even without additional contributions, your $8,000 IRA (at 8%) will grow to nearly $335,000 by the time you're 65!

Give a Gift

An individual can make a $10,000 tax-free gift each year to another individual. A married couple can double that and make it a $20,000 gift. Under conventional wisdom, grandparents are the ones who take advantage of this tax wrinkle to help their smart grandchildren with college. Under unconventional wisdom, parents might consider making an annual gift to grandparents. The purpose: To reduce their own asset position for need analysis and pay less for college. The money, meanwhile, really did not leave the family. A gift of securities is especially advantageous. If they have appreciated, you avoid paying tax on the gain. And, if they continue to appreciate after they have been transferred, they can be inherited at this higher value, and still no one has had to pay tax on the gain.

Start an Educational Benefit Trust

Small, closely held corporations can establish trusts to pay the college expenses of employees' children—that means all employees—the president's as well as the staff's. The corporation makes regular payments to the trust. Once an eligible person reaches college age, a predetermined amount of tuition money is withdrawn. This disbursement must be treated as a taxable benefit by the student's parents. Thus, the president who is in a higher bracket will probably gain less than a member of the staff.

Start a Company Scholarship Program

This is not as complex as a trust. Still, the program must meet an IRS test to qualify as a business expense. The test usually involves a set of standards. For example, beneficiaries must have a B average; their mother or father must have worked for the company at least five years. A second part of the test deals with eligibility. All employees' children must be eligible. If too many scholarships go to the children of corporate officers and directors, the company will flunk the test.

CHAPTER 8

LONG-RANGE PLANNING: COLLEGE IS YEARS AWAY

How Much You Need to Save

You've seen them. Charts that tell you to save $800 a month from now until your newborn turns 18 if you want to afford college in the year 2015 (to say nothing of the savings requirements for families with two or three children). You are best advised to ignore these charts and any other "scare-the-pants-off-you" marketing strategy employed by organizations who, of course, will be pleased to help you save (and invest) that $800 per month. Instead, you should save as much money as you can afford, do it systematically, but be realistic, and remember, when your student enters college, your savings can be supplemented by a contribution from your earnings, their earnings and a manageable loan.

If you feel you absolutely must use one of those "How Much You'll Need to Save" charts—a better goal might be to save enough to cover half the cost of college. Also remember, you don't have to have the entire amount saved by the time your student first enrolls. He or she will be there for at least four years—make certain the chart reflects this expanded time frame.

Another option is to calculate your EFC today, project that amount into the future, set that as your savings goal, and hope student aid picks up the balance. Example: Your EFC today would be $5,000. Five years from now, assuming 8% increases in your income and asset situation, your first year EFC would be $7,346 (calculation: $5,000 x 1.08 x 1.08 x 1.08 x 1.08 x 1.08). Over four years, that projects to around $33,100. Now, how does that amount compare to what you have on hand?

Still nervous? Think about buying a $200,000 home. Do you wait until you've saved the entire $200,000? Or do you think in terms of saving enough for the downpayment?

How Your Savings Grow

Heed the advice above, then head for *Kiplinger's Magazine* (http://www.kiplinger.com) or *FinanCenter* (http://www.financenter.com) to watch how your savings grow. Hundreds of companies offer free, on-line calculators, but a quick site-seeing tour showed these to be the most comprehensive, sophisticated (and fun) options. Under "Savings" you'll find "What will it take to save for a college education?"

If you aren't yet on-line, the chart below shows how your fund grows if you stash away $100 per month. In the short run, the rate of return makes very little difference. Over 20 years, however, the difference between 7% and 12% comes to $47,510. Lesson: Start saving early. Take a chance on riskier investments. Let compound interest work for you. Switch to safe investments when college bills loom near.

	7%	8%	10%	12%
Year 1	$1,245	$1,250	$1,267	$1,281
Year 2	2,580	2,610	2,670	2,725
Year 3	4,020	4,080	4,215	4,350
Year 4	5,550	5,675	5,920	6,185
Year 5	7,200	7,400	7,810	8,250
Year 7	10,860	11,285	12,195	13,200
Year 10	17,410	18,415	20,655	23,235
Year 12	22,600	24,210	27,875	32,225
Year 15	31,880	34,835	41,790	50,460
Year 20	52,400	59,290	76,570	99,910

Rule of 72

For novice investors, the Rule of 72 is a quick way to see how fast your money will grow. If you divide 72 by your investment's expected rate of return, the resulting answer is the length of time it will take for your money to double. For example, your $10,000 investment is earning 6%. In twelve years (72/6) it will be worth $20,000. At 8%, your $10,000 will equal $20,000 in just nine years.

Tax Planning vs. College Aid

When college is still years away, the name of the game is to accumulate enough money to help with the inevitable bills. Unfortunately, plans to minimize tax liability sometimes run counter to plans to maximize financial aid eligibility—making decisions about saving money more complex. The trick is knowing when tax planning and college planning run counter to each other, and when they are complementary. Of course, constantly changing tax laws and financial aid regulations, means no one can predict with certainty what rules will be in effect when your tuition bills come due—5, 10, 15 or 20 years from now.

Example 1: The first decision a family must make is whether to save money in the parents' or the child's name. For tax purposes, unearned income derived from parental assets can be assessed at a higher rate than unearned income from a child's assets. (For children under 14, the first $700 in interest or dividend income is tax-free. The next $700 is taxed at the child's rate. And any unearned income in excess of $1,400 is taxed at the parents's rate.) For financial aid purposes, however, parental assets are currently assessed at no more than 5.6% while student assets are assessed at a flat 35%. There's a chance these rates may change for 1999/2000; assuming they don't, this differential wipes out all the tax advantages previously received. The lesson? If the family has any chance of qualifying for financial aid, it should save in the parents's name.

Example 2: In saving for retirement, 401(k)s, 403(b)s, Keoghs, SEPs and IRAs all grow tax-deferred year after year. For financial aid purposes, they are excluded from need analysis. All this makes saving for retirement one of the most effective ways to accumulate money and lower your expected contribution to college costs.

Example 3: Middle income families can choose one entree from a menu of college-related tax incentives, the Hope Scholarship Credit, the Lifetime Learning Credit and the Education IRA. Which one is most beneficial to you? The answer will vary depending on the cost of your school, the number of years before tuition bills come due, and your annual income.

Getting Good Financial Advice

Where do you go to get good advice on maximizing savings, both for college and for retirement? Most people can get all the information they need by clipping articles from consumer-oriented personal finance magazines like *Kiplinger's, Money, Smart Money,* and *Forbes*. Other people rely on a stockbroker for advice about the marketplace, an accountant for tax strategies, and an attorney for the latest on trusts and estates. Between these three groups of professionals, families can get a lot of sound advice on financial planning. There is, however, another group of professionals who should be able to combine the advice you get from your broker, your accountant and your lawyer—that is the certified financial planner.

Financial Planners to the Rescue

Personal finance experts appear under many guises—stockbrokers, financial planners, bankers, accountants, and insurance agents. Most of these people are bright, resourceful professionals who can be of genuine help in the college planning process. Unfortunately, some of them are better at planning only one thing—their own lucrative retirement. Before you enlist in their services, learn something about investing, write down your objectives, and ask questions.

Are they fee only planners or do they work on commission? About how much are you going to pay for their services? Fee only planners charge by the hour. Comprehensive financial plans can cost you from $1,500 to $3,500. While this may be more expensive in the short-run, fee only planners point out that their counterparts don't always have real incentives to provide you with totally unbiased service (i.e., some planners will give you nothing but a glossy sales pitch for whatever products bring the largest commission). If possible, find out how much of the planner's income comes from each of four sources: commissions, fees you pay for advice, fees you pay for them to manage your funds, and fees they receive from companies that pay them to sell their products. And don't confuse fee-only planners with fee-based planners who charge both fees AND commissions.

What is their field of expertise? Their investment strategies? Are they selling you boilerplate from a parent company or is truly a personalized plan? Your planner should be familiar with investment strategies of all types—traditional advice on retirement planning and estate planning is not necessarily compatible with sound college planning. Your advisor should be able to explain these possible conflicts and help you maximize your resources (while minimizing your tax consequences). And, your planner should be a good listener, incorporating your tolerance for risk into your financial plan.

What is their prior work experience? Did they start out in law? Accounting? Insurance? Stock market? A college financial aid office? Charm school? How long have they been in business? How many clients do they have? How many new clients per year? Unless the firm specializes in short-term college planning, heavy turnover is a bad sign!

What are their professional credentials? Do they still have ties to an insurance company or brokerage house? Are they with an established company such as American Express or Waddell & Reed? Have they been certified by a reputable group such as The Institute of Certified Financial Planners?

Is the planner providing you with a service you can't get from your accountant, your stockbroker or your lawyer? There is no sense in paying for the same service twice.

Finally, ask for references. Reputable planners will be happy to oblige. Most will be registered as investment advisors with their home state or the Securities and Exchange Commission. Ask for a copy of your planner's state or SEC disclosure form (Form ADV). It will tell you all about his or her academic, professional and work history. For the number of your state commission, call the North American Securities Administrators Association, 888/846-2722. For a check on your planner's CFP designation, call 888/CFP-MARK or click http://www.cfp-board.org.

For more information, or to find a planner in your area:

- *American Society of CLU and ChFC,* 800/392-6900. Insurance agents and planners with an insurance orientation, these chartered financial consultants must also have at least three years experience in the field.
- *Institute of Certified Financial Planners,* 800/282-PLAN. Professional membership organization of 11,000 CFPs.
- *National Association of Personal Financial Advisors,* 888/333-6659. Trade group of fee-only planners, http://www.napfa.org.
- *International Association for Financial Planning.* 800/930-4511. Trade group that requires its 13,000 members to have a state license, or SEC registration.
- *American Institute of Certified Public Accountants,* 888/999-9256. Personal Financial Specialists, or CPAs who have passed a financial planning test and have practical planning experience, http://www.cpapfs.org.

Seeing the Sites

Professional money managers no longer have the same information advantage they used to. Personal finance sites litter cyberspace, and with a few mouse clicks you can find everything from full research reports to financial news headlines to mutual fund prospectuses to ten-minute stock tickers. Look for:

- Investment houses (for example, www.lehman.com, www.jpmorgan.com)
- Brokerage firms (for example, www.schwab.com, www.merrill-lynch.ml.com)
- Personal finance magazines (for example, www.smartmoney.com, www.moneymag.com, www.kiplinger.com)

- Mutual fund companies (for example, www.scudder.com, www.janus.com, www.templeton.com, www.morningstar.com, www.fidelity.com, www.vanguard.com, www.troweprice.com)

They all have little treats for you.

Of course, most site sponsors give you this free information because they want you to subscribe to their publications or give them all your money to invest, but that's no reason to forsake their largess. Just be a savvy surfer.

For a more general start place, try Yahoo!'s personal finance link at www.yahoo.com. Even better: The Syndicate, www.moneypages.com. Its partially-annotated links take you to stock sites, bond sites, mutual fund sites and 1,600 other finance-related sites, ranging from accounting to forecasts to newsletters to taxes.

If you're primarily interested in mutual funds, try Mutual Funds Interactive,www.brill.com. If you're looking for a specific company, try CompaniesOnline (www.companiesonline.com)

If you have months with nothing to do other than click through investment sites, try Invest-o-rama (www.investorama.com) with its 4,300 links, or Investor Guide (www.investorguide) with its 1,000 questions and answers.

If you want a more cooperative experience, and a wider range of "expert" opinions, join Motley Fool's rapidly growing club www.motleyfool.com). Investment advice comes from former stockbrokers, as well as 750,000 monthly site visitors with unknown credentials.

If you're serious about investing try Riskview.com (www.riskview.com). Thanks to a Dow Jones-IBM-Infinity Financial Technology partnership, you can now measure total returns and estimate portfolio risk with the best of them!

If you're willing to pay for investment advice, The Street (www.thestreet.com) employs dozens of market analysts who will keep you up-to-date with breaking news and sophisticated discussions.

Savings Philosophies

Ask ten financial advisors to recommend the best way to save for college and you're likely to get ten very different answers. Why? Because it's very difficult to offer sound investment advice in a vacuum, i.e., without knowing how much risk a family is comfortable with taking. As a general rule, the safer the investment option, the lower the return. The riskier the option, the greater the return (as well as the potential for a huge loss). Most of the plans described in this chapter are safe, or as some would say, plain vanilla, and don't require professional fund managers to turn a profit.

How can you tell if your portfolio is too risky? If you consistently wake up in the middle of the night concerned about a price drop in your stock or bond fund, then rethink the composition of your portfolio.

How else can you tell if an investment is right for you? If you don't understand the investment, its liquidity, its true costs, or how it works, then stay away.

Sample Portfolios

The composition of your portfolio should change with the age of your children. When they are young, you can afford to take more risks than you can when tuition bills are just around the corner. Here's one example:

The Early Years (Under 6). Time is on your side. About 90% of your money should be in stock funds, split between aggressive growth (the most risky) and growth and income (less risky). The other 10% should be in something safe like a money market or CD.

The Middle Years (6 to 13). Keep about 90% in stock funds, but as your college-bound student ages, gradually shift the money out of aggressive growth and into more conservative growth and income.

The Pre-College Years (14 to 17). According to personal finance expert Jane Bryant Quinn, money you'll need within four years shouldn't be invested in a mutual fund, because historically, that's how long it takes for stocks to drop from a peak and rise back to the original price. Our advice? During these years, aim to keep 25% of your money in growth and income funds, and move the rest (over the next four years) into CDs, money market fund, or US Treasury strips that mature during your student's first two years of college.

If you think you're going to qualify for financial aid, time these sales so the income figures you must submit for need analysis aren't inflated with capital gains.

If you don't think you're going to qualify for financial aid, consider switching money from your name into your child's. If you transfer appreciated stock funds into your child's account before you convert them into safer investments, the profit will be taxed at the child's lower rate.

The College Years (18 to 21). Remember, you have to pay tuition bills for four years. Keep your money safe. Some planners recommend putting everything in CDs and money markets. *SmartMoney* recommends treasury strips that mature during your student's last two years of college (while still keeping 20% in low-risk funds).

Pay Yourself First

The best way to accumulate money is to pay yourself first, and use an investment strategy called Dollar-Cost-Averaging. The premise is simple. You have a fixed amount of money withheld from your paycheck each month and invest that money in something like a mutual fund; you don't have to worry about whether the market is up or down, and you're pretty certain to be safe from financial disaster. In fact, you'll probably do better than most professional fund managers. Why does this work? Let's say you have $200 withheld from your paycheck and wired into a brokerage account each month where it buys shares of your favorite mutual fund. When the market is up, your $200 buys relatively fewer shares than when the market is low, so the average cost of your shares is lower than the average price during the period.

	Monthly Investment	Price per Share	Shares Purchased
	$200	$25	8.00
	$200	$25	8.00
	$200	$30	6.66
	$200	$25	8.00
	$200	$20	10.00
	$200	$25	8.00
Totals	**$1,200**	**$150**	**48.66**

Your average cost per share is $24.66 ($1,200/48.66) while the average market price per share is $25 ($150/6). You win! Here's another way to look at your smart investment: Had you simply purchased eight shares each month, you would have only 48 shares for your $1,200. Now you have 48.66. You win again! This method of regular, systematic savings allows you to accumulate funds fast, especially if you start when your children are very young!

Are you doomed if you aren't this disciplined? Of course not. What's important is that you save. An alternative approach is to put all your "surprise" money into a college savings account, for example, tax refunds, year-end bonuses or gifts from grandma.

Custodial Accounts and Trusts

Families that want to save money in the child's name have two main choices—custodial accounts and trusts.

Custodial Accounts

Custodial accounts under the Uniform Gift to Minors Act (UGMA) accept money. Custodial accounts under the Uniform Transfer to Minors Act (UTMA) also accept property. Both are irrevocable gifts to a child where a custodian is responsible for managing the funds until the minor reaches the age of majority. The money accumulates under the minor's lower tax liability. UGMA and UTMA accounts are easy to set up (just call your banker or broker), but they have one major drawback. Once the funds are turned over (as early as age 18), the child can do whatever he or she wants with them. Pay for college, pay for a new car, pay for a lifetime supply of jelly donuts...

Individuals may make a tax-free gift worth up to $10,000 to either of these two accounts

Minority Trust

Under section 2503(c) of the tax code, families can establish an inter-vivos (living) trust for a minor, provided the funds are used solely for the benefit of that minor. This trust has one main advantage over a UGMA. The trustee has control over the funds until the "donee" is 21 years old—well into the college paying years

Individuals may also each make a tax-free gift of up to $10,000 to a trust. The drawbacks? You'll need an attorney, and as much as $2,500 in attorney fees to set up a trust and, you'll have to file separate income tax returns for them. Worst of all, trust income is taxed more heavily than individual income. The idea was to nab the rich. Unfortunately, many of the affected trusts are those set up to care for the disabled or to pay for college. The first $1,700 in trust income is taxed at 15%; the next $2,300 is taxed at 28%; the next $2,100 is taxed at 31%, the next $2,250 at 36% and anything above $8,350 is taxed at 39.6%.

Charitable Remainder Unitrust

You donate a set amount of money (usually at least $50,000) to a college or a charitable institution, such as your alma mater or local art museum, but stipulate that from 5% to 10% of the value of the gift, be paid out each year as income to a fund for your college-bound student. At the end of a designated time frame, the principal goes to the college or charity. Meanwhile, you, the donor (1) receive a substantial tax deduction (2) build a college fund for junior and (3) give money to a favored charity. Many people choose to donate an appreciated asset for the trust to sell, because that way they avoid paying tax on the appreciation, yet they get to deduct the full market value of the item. You'll need professional help to set up such a trust.

CDs and T-bills

Some of the safest, and easiest ways for parents to save money are through short- and long-term Certificates of Deposit, Treasury bills (which mature in 13, 26 or 52 weeks), Treasury notes (which mature in 1 to 10 years), Treasury bonds (which mature in 10 to 30 years), and US savings bonds. As you shop around for rates, remember brokerage firms can usually get you the highest rates on CDs and money-market funds. In August, 1998, you could get six-month CDs that yield 5.89%, five-year CDs that yield 6.36%, three-month Treasury bills at 5.02%, one-year bills at 5.21%, two-year Treasury notes at 5.31%, five-year notes at 5.34%, ten-year notes at 5.39%, and 30-year Treasury bonds at 5.54%. Treasuries are exempt from state and local taxes, so for most families, these yields are even higher.

EE Savings Bonds

Parents who purchase EE savings bonds will not have to pay tax on the accrued interest, provided they use the proceeds for their children's education. To qualify, they must pay the money directly to an eligible institution, or to a state tuition savings plan. Full benefits are available to couples with incomes of $78,350 or less and to single parents with incomes of $52,250 or less when it's time to redeem their bonds. The exemption tapers off for families with incomes above these limits, and disappears completely for couples with incomes above $108,350 and single parents with incomes above $67,250. Income limitations will be indexed for inflation, so, by the time you redeem your bonds, the income ceilings may be much higher. One Catch: Your income for the year in which you plan to redeem your bonds includes all the interest the bonds have earned! This additional income may push some families right past the income cut-offs and ironically eliminate their exclusion!

Bonds may be purchased at any time during the year, but the purchasers must be at least 24 years of age. In other words, families with incomes too high to benefit from the tax break may not have their children take advantage of the benefit by buying the bonds themselves. For the same reason, grandparents and couples who file separate tax returns are also ineligible to participate. If you mistakenly bought bonds in your child's name, you can plead your case by filing a reissue request on Public Debt Form 4000 with the Bureau of Public Debt, Savings Bond Operations Office, Division of Transactions and Rulings, Parkersburg, WV 26106-1328.

EE Bonds equal 90% of the average yield of five-year Treasury securities over the preceding six months. Rates are adjusted twice a year (May 1 and November 1) and currently stand at 5.06%. To encourage long-term saving, investors who cash in within five years of purchase will forfeit three months worth of interest. For rate information after November 1, call 800/4US BOND.

Bonds are available through payroll deductions and at most banks and credit unions. They will soon be available on-line. For more information, get *The Savings Bond Question and Answer Book* and *Questions and Answers About Education Savings Bonds* from the Department of Treasury, Savings Bond Operation Office, Parkersburg, WV 26106, or visit the Savings Bond Home Page, http://www.savingsbonds.gov.

Inflation Bonds

For people who worry about the impact of inflation on the value of their bonds, Uncle Sam has introduced bonds which have yields pegged to the inflation rate. The ten-year bonds, officially known as Treasury Inflation Protection Securities (TIPS) will soon be available in denominations ranging from $50 to $10,000 and (based on the last auction) carry a fixed interest rate of 3.77%, plus inflation. For example, during a year when inflation is 3%, the principal of a $1,000 bond will increase to $1,030. Interest will be calculated based on the revised principal. In this example, interest payments would equal $38.83 making the total return (6.883%) better than the non-inflation indexed 10-year treasury (5.41%).

On the downside, TIP holders cannot collect any principal until the bond matures. Also, they have to pay annual federal taxes on their interest income as well as on any additions to principal. On the upside, the bonds are very safe, which means purchasers can devote a greater percentage of the rest of their portfolio to high yielding stocks without increasing their portfolio's overall risk. You can buy TIPS by opening a free Treasury Direct Account (for information, call 202/874-4000).

Mutual Funds

The best way for small investors to play the market is via a mutual fund. By having your money pooled with money from lots of other investors, you gain the advantage of diversification and professional fund management. Mutual funds are usually categorized by investment goal. For example:

Growth Funds aim to increase the value of your investment rather than provide you with a large stream of dividends. Growth Funds generally invest in stocks and are best suited for people who plan to hold on to the fund for a longer period of time, for example, people who won't need to tap their college fund for many years.

Income Funds focus on providing investors with high current income (i.e., large dividends). Income funds generally invest in corporate and government bonds, or stocks with good dividend-paying records. They bring higher yields than money market funds, but their share price can move up or down, making them a little riskier.

Money Market Funds are very safe, and accordingly, offer the lowest return. Money Market Funds generally invest in high quality securities with short maturities (e.g., bank CDs, US Treasury bills).

Other types of funds include hybrids of the above, for example, Aggressive Growth, Balanced Growth, and Growth and Income. Investors will also find specialty funds grouped by company type (for example, energy, environmental, health care, real estate, utilities, etc.).

To simplify your taxes, set up four separate funds. Then, to cover each year's college expenses, sell one fund. Also remember, as students approach college age, families should lower their investment risk by shifting the balance of their savings from aggressive growth funds to growth and income funds, and finally, to money markets.

You can either buy funds yourself (using data from the *Wall Street Journal*, or magazines like *Smart Money, Kiplinger's* and *Money)* or, work with a broker. You can even buy "Life-Cycle Funds" which are pre-fabbed allocation pies sold by mutual fund companies; there's a pie for every investment goal.

Educate America

So how do you choose "the best" mutual fund or annuity from the thousands (and thousands) of options? Harris Insight Funds and the College Life Insurance Company of America hope their newly-launched *Educate America* program will convince you to give their companies a closer look. Parents (or grandparents) who invest with Harris or College Life will earn an undergraduate tuition reduction equal to 5% of their average annual account balance to a maximum of $13,800 or one year's tuition, whichever is less (of course, they receive their investment gains as well). Students may use this reward at any of 100 participating schools—mostly small, liberal-arts colleges in the East and Midwest. Example:A $20,000 balance held for one year would earn a tuition reduction reward of $1,000.

As an added bonus, *Educate America* offers a "Total College Readiness Package" including a quarterly newsletter and a college application workbook, something you might need, since admission to participating colleges is not guaranteed. (If your student does not attend a participating college, you don't get the discount, but you do keep your initial investment plus any gains.)

Participants pay $39.95 per child to join the program, $19.95 per child per year up through 7th grade, and $39.95 per child per year from 8th grade on. For more information, contact Sage Scholars, Inc., 100 Four Falls Corporate Center, #209, W. Conshohocken, PA 19428, 888/222-0550, or click to http://www.student-aid.com.

Is it a Trust? Or a Mutual Fund?

Royce Gift Shares (800/221-4268) and American Century Gifttrust (800/345-2021) can be set up to allow withdrawals for undergraduate or graduate education. If you don't use the money for college, you can specify when the beneficiary may next have access to the money, for example, when he or she turns 25 or 30 or 65. It's much simpler to set up than the trusts discussed earlier (i.e., you shouldn't need a lawyer), however, the trust does pay taxes at the trust's rate. Royce's minimum investment is $2,500. American Century's minimum investment is only $500. Both are irrevocable, and have a history of volatility.

Zero Coupon Bonds

These are bonds stripped of their interest coupons. Owners receive no income while holding the bonds. Instead, income compounds and reinvests semi-annually. At some future date, you receive a fixed sum that is much larger than your purchase price. For example, a 7.4% zero maturing in 2008 will cost you $486 per thousand (you pay $4,860 today to get $10,000 ten years from now). Zero coupons are seldom called "zero coupons." Instead, investors should look for them under acronyms like STRIPS (Separate Trading of Registered Interest and Principal of Securities).

Many families like to use zeros to save for college because they can time maturity dates to coincide with tuition bills. Also, they know exactly how much money they will receive when those bills come due, a certainty that for some families is more important than taking chances with a riskier portfolio. Zeros have, however, several drawbacks which families should consider before deciding on this type of long-term investment.

- Corporate bonds and municipal bonds may be called before they reach maturity, and if you miss the call, you may be in for a nasty surprise when you go to claim your money. Here's why. When a bond is called (usually because of declining interest rates) interest stops accumulating, and its value freezes. The $10,000 face value you thought you were getting could turn out to be little more than the bond's original cost. Treasury bonds are safer, as they carry a no-call provision.

- No income is distributed, yet tax must be paid yearly on the accrued interest. The exception is for tax-free zero-coupon municipals.
- There is no way to know the value of the money when the bond matures. If interest rates rise, the bond value drops. If interest rates drop, the bond value rises.
- Will the bond's issuer will be around in 20 years for the big payoff? To be safe, avoid risky bonds and those issued by small municipalities (AAA is good, DDD is not).

State-Based College Savings Programs

To encourage early planning for college, over forty states sponsor (or will soon sponsor) college savings programs. These plans have taken-off thanks mostly to Section 529 of the tax code which clarified that money in state-sponsored tuition plans could grow tax-deferred, with families paying federal tax (at the student's rate) on the appreciation when they redeem the money for college. The 1997 Taxpayer Relief Act expanded the scope of these plans so they may now cover room and board, as well as tuition and fees. Furthermore, families can contribute up to $50,000 in a lump sum without incurring a gift tax.

One caveat: A student may be the beneficiary of both an education IRA and a state prepaid tuition plan, however, no contribution may be made to that student's education IRA during the same year a contribution is made to his or her state plan.

Prepaid Tuition Plans

Eighteen states have Prepaid Tuition Plans in which parents can guarantee four years of tuition at any of the state's public (or in some cases, private) colleges by making a lump sum investment or periodic payments. No two plans are the same, but most operate under the same assumptions: The investment amount depends on the child's date of entry into college, the percentage of costs the family wants to cover, and the degree of flexibility parents desire in withdrawing funds. The state invests the money and pays the student's tuition when he or she enters college, and takes the risk of actually guaranteeing tuition.

Smaller tuition increases have eroded the value of prepaid tuition plans so even less-sophisticated investors can usually earn greater returns on their own. Most families, however, are not comfortable playing investment games. They want an easy way to guarantee they'll have enough money for their children's education, and are happy to sacrifice a percentage point or two of interest to buy that security.

Savings Plan Trust

The real growth, however, is in state-sponsored education savings accounts. Twenty-five states are crafting programs that give families big incentives to save for college, and several advantages over prepaid tuition plans. First, they offer families greater flexibility. Families are not restricted to in-state schools, but can frequently use their investment at any US college. Second, they offer potentially greater returns. State savings plans do not "guarantee" that they will keep pace with tuition increases, however, they typically invest in stock- and bond-markets, which currently earn a much higher return than 5% (the average tuition increase over the past few years). Many of these plans are not even restricted to state residents, so shop around!

For more information about both types of state-based savings plans (and a state listing), contact the National Association of State Treasurers, College Savings Plan Network, PO Box 11910, Lexington, KY 40578, 606/244-8053 (fax), http://www.collegesavings.org.

Life Insurance

Many people are completely (and justifiably) confused by the endless variety of life insurance options. Essentially there are two types: Term, which provides protection for a fixed period of time but has no cash value (unless you die); and Permanent, which provides lifelong protection, including a death benefit and savings component and does have a cash value if you decide to give up your policy. This second type of insurance is frequently touted as a good vehicle for long term saving needs (like college) and comes in three forms:

- Whole Life—premiums remain constant over the life of the policy;
- Universal Life—premiums are flexible subject to certain minimums and maximums
- Variable Life—death benefits and cash values vary with the performance of your portfolio.

Variable Life gets the most attention from consumer-oriented investment writers since it provides investors with the most flexibility. It is also, however, the riskiest. In fact, you should only use insurance products to save for college if you're certain to maintain the policy for a long time, otherwise fees and commissions will probably make the surrender value worth little more than your initial investment. *And don't decide to invest in life insurance while under pressure or because of financial aid rules that place the value of your insurance outside the need analysis formula.*

Variable Annuities

Best described as "mutual funds bundled in an insurance wrapper," annuities let you stash an unlimited amount of money into a tax-deferred account which also escapes the eye of need analysis. But before you invest all your money in this way, consider the possible impact of 1997's Taxpayer Relief Act:

- Pre-retirement withdrawals for college expenses are more easily made from an IRA. In other words, unless you have lots of money to put away or will be older than 59 1/2 when your student begins college, IRAs (which currently also escape the eye of need analysis) are probably a better place for your college savings.
- Annuity earnings won't benefit from the new, lower capital gains rate. Annuities convert capital gains into ordinary income, therefore, instead of paying 20% on your earnings, you could pay up to double that amount.

Useful Resources

Some insurance companies provide advice on college selection and financing. Although they'll probably be happy to sell you insurance (if you need it), the planning service is free, as is the phone call: American National Life Insurance (800/777-2372) sponsors a Collegiate Planning Center, and will refer you to lenders for the Stafford Loan.

Tax Payer Relief Act Of 1997

As soon as you figure out how to make wise investment decisions based on new capital gains rates and IRA options, Congress will change the rules. In the meantime, here are some points to consider.

Capital Gains, Capital Pains

The top rate on long-term capital gains is now 20% (10% for those in the 15% tax bracket). While new tax rules shouldn't be your only consideration, here are some ways to benefit from this new, lower rate:

- Avoid frequent trading. You must hold an asset for at least 18 months to benefit from lower capital gains rates (although Congress has already approved reducing this holding period to 12 months).
- When choosing a mutual fund, ask about "turnover rates." The higher the rate, the more likely it is to generate short-term gains (which are

taxed at ordinary rates). 100% means the fund (on average) holds a stock for one year before selling; 50% means the fund holds it for two years.

- Invest in stocks and mutual funds that focus on growth rather than dividends. Dividends, too, are taxed as ordinary income.
- Keep stocks in taxable accounts and bonds in tax-deferred accounts (annuities, IRAs and 401 (k)s). All investment earnings in tax-deferred accounts get taxed as ordinary income when withdrawn, even if the earnings came from capital gains.

Roth IRAs

Your contribution to these new IRAs is not tax deductible, however, your money does grow tax-free. The benefit is phased out for single taxpayers with incomes between $95,000 and $110,000, and couples with incomes between $150,000 and $160,000. You may withdraw money penalty-free to pay for college tuition, however, the withdrawal is tax-free only if the account has been open at least 5 years, and the holder is at least 59 1/2. Otherwise, you may withdraw only your original contribution tax-free.

In Whose Name—Parent or Child?

Sure, you might still save a few tax pennies by keeping money in your child's name, but you can also lose control of the money and eliminate yourself from consideration for low-interest student loans.

Let's attach some numbers. A family in the 35% bracket (this includes an allowance for state taxes) elects to make a yearly gift of $1,000 to a child, starting at birth. They invest the money at 8%. At the end of 18 years, the kitty will be worth $34,892. Had the family added $1,000/year to a parental account, also invested at 8%, the money, under higher taxation, would have grown to only $28,662. (If you had taken advantage of new tax-deferred IRA options and/or new 20% capital gains rates, the difference between accounts wouldn't be nearly that great.)

Now it's need analysis time. For each of the next four years, the student's kitty is depleted by 35% of its value. The parental kitty, on the other hand, is depleted by only 5.6%. At the end of four years, the child's kitty has shrunk by $28,664 to $6,228. The parental kitty has shrunk by only $5,904 and is still a respectable $22,758.

So what should you do?

If there's no chance your family will qualify for aid, save in the child's name, the money will accumulate more quickly. To take advantage of the fact that all unearned income of children over 14 is taxed at the child's rate, if you have young children, give them tax-deferred investments such as fast-growing stocks. Once the child reaches 14, sell the stocks, and place the proceeds in a safe, but high yielding investment. Then spend it all on tuition.

If there is any chance for getting financial aid, save in the parents name.

Of course, predicting aid eligibility is no easy task. Constantly changing tax laws and student assistance laws confuse professionals, to say nothing of those whose jobs do not depend on keeping up with Congressional activity. Here's what we advise. Assume the ratio between present earnings and assets and present college costs will hold for the future. Run your family through the Federal Methodology in Appendix 1. Compare the estimated family contribution with the current costs of colleges of interest. If your family contribution is less than the cost of college today, you may qualify for aid in the future. Remember to divide the parental contribution by the number you will have in college at least half-time at any one time.

CHAPTER 9

THE COLLEGES

Rethinking Your Ideas About Admission

Unless you plan to attend one of the few highly selective colleges, banish the thought that it's hard to get into college. It's easy. Over 90% of all students attend their first or second choice school. In the old days, you applied to five or six schools; one or two where your odds were fifty-fifty, a couple where you had the edge, and a safety school that was sure to take you. Today your selection strategy needs to be based on factors other than the possibility of rejection. First and foremost you should consider quality of education and your fit with each school, but then you should consider its financial aid offerings. Look for:

- Schools with innovative payment plans. These can ease cash flow problems.
- Schools with innovative aid programs. These can funnel money toward "desirable" students.
- Schools with mountains of cash. These can usually handle your need.
- Schools with a reputation for leadership in your selected field of study. They are likely to be well-endowed in your field.

Financial Aid in the Admission Process

If students can't afford the school, they aren't going to enroll! This simple truth means the line between financial aid and admission is beginning to disappear. New experiments in "enrollment management" and the intense competition for quality students translate into "no-need" awards and "preferential packaging." In other words, aid administrators are being pressured to reassess family contributions and the contents of aid packages for certain students to help the school meet enrollment goals. Here are some things to consider as you plan your college selection strategy.

1. Apply early for financial aid. Most schools have limited resources so the first people in line are more likely to have their need met than the last.

2. Forget about "Early Decision" if you need financial aid. Your admission chances may be better, but since the school knows you're committed to attending, it doesn't need to sweeten your aid package.
3. Apply to colleges where your qualifications place you in the upper 25% of the applicant pool. That standing will have a strong impact on the composition of your aid package. Schools make no bones about that. Oberlin (OH), for example, says its "policy is to award aid packages with larger portions of grant aid to those students who show great academic promise or who can contribute to the College's diversity. This policy is consistent with Oberlin's goal of maintaining a high-quality academic program and attracting a talented and diverse student body."
4. For better leverage, pair your applications. Apply to two four-star schools; and two three-star schools; not just one of each. You might pay more in application fees, however, when you receive acceptance letters from schools of similar prestige, you may be able to improve your aid package. Schools may not mind losing you to lesser or higher regarded colleges. But they will fight to keep you away from direct competitors. Even Harvard says, "We expect that some of our admitted students will have particularly attractive offers from the institutions with new aid programs, and those students should not assume that we will not respond."

It Doesn't Hurt To Ask

The financial aid sections of college catalogues are often very vague. Pious generalities outnumber hard facts while the tone is reminiscent of sweepstakes notices. Why do schools do this? First of all, vagueness about financial aid is important when you know Uncle Sam will release some enormous rule change two days after 500,000 copies of your school's materials come back from the printer. Second, it's hard to be precise about what kinds of aid a student might expect when decisions vary from student to student depending on their income and asset situation and their admission qualifications. And third, the "you may be a grand prize winner" attitude is essential for colleges trying to convince students not to worry about the $25,000 bill they'll face if they enroll! While it's true that aid packages at many schools are quite generous (Princeton, for example, awards $19 million per year from its own scholarship funds), frequently, that generosity takes the form of loans, which you must repay.

There are exceptions. Saint Olaf (MN) says, "We believe the primary responsibility for meeting college costs rests with the student and the family. Because going to college is an experience that is out of the ordinary, it sometimes also requires some out of the ordinary financial sacrifices." And Central College (IA) made no bones about using aid for recruiting. "Frankly, we're out to attract talented and academically-ambitious students and we'll reward them for their past performance as well as for their potential."

But such candor is seldom found. To get answers, you will have to write. Don't be bashful. You have the right to ask colleges as many questions as they ask you. Find out about innovative payment plans of the type illustrated in the next two sections. And get answers to the following:

1. Do you guarantee to meet a student's financial need (or a certain percentage of a student's need)? *Reason*: Under the Federal Methodology, most families are eligible for financial aid. Unfortunately, there's not enough federal money to help all these eligible families.
2. Do you guarantee to meet need (or a certain percentage of need) for all four years? *Reason*: A handful of colleges do a bait and switch—offering generous grant-filled aid packages to lure new students, then deserting them (or giving them loans) in post-freshman years. Even if the school promises you a fixed size grant for all four years, remember, tuition will increase each year, and that generous package that met your full need in Year One, may not come close by Year Four.
3. Do you have a per-student-limit on the aid you provide? *Reason*: Some schools set ceilings, such as a $10,000 per student maximum.
4. Do I have to demonstrate a minimum amount of need to qualify for aid? *Reason*: Some schools won't consider students for aid unless they have at least $500 need.
5. Do you have a standard "unmet need" figure for each aid recipient? *Reason*: Some schools will leave each person $500 short.
6. What is your expected "student earnings" figure? *Reason*: Regardless of need analysis, some colleges expect students to contribute a certain amount (which can be as high as $1,700 per year), whether it comes from the student's contribution or the parents' contribution.
7. Is there an application cut-off date for meeting a student's need? *Reason*: Some colleges say they can meet all need for students whose applications are received prior to Date X. But no such guarantee extends to students who apply after that.
8. Do you maintain financial aid "waiting lists" or accept students on an "admit-deny" basis? *Reason*: These practices mean financially needy students are welcome but they will not receive financial aid.

9. If I don't apply for aid in my freshman year, can I apply in subsequent years? *Reason*: You can't be prohibited from applying, however, you may get nothing because many colleges give priority to "continuing recipients."
10. What percentage of alumni contribute to the school's annual fundraising campaign? *Reason*: If you are worried about the college's financial survival, you can't ask for a corporate balance sheet. But you can check with the college's development office to learn whether the school has strong alumni support. At some schools, it's as high as 65% and when colleges have this kind of loyalty, they are not going to fold.
11. Will my request for financial aid have any impact on my admission chances? *Reason.* In an effort to meet 100% of financial need, some colleges are having to base their last few admission decisions on the family's ability to pay the bill.
12. Do you place any time limits on financial aid? *Reason*: With fewer and fewer students finishing their degrees in four years, Uncle Sam, the states and the colleges are all looking for ways to hurry students along.
13. How do you package "outside scholarships?" *Reason*: Different colleges have different "aid philosophies." One school in New York will take the first $300 of the outside scholarship and 20% of the rest and use it to replace a loan. What's left reduces the student's grant from that school. At other colleges, the outside scholarship merely replaces, on a dollar for dollar basis, collegiate grants, causing the poet Leider to ponder from her garret:

You found a nifty scholarship,
To loosen the tuition grip.
But does this change what you must pay?
Or do they take your grant away?

Don't expect outside scholarships to lower family contribution (unless, as explained in Chapter 7, the scholarship exceeds your financial need). But do search for a policy that at least permits it to replace part of the package's self-help component (loans and work-study).

The Taxman Cometh

Uncle taxes the portion of a scholarship that exceeds tuition, fees, books and equipment as ordinary income. This means room and board scholarships may be taxed. If you've received a large grant, use it to pay the tax-free items first, and keep track of everything left over. You're usually on your own to report your good fortune to the IRS.

Sixteen Innovative Payment Plans

1. **Installment Plans.** Not many people can write a $5,000 or $10,000 check at the beginning of each semester, so many colleges soften the blow by letting families spread out the payments. Furthermore, by using installment plans, you may not have to borrow as much as you originally thought. If a college doesn't have a plan of its own, ask whether it works with Academic Management Service (800/635-0120), Key Education Resources (800/540-1855), Tuition Management Systems (800/722-4867), or USA Group (800/348-4607). AMS alone has contracts with 1,500 schools. Here are variants you may encounter.
   - Interest: (1) No interest (2) Fixed interest (3) Interest on the remaining balance (4) No interest, but a one-time fee.
   - Down Payment: (1) No down payment (2) Down payment of 1/4.
   - Payment Frequency: (1) Ten monthly installments (2) Two installments per semester (3) Four installments per semester.
2. **Prepayment Discount.** Pay a year all at once, and your tuition is discounted, sometimes by as much as 10%.
3. **Advance Payment Bonus.** Place money into your account before it's due and the college adds a bonus to your balance. It can be a set dollar amount (e.g., $100) or a percentage of the amount on deposit (e.g., 2%).
4. **Adjustable Rate Loans.** First we had adjustable rate mortgages; now colleges offer adjustable rate tuition loans. Sometimes your monthly payment changes with the rate. Other times, your monthly payment remains the same, but since tuition costs and interest rates fluctuate—borrowers will not know how long they must make their payments. All they know is that the payments will continue long after graduation.
5. **Tuition Freezes.** Guarantee that tuition will hold for a set time or won't increase by more than a fixed percentage (e.g., 3%). Schools may use freezes to improve retention and limit them to upperclassmen.
6. **Guaranteed Tuition Plans I.** No Prepayment. Guarantees students that tuition will not increase in their sophomore, junior, and senior years.
7. **Guaranteed Tuition Plans II.** Deposit Required. Same as preceding plan, but the college requires you to maintain a set sum on deposit—anywhere from $500 to $3,000.
8. **Guaranteed Tuition Plans III.** Prepayment Required. Pay four years tuition in advance, at the rate which prevails your freshman year. Parents who can make an out-of-pocket prepayment must decide whether the tuition increases they will be spared are worth more than what their money could earn if it had not been used for prepayment.

9. **Guaranteed Tuition Plans IV.** Other Types. At some schools, the guaranteed tuition plan covers as many years as parents can pay in advance—one, two, three, or four. At others, the school will sweeten the pot by rebating say 10% of the payment at the end of each year.
10. **Stretched Payments.** Similar to a loan. Parents who do not qualify for aid defer a fixed amount of their tuition bill. They have two years to pay the deferred amount and are charged a slight interest rate.
11. **Barter.** You provide a usable service in exchange for tuition.
12. **Three-Year Option.** Some colleges offer a "time-shortened degree" that lets students graduate in three years, saving one year in tuition costs.
13. **Two Degrees in One.** Students can also save a year's tuition by finding schools that offer joint undergraduate-graduate degree programs. For example, students can receive their BA-MBA in five years instead of the usual six, or a BA-MA in four years instead of the usual five.
14. **Choice of Accommodations and Meal Plans.** Do you need a spacious room with a spectacular view, or are you happy contemplating the backside of a dumpster? Do you need 21 meals a week in the dining hall or would you rather fend for yourself when the menu reads "Chef's Surprise" or "Mystery Meat?" Colleges give you options. Housing contracts can vary up to $2,000 per year, depending on location and type of room. Meal plans can vary from $25 to $1,000 per year, depending on how often you want to eat dining hall food. If a college is having trouble filling dorm rooms, you might even get a "buy two, get two free" offer. This keeps upperclassmen from moving off-campus, makes college more affordable and doesn't cost the school much of anything.
15. **Use of Credit Cards for Bill Payment.** Provides credit card holders with some flexibility but can cost them dearly in finance charges. If you pay by this option, use an "affinity" credit card that at least gives you a bonus, like frequent flier miles. Or, use the college's own card.
16. **Use of Electronic Bank Transfers.** A set amount is transferred directly from your account to the college each month.

Forty Innovative Aid Programs

1. **Academic Scholarships.** Over 1200 colleges offer scholarships—generally of the "no-need" type—to students who meet special criteria in grade point averages, SAT/ACT scores, or class standing. See *The A's & B's of Academic Scholarships* (inside back cover).
2. **Research Assistants.** Some (hoity-toity) colleges claim not to offer merit-based awards, because if they did, "all their students would

deserve one." Some of these schools do, however, lure preferred applicants with financial incentives—for example, research jobs with choice faculty (complete with large stipends) or high-paying internships.

3. **Merit Scholarships.** The National Merit Scholarship Corporation names over 7,000 "Merit Scholars," but only gives out 2,000 scholarships. What do the other 5000 "winners" get? Nothing, unless they attend one of the 200 colleges that give scholarships to merit finalists (or their parents who work for one of the 340 sponsoring companies).
4. **Honors Colleges.** Many schools have created Honors Programs or Honors Colleges which offer elite, small-college benefits—smaller classes, closer contact with professors, etc.—but at half the price.
5. **Low-Interest Loans.** Many colleges have become low-interest lenders to offset Uncle Sam's yo-yo student aid policies and provide parents with financial planning stability. Others have negotiated good deals with private lenders, by agreeing to share financial risks (i.e., they're betting you'll be a successful graduate and repay your loan promptly).
6. **Quickie Loans.** Many colleges offer short term loans to tide students over in times of temporary financial crisis. These loans usually run from $100 to $500, but sometimes students can get up to $5,000.
7. **Replacing Loans.** Many schools let you use outside scholarships to replace loan components of your aid package. Some schools limit this bonus to bright students, or convert your loan to a grant only if you maintain a certain GPA. Others make the switch only if you find the scholarship before your loan gets processed. You should also ask if the school has a limit (e.g., $2,000) on the total amount it will replace.
8. **Forgiving Loans.** Some schools repay your loans if you do worthwhile (low-paying) things after graduation. Most likely beneficiaries: Health workers who practice in areas of "critical need" (especially in low-income communities) and attorneys who sign up with non-profits or public-interest firms.
9. **Middle Income Assistance Programs.** Special loans and scholarships for middle-income families.
10. **Asset-Rich Families.** Land-rich families whose "non-liquid" holdings disqualify them for assistance can sometimes get special consideration.
11. **Family Plans.** Lower tuitions when more than one family member enrolls—not only brother and sister, but also Mom, Dad and Grandma.
12. **Faculty and Staff Discounts.** Do you or one of your parents work for a college? Is it your dream school? If not, dream again. Most schools allow faculty and staff members, and their children to attend classes at

reduced tuition. Discounts range from 50% to 100%. Some schools offer "professional courtesy" by extending this discount to dependents of faculty and staff at other institutions.

13. **Alumni Children.** Tuition breaks for alumni kids are also common. Colleges like to establish multi-generation relationships with families. That's how chairs get endowed and buildings get built.
14. **Peace of Mind.** Some schools waive (or reduce) tuition if the person primarily responsible for your support dies or suffers total disability.
15. **Incentives for Academic Achievement.** Many colleges have special awards for the top enrolled (continuing) students. Other schools offer academic awards to any student who was in the top 10% of their high school class. Finally, some schools will convert part of a student's loans to grants if the student maintains a high GPA.
16. **Matching Scholarships.** Some schools match church scholarships. Other schools match state awards, or Dollars for Scholars awards.
17. **Remissions for Student Leaders.** Many colleges provide discounts to campus leaders—class officers, school newspaper editors. You won't get this money your first year, but you should know about it so that you can start planning your campaign for student body president.
18. **Remissions for Work.** At Warren Wilson (NC) and Blackburn (IL) students get free room and board. But they must put in fifteen hours of campus work every week. Berea (KY) charges no tuition to students of limited means, but requires them to work ten hours/week. Many other schools provide room and board for residence hall assistants. You may not qualify your first year, but you should know about the opportunity.
19. **Emphasis on Student Employment.** Many colleges have beefed up their placement offices to help students find on- and off-campus employment. They also use their formidable alumni networks to locate summer work opportunities.
20. **Off-Hour Rates.** Look for lower charges for off-hour courses—those on evenings, weekends and summers. The difference can be as high as $300 per course or a 50% room rate reduction (for summer school).
21. **Moral Obligation Scholarships.** Not a scholarship. Not a loan. The college loans you money and attaches a moral—not legal—obligation to repay it after graduation. A special sweetener: The payback becomes a gift to the college and a tax deduction to the former student.
22. **Trial Attendance.** Some colleges say, "Try us you'll like us" and will offer new students a discount on their first few credits. For example, the school may offer free classes to high school juniors and seniors, it may

let some students try the school for one semester for a low fee (e.g., $25), or it may run a free summer program to give students a little taste.

23. **Bucking the Trend.** Some colleges seek to win the enrollment competition by freezing or even lowering tuition.
24. **Special Scholarship Drives.** Some schools have launched special fundraising drives aimed at increasing their in-house financial aid kitty. Columbia University (NY) raises $100,000 a year from Visa and Master card users through a collaboration with MBNA America Bank.
25. **Helping Students Find Scholarships.** Hundreds of schools have special offices to help students find grants, scholarships, etc.
26. **Older Student Remissions.** If you are over 24, some schools will give you a discount on tuition, however, at most schools, "older" means 50 or 60. In fact, many public schools offer free tuition to senior citizens as long as they are state residents and attend on a space available basis.
27. **Special Students.** Colleges look for students with unique interests. Many give scholarships to National Honor Society members or future math or science teachers. Grand Canyon (AZ) is looking for Eagle Scouts. Tarleton State (TX) offers rodeo scholarships. And, Arkansas College (AR) will pay you to play the bagpipes.
28. **Persistence Awards.** Schools used to worry about retention rates. Now they worry about persistence. The name may have changed (in an effort by educators to shift responsibility for retention from school to student) but the concept hasn't. To recoup the money they spend recruiting new students, schools must keep them enrolled (and paying at least some tuition) for four years. Accordingly, to keep you from transferring or dropping out, some colleges offer financial inducements such as senior class trips, loan cancellation or scholarships for returning students.
29. **Travel Awards.** Some schools will reimburse you for campus visits or, if you are enrolled, for commuting costs.
30. **Loan Origination Fee.** Some schools pay your student loan origination fees.
31. **Adopt-a-Student.** At some schools, local churches, businesses and community groups help students with scholarship money.
32. **Students Helping Students.** When that happens, it's a sign of good student morale and a friendly campus. For example: DePauw (IN) students raised $134,00 for scholarships in a phonathon. Brown (RI) put $4 in the college's scholarship fund for every hour student volunteers spent picking up litter on campus. Notre Dame (IN) students waived return of room-damage deposits, electing to contribute the money to a

scholarship fund. Fitchburg State (MA) deposited all parking fines in a scholarship fund. And Davidson's (NC) senior class gift to the college was a $100,000 scholarship fund.

33. **Running Start.** High school students can spend their senior year, or the summer before their senior year on a campus, taking regular college classes. Colleges look on such students as a farm club. For example, at Wesley (DE), local students in the top 40% of the HS class may take (and receive academic credit for) up to two free courses each semester. At Simon's Rock College (MA), high school students may complete a two year "Acceleration to Excellence" program, then finish their BA at Simon's Rock for the cost of attending their home-state public university. No matter what program is offered, here are some questions to ask: Are the courses for college credit? If so, are the credits good only at the offering college or are they transferable?
34. **Help for the Unemployed.** Some schools offer free tuition to students from families whose major wage earner is unemployed.
35. **Free Tuition for Farmers.** Some schools offer a year of free tuition to farmers who have had to quit farming because of financial hardships.
36. **A Birthday Gift.** To celebrate its 100th anniversary, Dana (NE) let each graduating senior award a $4,000 scholarship to any incoming student. Goucher (MD) celebrated its 100th birthday by allowing selected students to pay 1885 tuition rates, $100/year. Note: These opportunities have passed, but keep your eyes open for similar "celebrations."
37. **Guaranteed Degree.** Graduates who are unhappy with their major (because, for example, they couldn't find a job) may return to the alma mater and major in another field, tuition-free.
38. **Tuition Equalization.** To compete more effectively with public schools for top students, some private colleges offer their own tuition equalization programs. At Bard College (NY), top high school grads pay only as much tuition as they would have paid had they gone to their home-state school. The University of Rochester gives alumni children and all New York state residents a $5,000 discount.
39. **Toll-Free Numbers.** Most schools have toll-free numbers and financial counselors with whom to discuss your financing options.
40. **Reward for Community Service.** Many schools encourage students to participate in community service. Some give course credit. Campus Compact, c/o Brown University, Box 1975, Providence, RI 02912 is a coalition of 520 colleges serving 140,000 students. Campus Outreach Opportunity League is a coalition that serves students at nearly 650

schools. (COOL, 1511 K Street NW, #307, Washington, DC 20005, http://www.cool2serve.org/)

The Rich Schools

There is no proven relationship between the size of a school's endowment and the pool of money it makes available for student aid, however, rich schools generally spend more on student aid than poor schools. At some, the average need-based grant ranges from $10,000 to $15,000! Rich schools also have greater flexibility in making financial aid awards. It's their money, so they are better able to take individual circumstances into account than schools that dispense, in the main, public funds. Here are schools with mountains of money:

Over $10 billion: Harvard

Over $3 billion: U. of Texas System, Yale, Princeton, Stanford, Emory, U. of California, MIT, Columbia

Over $1 billion: Texas A&M System, Washington U., U. of Pennsylvania, Rice, Cornell, U. of Chicago, U. of Michigan, Northwestern, Notre Dame, Vanderbilt, Dartmouth, U. of Southern California, Case Western, Johns Hopkins, Duke, U. of Virginia

Over $500 million: U. of Minnesota, CalTech, Brown, U. of Rochester, Purdue, New York U., U. of North Carolina, Georgia Tech, Ohio State, Grinnell, Swarthmore, Texas Christian U., Wellesley, Smith, U. of Cincinnati, U. of Richmond, U. of Delaware, Boston College, U. of Pittsburgh, Southern Methodist, Washington and Lee, U. of Kansas, Williams, Wake Forest, Indiana U., Carnegie-Mellon, Pomona, Nebraska, U. of Tulsa, George Washington, Middlebury, Yeshiva, U. of Washington, Berea, Lehigh, and Saint Louis U.

Leadership in Selected Fields

Colleges that are acknowledged leaders in selected disciplines (e.g., the Midwestern colleges in agriculture; the western schools in mining and geology) are usually heavily endowed by private sponsors in the areas of their special expertise. You are far more likely to find an agriculture scholarship at Iowa State than at Baruch College in New York City, or a petroleum engineering scholarship at the University of Oklahoma than at the University of the District of Columbia.

For opinions on who is best in what, ask the guidance office or school library to pick up a copy of **Rugg's Recommendations on the Colleges** ($20.95, Rugg's Recommendations, 7120 Serena Court, Atascadero, CA

93422). Another (perhaps better) way to get this kind of information is to speak with people you respect in your intended academic/career field. Find out where they went to school, and ask if they have any recommendations.

A tip: Strong departments usually have funds they control themselves rather than the financial aid office. Consider dropping a note to the department head and ask about the possibility of departmental assistance.

Working With Financial Aid Administrators

The median salary of financial aid directors in 1997/98 was $48,450. You might keep that sum in mind as you get ready to explain how your $100,000 income has been ravaged by inflation to the point of making it impossible—absolutely impossible—to handle your family contribution. You might also remember that the purpose of financial aid is to make college affordable, not to give families a free ride.

Financial aid administrators primarily dispense public funds—tax money—and such expenditures are usually strictly controlled by law and regulations. They have more flexibility in awarding the colleges' own funds and in treating changed circumstances—such unfortunate events as death, disability, disaster, and divorce, as well as newfound expenses like medical bills, private secondary school tuitions, prior education loans, failing businesses, or upcoming retirements.

"Responding to New Information"

Only 1-2 % of all aid administrators say they adjust packages to meet other institutional offers, but over 70% will "respond to new information." That doesn't mean they'll haggle over price. But they will listen if your situation prevents you from writing a tuition check. After all, aid administrators won't know about your problem unless you tell them. Some even welcome the opportunity to discuss aid packages. It gives them the chance to help families understand the EFC calculation. At the same time, families can help FAAs understand what special circumstances they have that may impact on their ability to pay.

The Professional Judgment Process

As schools grow tired of "let's make a deal," they're beginning to formalize their "professional judgment" process. Over half now have written policies, and stick to them. In other words, you might be better off honing your negotiating strategy with your accountant, rather than the neighborhood car dealer.

One large university, for example, found that too many students knew which financial aid counselors would be most sympathetic to their cause, and would schedule their appointments accordingly. To correct the imbalance, the school now has a formal appeals process. Here's how it handles the question of dependency:

First, students complete a standard form which asks them to:

- Identify the location of their parents.
- Describe their last contact with their parents (including "when" and "where").
- Explain why they should receive a waiver. Expect this to be open-ended—schools don't want students to parrot back some approved definition of "unusual circumstance."
- Describe how they've been self-supporting (and for how long).
- Provide statements of support from two responsible adults who are aware of their situation (guidance counselor, social worker, clergy member, etc.).
- Provide copies of any relevant court documents.

Next, two separate counselors will review the forms independently and render judgment. If counselors vary in their decision, a third counselor will break the tie. Students unhappy with the decision may request an interview with the financial aid director.

Finally, the financial aid director will review the decision to make sure the process remains consistent. In subsequent years, students simply submit a letter saying "the situation has not changed."

The Lesson?

If you feel the college should change any part of your award letter—the expense budget, your family contribution, or the mix of aid—then go ahead and call the office. But do so with sound reasons and documentation. Don't try to "cut a deal." Aid administrators are professionals who must stick to certain budget goals. If they agree to increase your award, it could be at the expense of another's. The FAA will not make that decision lightly, and never without good cause. So before you bully your way into the aid office demanding a recount, document your case carefully and remember, you catch more Drosophila Melanogaster with honey than with vinegar.

CHAPTER 10

UNCLE SAM

Meet Your Uncle—Uncle Sam

For many students, applying for financial aid represents their first encounter with Uncle Sam. One thing will become apparent very quickly. Getting things from Uncle Sam is no more pleasant than giving him things, like your money at tax time. Here is what you should expect:

Uncle Sam likes forms. Lots of forms. Most have an awkward layout, an illogical sequence, and poorly written instructions.

Uncle Sam makes a sharp distinction between "authorizations" and "appropriations." A program may be authorized, but that doesn't mean a nickel will be spent (appropriated) for it. A new $10 billion student aid program does no good unless money for the program actually gets appropriated.

Uncle loves semantics and fine distinctions. His authorization bill may promise a chicken in every pot. But the enabling legislation may define "chicken" as "any part of the bird," a claw, a feather... Or the definition may emphasize the avian nature of a chicken. The operative word then becomes "bird" and any bird can be substituted for a chicken—pigeon, crow...

Uncle is a social engineer. After redefining chicken, he will turn his attention to the pot. He may rule that anybody who owns a pot large enough to hold a chicken is too rich to qualify for a fowl. Only owners of small pots can get birds—the smaller the pot, the bigger the bird will seem.

Uncle's promises don't hold for very long. Any program can be supplemented, altered, filibustered, modified or rescinded in mid-year or near election time when it becomes important to hold down expenses and balance the budget.

Uncle likes to arm wrestle with himself. If the Administration doesn't like what Congress has mandated (or vice versa), it will miss dead-lines, base its case on budget figures that have already been rejected (but not yet replaced), blow smoke over the issues, hold up regulations, or tie up appropriated funds.

Uncle's timing does not correspond to the academic cycle. When you want to start planning for the next year, Uncle is not ready for you. By the time he can tell you what he will do for you, you've already made your plans.

But when all is said and done, Uncle Sam is still your main source of financial aid. Warts or no warts, you had better learn to live with him and like him.

More Money, More Complexity

One of the nation's top five worries is that a good college education is becoming too expensive. Accordingly, the House, the Senate AND the Administration have agreed to attack the problem from two sides: new tax initiatives to benefit middle income students and new budget initiatives to benefit the most needy. The end result? A cobbled together package that requires advanced legal and accounting skills to decipher. The first part of this Chapter focuses on student aid from the Department of Education. The second part explains how the taxman can become your new best friend.

	Level of Study		Need-Based		Part-Timers		
Program	**Undergrad**	**Grad**	**Yes**	**No**	**Yes**	**No**	**Need Analysis**
Pell Grant	X		X		X		FM
Stafford Loan	X	X	X			X	FM
PLUS Loans	X			X		X	none
Direct Stafford	X	X	X			X	FM
Direct Plus Loan	X			X		X	none
Unsub. Stafford	X	X		X		X	FM
SEOG	X		X		X		FM
Work-study	X	X	X		X		FM
Perkins Loans	X	X	X		X		FM

The Big Six Today

Most of Uncle's student aid flows through six gigantic programs. Three are student based—Pell Grants, Family Education Loans (Stafford and PLUS), and Direct Student Loans (Direct Stafford and Direct PLUS). You apply for assistance under these programs and the money comes to you.

The other three programs—Supplemental Educational Opportunity Grants, Work-Study and Perkins Loans—are campus-based. This means Uncle funds the programs, but gives the money to the colleges to dispense in accordance with federal guidelines. Most of the money goes to full- and half-time students, however, if the financial need of part-timers is at least 5% of the need of all the students at the school, then at least 5% of campus-based funds must be offered to these students.

Uncle also funds several smaller programs—Byrd Honors Scholarships, AmeriCorps, and LEAP (Leveraging Educational Assistance Partnership, formerly SSIG). This last program is administered by the states, and is described in Chapter 11.

Useful Phone Contacts

For information about federal programs, call the Federal Student Aid Information Center, 800/4-FED-AID, Monday through Friday between 9:00 a.m. and 8:00 p.m, EST (TDD: 800/730-8913). Trained staff can help families complete the FAFSA, explain Expected Family Contribution and answer questions about eligibility. You may also request Uncle's free book, *The Student Guide: Financial Aid from the Department of Education*. The number is NOT to be used for financial counseling, to change information in your file, to interpret policy, or to expedite application processing.

To check on the status of your application, or to request a duplicate Student Aid Report, call 319-337-5665. If you suspect fraud or abuse involving federal student aid funds, please call the Inspector General's Office at 800/MIS-USED.

To learn about the GI Bill and benefits for dependents of deceased or disabled veterans, call the Department of Veteran's Affairs, 800/827-1000.

Useful Web Contacts

Project EASI (Easy Access for Students and Institutions, http://easi.ed.gov) is supposed to be a collaborative effort between the postsecondary "community" and the Department of Education to "use cutting-edge technology to transform the administration of financial aid and access to financial aid information." It's been VERY slow going, but the site is easy to navigate and has made progress from last year. Take a look. You'll find links to the following:

- FAFSA on the Web (http://www.fafsa.ed.gov) and FAFSA Express (http://www.ed.gov/offices/OPE/express.html) let you submit your FAFSA electronically.

- FAFSA Help (http://www.ed.gov/prog_info/SFA/FAFSA) provides very detailed FAFSA instructions.
- On-line editions of *The Student Guide: Financial Aid from the Department of Education.* (http://www.ed.gov/prog_info/SFA/student guide) and *Funding Your Education* (http://www.ed.gov/prog_info/SFA/FYE) answer all your basic questions about federal student aid.
- Students' Site Grading Service (http://easi.ed.gov/html/ssgs.html). This feature lets you rate any site linked to EASI, or just see which sites other students have found useful.

Pell Grants

These make up Uncle's largest gift program. In 1999/2000, $7.5 billion in Pells will be dispensed to four million students. They are the foundation of student aid, the bottom layer of the financial aid package. But they can also be called Pinochio Grants because Uncle seldom holds to the award range that he promises; Pells are a big part of the Education budget and increasing or decreasing four million grants by $50, $100 or $200 can make a big difference in the balancing act.

So what will the award range be for 1999/2000? House leaders budgeted for $3,150. The President called for $3,100. So pay no attention to bills that authorize maximum Pells of $4,500 or $5,000 and assume only $3,100 will come through. Why are we so pessimistic? Every year, people clamor for larger Pells as a cure-all for removing barriers to higher education. Lawmakers oblige by setting ever-higher Pell limits—unfortunately, budget realities preclude funding these lofty limits. Families are getting $31 billion in new education tax credits over the next five years. That's $31 billion less Uncle can spend on other programs, and still meet his balanced budget goal. Again, remember, the difference between authorization and appropriation.

How large a Pell will you get? It varies with your expected family contribution, the cost of education at your school and your student status. If you are a part-time, half-time or three-quarter time student, you receive 25%, 50% or 75% of your award, respectively. Uncle publishes tables with exact levels of Pell funding, but to get an estimate, if the cost of college exceeds the maximum Pell (e.g., $3,100), just subtract your EFC from the maximum grant. For example, assuming an award range of $200 to $3,100, an EFC of $1,000 translates into $2,100 for full-time students ($1,050 for half-time students); an EFC of $3,100 gets you nothing.

For Whom the Pell Tolls

You apply for a Pell by completing the FAFSA. Make certain to go this route, even if you know you aren't eligible. Colleges and the states expect you to do so and won't consider you for other awards until they know your Pell status. The only way for them to know your Pell status is by seeing results from your FAFSA.

Family Education Loans and Direct Student Loans

Uncle Sam now runs two parallel student loan programs:

Federal Family Education Loans: Subsidized Staffords, Unsubsidized Staffords and PLUS. These loans are made by commercial lenders.

William D. Ford Federal Direct Loans: Direct Subsidized Staffords, Direct Unsubsidized Staffords, and Direct PLUS. These loans are made by Uncle Sam.

Interest rates, annual and aggregate loan limits, fees, deferments, cancellations, and forbearance terms are essentially the same. Repayment options vary slightly. The main difference, as far as the student is concerned, is who lends them the money. So why are there two different programs? Politics, as usual. Can you borrow under both? No! Your college will usually tell you which program it prefers.

The Direct Lending Debate

Right now, there are thousands of lenders making loans, nearly a hundred secondary markets buying up the loans, and dozens of guaranteeing agencies administering loans. The Administration hoped the loan process would run more smoothly and at less expense by eliminating the middlemen. Under Direct Lending, there are no middlemen (just giant government contractors). Uncle is the only lender, wiring money straight to the colleges. Students then repay the Treasury directly.

While many agree the loan process could be simpler, there is no guarantee that turning the Department into one of the country's largest banks wouldn't spawn a clumsy and expensive bureaucracy to keep tabs on the $100 billion or so in outstanding loans. Also, the Department does not have the (profit) motive of the private sector; a motive that usually contributes to efficiently run, quality programs and lets students shop around for the "best deal." In fact, the threat of direct lending brought the private lending community together to improve delivery systems and introduce more creative (less costly) repayment options. Since competition has resulted in better loan products for students, both programs will survive reauthorization.

Stafford Loans

Formerly called Guaranteed Student Loans, the program was renamed in honor of retired Senator Robert T. Stafford (R-VT). Stafford Loans are low-interest loans to undergraduate and graduate students enrolled at least half-time. They are available to all families without regard to financial need.

Which Stafford Loan is for you?

Students with financial need may receive a subsidized Stafford in which Uncle pays the interest while they are in school and during any deferments.

Students without financial need may receive an unsubsidized Stafford in which interest accrues while they are in school and during any deferments.

Students with partial financial need may receive a combination of the two, depending on their status (dependent vs. independent) and level of need.

Loan Limits:

Dependent Undergraduates: Freshmen may borrow up to $2,625 per year. Sophomores may borrow $3,500 per year. Juniors, seniors and fifth year undergrads may borrow $5,500 per year. The maximum undergraduate loan amount is $23,000. These limits apply whether the money comes from the subsidized or unsubsidized program (or a combination of the two). For example, a freshman who receives a $1,500 subsidized Stafford may also borrow $1,125 under the unsubsidized program.

Independent Undergraduates: Freshmen may borrow $6,625 per year. Sophomores may borrow $7,500 per year (in both cases at least $4,000 must come from the unsubsidized program). Juniors, seniors and fifth year undergraduates may borrow up to $10,500 per year (of which at least $5,000 must come from the unsubsidized program). The maximum an independent student may borrow during his or her undergraduate years is $46,000.

Graduate Students may borrow up to $18,500 per year (of which at least $10,000 must come from the unsubsidized program) to a maximum of $138,500 ($65,500 in subsidized loans, $73,000 in unsubsidized loans). This limit includes any money they borrowed as an undergraduate.

Additional Limits: Students who could have borrowed under the Health Education Assistance Loan (see Chapter 20), but now can't (since

Uncle eliminated HEAL) may receive additional annual (but not aggregate) unsubsidized Stafford money. Also, in no case may a Stafford Loan exceed the cost of attendance at your school minus any other financial aid you receive.

Prorated loan limits: Borrowing limits are prorated for programs of less than a full academic year. For example, students attending the equivalent of 1/3 of an academic year are eligible for 1/3 the maximum annual loan amount.

Loan Origination Fee and Insurance Fees. Commercial lenders subtract a 3% loan origination fee and a 1% insurance fee. As an extra incentive to borrow from them, some lenders pay your origination fee saving you as much as $1,000. If your loan comes from Uncle, you pay a combined 4% instead. No deals.

Interest Rate. The in-school rate equals 1.7% more than the 91-day T-bill with an 8.25% cap. This year, it is 6.86%. During repayment, the rate equals 2.3% more than the 91-day T-bill with an 8.25% cap. This year, it is 7.46%. This rate structure was part of a temporary student loan provision and expires on October 1, 1998. Both the House and Senate are pushing for the rates to become permanent, although we expect to see market-based rates down the road (like car loans and house loans).

Interest Subsidy. For families with demonstrated financial need, Uncle Sam pays interest on the loan while the student is in school and for a six-month grace period after the student completes his or her studies.

Minimum Annual Repayment. $600.

Years to Repay. 5 to 10.

Who Makes Loans? Private lenders—Banks, Credit Unions, Insurance Companies. Also Uncle Sam (for students attending Direct Lending schools). If you can't find a lender (it's usually pretty easy), contact your state's loan guaranty agency; it must either designate a lender, or act as a lender of last resort. (You can get the address from your high school counselor, or your state agency in Chapter 11).

Entrance Counseling. Before you may receive any Stafford money, you must go through "Entrance Counseling" to learn about your responsibilities as a borrower. Some schools let you complete this requirement on-line. Other schools insist on an in-person interview.

Under certain circumstances, loans can be deferred, postponed, canceled or considered for forbearance. Usually these circumstances are unpleasant things like death, permanent disability, or economic hardship.

PLUS Loans

PLUS loans are not based on need so you may use them to cover your expected family contribution. In fact, creditworthy parents may borrow an amount equal to the student's total cost of attendance less any aid received.

If a parent is deemed uncreditworthy, the student may borrow an additional amount under the unsubsidized Stafford; freshmen and sophomores get an extra $4,000; juniors and seniors, an extra $5,000 (these amounts correspond to the higher borrowing limits for independent undergraduates).

Loan Origination Fee and Insurance Fees. Lenders may subtract a 3% loan origination fee and a 1% insurance fee. If your loan comes from Uncle, you pay a combined 4% instead.

Interest Rate. The rate equals 3.1% more than the 91-day T-bill and carries a 9% cap. Currently, it is 8.26%. This rate was part of a temporary student loan provision and expires on October 1, 1998. Both the House and Senate are pushing for the rate to become permanent, although we expect to see market-based rates down the road (like car loans and house loans).

Interest Subsidy. There is no interest subsidy to borrowers.

Repayment begins within 60 days after the final loan disbursement for the academic year and extends from 5 to 10 years. Under certain circumstances, loans can be deferred, postponed, canceled or considered for forbearance. Usually these circumstances are unpleasant things like death, permanent disability, or economic hardship.

Who Makes Loans? Private lenders—Banks, S&Ls, Credit Unions, some states, and Uncle Sam (for students attending Direct Lending schools).

Supplemental Educational Opportunity Grants

Uncle will give the colleges $700 million for SEOGs next year.

Size of awards. From $100 to $4,000 per year of undergraduate study.

Criteria for Selection. Need and fund availability. Be smart. Apply early. Nearly one million SEOG recipients each year; priority goes to those receiving Pells.

Work-Study

Uncle will give colleges about $1 billion for work-study next year.

Eligibility. One million participants each year, undergrads and grad students.

Criteria for Selection. Need and fund availability. Work-study students are more likely to stay in school and graduate with less debt. Be smart. Apply early.

Program Description. On- and off-campus employment. Salary must at least equal minimum wage. You cannot earn more money than your award stipulates. Thus, if you receive a $1,000 award, your employment lasts until you earn $1,000 and then it terminates for that academic year. Employment may not involve any political or religious activity nor may students be used to replace regular employees.

Schools are also being encouraged (bribed?) to use work-study money to pay for 100,000 "America Reads" tutors. Uncle will pay 100% (instead of the more usual 75%) of work-study wages earned by students employed as reading tutors for preschool and elementary school children. Over 1,000 colleges have joined the effort. For more information, visit America Reads, http://www.ed.gov/inits/americareads/training.html.

Perkins Loans

The college acts as lender, using funds originally provided by the federal government. Uncle adds about $160 million per year, and there is now $1 billion in "revolving fund" capital (money paid back by borrowers). About 725,000 students receive an average of $1,342 each.

Eligibility. Undergraduate and graduate students.

Criteria for Selection. Need and fund availability. Be smart. Apply early.

Loan Limits:

Undergraduate: $3,000 per year to a maximum of $15,000.

Graduate students: $5,000 per year to a maximum of $30,000 (less any Perkins money borrowed as an undergraduate).

Expanded Lending Option (ELO): Students who attend schools with low default rates may qualify for a little extra under ELO. Undergraduates may borrow up to $4,000 per year to a maximum of $20,000; graduate students may borrow up to $6,000 per year to a maximum of $40,000 (less any Perkins money borrowed as an undergraduate). As a result of reauthorization, all Perkins loan limits may increase to equal those under ELO.

Minimum Annual Repayment. $480.

Interest rate. 5%.

Interest Subsidy. Student pays no interest while in school or during a 9-month grace period following graduation.

Repayment. 10 years. Under certain circumstances, loans can be deferred, postponed or considered for forbearance. Usually these circumstances are unpleasant reasons like death, permanent disability, or economic hardship. Loans can also be forgiven or canceled if you do worthwhile things after graduation, like serve in the Peace Corps or teach in an under-served community.

On Defaulting

Uncle Sam rewards and punishes colleges for their ability to collect on loans. Schools with small default rates (under 7.5%) get an increased infusion of Perkins capital; schools with high default rates (25% +) for three years running may become ineligible for federal funds altogether. (No Perkins money. No Stafford money. No Pell money. No any kind of federal student aid money.) The national default rate is currently about 10.4% per year (generally lower at four-year schools and higher at trade schools). It may pay you to ask schools for their default rate before you apply.

Uncle Sam can also punish you if you are one of the defaulters, as he should, since in our book, defaulters eclipse even the most parasitic protozoa! He can notify credit bureaus which will damage your credit rating. He can withhold your tax refunds until your loan is repaid. He can take you to court. Or, he can garnish your wages (and fine your employer if he/she doesn't follow through). As Uncle gets tougher, the default problem gets better, but at some trade schools defaults still run as high as 85%.

Loan Repayment Options

Borrowers with multiple federal loans or borrowers who face larger monthly payments than they can handle under standard, ten-year plans, may want to consolidate their loans and/or use a longer-term repayment plan. Married couples may consolidate their individual loans if they agree to be jointly liable for repayment even if there's a "future change in their marital status." Again, Uncle is running two parallel programs, which we'll call regular consolidation and direct consolidation. Under all of these plans, your monthly payments will be smaller but the total amount you repay much greater than under regular (10-year) repayment. For more information, check with Uncle Sam or the institution that gave you your loan.

Extended Repayment

Repayment may extend for up to 12 years for students with under $10,000 in loans; 15 years for students with between $10,000 and $20,000; 20 years for students with between $20,000 and $40,000; 25 years for students with between $40,000 and $60,000; and 30 years for those lucky students with more than $60,000 to repay. Under regular consolidation, the interest rate cannot exceed the weighted average of all the loans rounded up to the nearest whole percent. Some lenders charge less than this maximum. Shop around. Under direct consolidation, the payback periods vary slightly and the interest rate cannot exceed 8.25% for Staffords and 9% for PLUS.

Graduated Repayment

Students repay their loan within ten years, but payments start small (when incomes are low), and increase over time (while incomes also rise). Borrowers with consolidated loans may repay their loan in this fashion within the extended time frame described above.

Income-Sensitive Repayment

This option is available only from commercial lenders. Students work with their lender to establish a more flexible repayment schedule than the ones above. Payments may be adjusted annually to reflect current and future earning potential.

Income Contingent Repayment

This option is available only under Direct Consolidation. Uncle Sam has developed a complex formula for determining repayment rates; they vary depending on your income and the size of your loan. For example, a single borrower with an income of $25,000 would begin repaying a $12,500 loan at $113 per month while a borrower earning $35,000 would repay that same loan at $133 per month. After 25 years, a borrower who has been repaying faithfully, but has not yet retired the loan, will have the rest of his or her debt forgiven. On the down-side, the IRS will count your forgiven loan as in-kind (and taxable) income. Also, PLUS loans may not be repaid using the Income Contingent option.

Borrower Bonuses

Private lenders frequently reward students who repay their loans faithfully. For example, some will lower your interest rate by 2% after receiving 48 on-time payments. They may refund your 3% loan origination fee, or lower your interest rate an additional .25% if you repay using automatic monthly bank transfers. A student with $10,000 in Stafford loans would reap $866 in saving; a student with $20,000 would reap $2,137. Before you take out a student loan, make certain your lender offers these bonuses; otherwise, you may want to look further.

Tip: Set up "overdraft protection" with your bank, so you can take advantage of these benefits without worrying about missing a payment. Contact Sallie Mae for a list of "Great Rewards" lenders (800/222-7182, http://www.salliemae.com) or USA Group for a list of "Choice" lenders (800/849-6510, http://www.usagroup.org).

Robert C. Byrd Honors Scholarships

$40 million program. No-need, renewable awards of $1,500 intended to promote student excellence. Each state establishes its own criteria and selects recipients.

AmeriCorps

Participants receive a minimum wage stipend and a $4,725 credit per year of full-time service (for up to two years). They may use the credit at any college or graduate school, or to pay down outstanding student loans. Furthermore, the money does not affect their eligibility for other federal student aid. Currently, 25,000 students serve in 450 different programs with Uncle providing most of the funding, but states and nonprofits doing the hiring. Prime projects are those that address unmet needs in education (assisting teachers in Head Start), the environment (recycling or conservation projects), human services (building housing for the homeless) or public safety (leading drug education seminars). Interested students should apply directly to a funded program (for a list, contact AmeriCorps, 800/94-ACORPS, http://www.cns.gov). While AmeriCorps is small in scope, its real importance has been to focus attention on our county's extensive network of service programs. With AmeriCorps adding new structure, and a solid core of workers, these programs have become a magnet for corporate "do good" money as well as for volunteers with only an hour to spare. The funded projects have brought huge economic benefits to the communities in which they operate as well as a heightened sense of personal and social responsibility for the AmeriCorps participants. Unfortunately, some Congressional critics want to snuff out AmeriCorps saying the government has no business creating a Department of Good Deeds. For now, however, AmeriCorps lives.

The Taxpayer Relief Act of 1997

Education can be the "Continental Divide" between those who will prosper economically and those who will not. Unfortunately, many families feel priced out of college, hence, the push to make tuition-payers the big winners in last year's Taxpayer Relief Act.

Education Tax Credits

The Hope Scholarship Credit allows taxpayers to claim a maximum annual credit of $1,500 per student for tuition expenses paid on behalf of the taxpayer, the taxpayer's spouse, or a dependent for the first two years of college; 100% of the first $1,000 of tuition, and 50% of the next $1,000. That $1,000 figure will be indexed for inflation beginning in 2002. The student must be enrolled at least half-time.

The Lifetime Learning Credit allows taxpayers to claim an annual credit equal to 20% of up to $5,000 in total tuition expenses (increasing to $10,000 beginning in 2003). Unlike the Hope credit, this is not a "per student" maximum. Also, part-timers are eligible, so are working-adults who are taking classes to improve their job skills.

The two credits will be phased out for single filers with incomes between $40,000 and $50,000, and joint filers with incomes between $80,000 and $100,000. Income levels are to be indexed for inflation beginning in 2002.

Note: Beginning in 1999/2000, the FAFSA will collect data on the size of your tax credits, and the Federal Methodology will be modified to provide offsets for them. Otherwise, these credits would have increased available income, which would have increased EFC, and decreased eligibility for other aid. And that was certainly not the tax writers' intent.

Education IRAs

These let you sock away up to $500 per year per student under the age of 18. Contributions are non-deductible, however, earnings accumulate tax-free, and remain tax free upon withdrawal if the proceeds go toward tuition, fees, books, room and board. The money must all be used by the time the "child" turns 30, or rolled over into a younger family member's account. Families may set up Education IRAs even if they've maxed out on their real retirement contributions, but no contributions may be made to a student's Education IRA in the same year he or she receives a contribution to a state tuition savings plan.

Benefits will be phased out for single filers with incomes between $95,000 and $110,000 and joint filers with incomes between $150,000 and $160,000 (limits to be indexed for inflation).

So Which Option Should You Choose?

Taxpayers cannot claim more than one of these three benefits for a student in any given year. They could, however, claim the Hope credit for expenses paid for one student and the Lifetime Learning credit for expenses paid for a second student.

Parents with incomes under $80,000 should take advantage of the Hope Scholarship Credit for college years one and two, and the Lifetime Learning credit for years three and four. If grandparents are around, and willing, you might ask them to set up an Education IRA for their smart grandchildren; that way at least someone in the family reaps the benefit of tax deferred earnings. Parents could even give grandparents $500 per year for each account. Of course, if your state has a tuition savings plan, you should probably fund that first, since those contributions can be substantially higher than $500 per year.

Deduction for Student Loan Interest

The Taxpayer Relief Act of 1997 also phases in a deduction for interest paid on "qualified education loans" over the next four years (this definition excludes loans from people related to the taxpayer). The maximum deduction is $1,000 in 1998, $1,500 in 1999, $2,000 in 2000, and $2,500 in 2001. The deduction will be phased out for single filers with incomes between $40,000 and $55,000 and joint filers with incomes between $60,000 and $75,000. Income levels will be indexed for inflation beginning in 2003.

You may only use this deduction for the first 60 months that interest payments are due; keep this in mind as you weigh the benefits of various repayment plans.

Good Politics or Good Policy?

Naysayers called it Torture By Taxation—the proposals bring little help and large headaches. They benefit families who would have sent their kids to college anyway, rather than those most in need. They drown the tax system in added complexity. And they make a mockery of the "forgotten middle class," who finally get their tax cut, but only if they spend money in ways Uncle deems desirable.

We say, give the proposals a chance! So what if every phaseout needs its own worksheet. Our current system is so full of disincentives to save or borrow for college, if this is what it takes to get more families to assume responsibility for tuition payments, we'll take it!

Every Student's Song

Do not forsake me, oh my Uncle,
before commencement day.
Do not change programs, oh my Uncle,
oh please, oh please—I say.
I do not know what costs await me,
I only know there will be more.
I need to have the grants you give me,
or be a drop-out, a lazy drop-out,
Or a starving sophomore.

CHAPTER 11

THE STATES

All states maintain extensive programs of grants, fee reductions and loans. Over 2 million students receive over $2.6 billion in need-based state grant aid and 250,000 share in $458 million of non-need-based grant aid. States award another $290 million in low-interest loans and work-study.

States making over 50,000 need-based awards: New York, Pennsylvania, Illinois, Ohio, California, Michigan, New Jersey, Minnesota, Wisconsin, Puerto Rico, and Massachusetts—in that order.

States spending over $50 million on student aid: New York, Illinois, California, Pennsylvania, Georgia, New Jersey, Ohio, Florida, Virginia, Minnesota, Michigan, Indiana, Washington, Massachusetts, Wisconsin and North Carolina—in that order.

States where tuition is most affordable when measured as a percentage of median family income: Hawaii (3.61%), Nevada (5.1%), North Carolina (5.39), Idaho (5.44%), Alaska (5.52%), Utah (5.62%), and Texas (5.96%). The national average is 8.82%.

States which give money to at least 25% of their students: Georgia, Vermont, New Jersey, New York, Ohio, Pennsylvania, Illinois, Maine, Washington DC, New Mexico, Colorado, Wisconsin, Florida, Maryland, Connecticut, Indiana, and Virginia.

Eligibility for State-Based Student Aid

States determine eligibility for need-based aid in one of four ways: (1) Twenty-one states use only the federal methodology; (2) Twenty-four states (including Puerto Rico and Washington DC) use the federal methodology for most of their grants and a hybrid methodology for a few other programs; (3) Two states (Montana and South Dakota) lets schools make the decisions regarding eligibility; and (4) Five states rely on their own system—Alaska, New York, Ohio, Oregon, and Pennsylvania.

So, how do you find out which forms to file? In almost all instances, to be considered eligible for state-based student aid, you must file Uncle Sam's

FAFSA (and on it, indicate your home state). Some states, those that use the institutional methodology, might ask you to use the College Board's PROFILE, and finally, some states have their own applications. Important: Many states have already noted that using the federal methodology to determine eligibility means more students are qualifying for aid. Unfortunately, state grants are not usually entitlement programs, so when the money runs out, too bad! Again, apply early!

A Summary of State Programs

The following summary table describes state programs other than state participation in federal programs like the Stafford and PLUS loans. With regard to Stafford and PLUS loans, most states have a guaranteeing agency to administer loans. Here is an explanation of the table's columns:

Column 1—In-State Study. These are need-based grants, generally restricted to undergraduates. Many of these grants are funded with help from Uncle Sam's State Student Incentive Grant (SSIG). Unfortunately, SSIG is a frequent target of over zealous budget cutters who feel state grant programs are now well established and no longer need matching funds from Uncle Sam for survival. States who rely on SSIG respond by saying that without the incentive of federal matches they may end their grant programs and transfer their money into other efforts. It looks like SSIG will survive in 1999/2000, and be re-named LEAP—the Leveraging Educational Assistance Partnership Program.

Column 2—Some Other States. Some states provide need-based assistance to residents attending schools out-of-state. These states make grants worth $17 million.

Column 3—Merit Programs. Generally, there are three kinds of merit programs. The first type is based on financial need; however, you must meet some academic threshold to be eligible. The second is based on academic accomplishment, but you must demonstrate financial need to qualify for a monetary award, otherwise, your recognition is honorary. The last is based solely on academic accomplishment. Your award is not affected by your finances. Funding for merit-based programs is growing much faster than funding for need-based programs because states don't want to lose their best students to other states.

Column 4—Special Loans. These loans are separate from any federal programs. For example, in Minnesota, first and second year students may borrow $4,500 per year at .75% above the 91 day T-bill rate (Juniors and Seniors may borrow $6,000 per year). In some cases, out-of-state students attending a school in the state underwriting the loans may benefit from the low rates.

Column 5—Teaching. To increase the supply of teachers, many states have instituted special loan programs, with "forgiveness" features if the students actually end up in classrooms. If the students don't go into teaching, they must repay the aid. Some programs limit their benefits to students who teach in a shortage area. This could mean a subject area like math or science. It could also mean a geographic area like rural America or the inner-city.

Column 6—Special Fields. This category covers a variety of programs designed to increase representation in other fields in which the state believes it has shortages. These fields may include medicine, nursing, special education, bilingual education, etc. At least 30 states also get money for loan forgiveness from Uncle's "National Health Service Corps." For more information, you'll have to contact your state's Department of Health Services, or Department of Public Health.

Column 7—Minority Group Programs. Beneficiaries must usually be African-American, Latino or Native American—Eskimo, Indian or Aleutian.

Column 8—Work-Study. State operated programs similar to the federal work-study or cooperative education programs.

Column 9—Veterans. Special state benefits to state residents who served in the Armed Forces, usually during times of hostilities. For more information, you may have to contact your state's Department of Veteran's Affairs.

Column 10—National Guard. State educational benefits for serving in the state's National Guard. These are in addition to federal benefits.

Columns 11,12, 13. Special benefits to state residents who are dependents of deceased or disabled veterans, POWs, MIAs, or police/firefighters killed on duty.

Column 14—Military Dependents. These states let military personnel and dependents stationed within the state, attend in-state universities at in-state rates.

Column 15—Tuition Savings Plans. Most states now encourage early planning for college. Income from "Baccalaureate Bonds" is tax exempt if used to pay college expenses. "Prepaid Tuition Plans" let parents make a lump sum investment (or periodic payments) to guarantee tomorrow's tuition (room and board) at today's prices. The guarantee is usually good at any of the state's public or private colleges. Increasingly, they are good out-of-state, as well. No two plans are the same. Mississippi gives state income tax deductions to families who make payments to these plans.

	1. In-State Study	2. Some Other States	3. Merit Programs	4. Special Loans	5. Teaching	6. Special Fields	7. Minority Gp Prgrms	8. Work Study	9. Veterans	10. National Guard	Dependent of			14. Active Duty	15. Tuition Savings Plan
											11. Disabled Vet	12. POW or MIA	13. Police/Fireman		
Alabama	X		X		X	X	X			X	X		X	X	X
Alaska	X	X		X	X										X
Arizona	X													X	
Arkansas	X		X		X	X	X			X	X	X	X	X	X
California	X		X		X	X		X					X	X	
Colorado	X		X			X		X	X	X		X	X	X	X
Connecticut	X	X	X	X				X	X		X	X		X	X
Delaware	X	X	X		X	X		X		X	X	X	X		
DC	X	X												X	
Florida	X		X		X	X	X	X			X	X		X	X
Georgia			X		X	X				X			X		
Guam			X	X	X	X								X	
Hawaii	X		X							X				X	
Idaho	X		X		X	X	X	X				X	X		
Illinois	X		X		X	X	X		X	X	X		X		X
Indiana	X	X	X				X	X						X	X
Iowa	X		X	X	X	X		X		X					
Kansas	X		X		X	X	X	X						X	X
Kentucky	X		X		X	X		X		X	X	X	X	X	X
Louisiana	X		X			X		X		X	X		X	X	X
Maine	X	X			X	X	X		X		X	X	X	X	X
Maryland	X	X	X		X		X		X	X	X	X	X	X	X
Massachusetts	X	X	X	X	X				X	X	X	X	X	X	X
Michigan	X			X		X	X	X	X	X	X	X			X
Minnesota	X		X	X			X	X	X	X	X		X		X
Mississippi	X		X		X	X	X			X	X	X	X	X	X
Missouri	X		X		X	X			X		X		X	X	X
Montana	X		X				X	X	X	X	X	X	X	X	X
Nebraska	X		X			X	X		X	X	X		X	X	
Nevada	X		X	X		X	X	X	X	X	X	X	X		X
New Hampshire	X	X		X		X			X		X			X	X
New Jersey	X		X	X		X							X		
New Mexico	X	X	X		X	X	X	X	X						
New York	X		X		X	X	X		X		X	X	X	X	
North Carolina	X		X		X	X	X	X	X	X	X	X	X	X	X
North Dakota	X		X			X	X			X	X	X	X	X	
Ohio	X	X	X			X					X	X	X	X	X
Oklahoma	X		X			X	X					X			
Oregon	X					X							X	X	X
Pennsylvania	X	X	X			X		X	X			X			X
Puerto Rico	X		X					X		X				X	
Rhode Island	X	X		X				X							X
South Carolina	X		X		X					X	X	X	X	X	X
South Dakota	X					X			X	X	X	X			
Tennessee	X		X		X		X						X		X

	1. In-State Study	2. Some Other States	3. Merit Programs	4. Special Loans	5. Teaching	6. Special Fields	7. Minority Gp prgrms	8. Work Study	9. Veterans	10. National Guard	Dependent of			14. Active Duty	15. Tuition Savings Plan
											11. Disabled Vet	12. POW or MIA	13. Police/Fireman		
Texas	X	X				X	X	X	X	X		X	X	X	X
Utah	X							X							X
Vermont	X	X				X					X				
Virgin Islands	X					X				X					
Virginia	X		X		X	X	X			X	X			X	X
Washington	X	X	X			X	X	X	X				X	X	X
West Virginia	X	X			X	X								X	
Wisconsin	X		X			X	X		X	X	X				X
Wyoming	X				X	X			X						X

North Carolina integrates a low-interest loan into its "College Vision Fund." Minnesota gives families a 15% match on annual savings. Recent favorable tax rulings are expected to spur millions of families to enroll in these plans—to the tune of $6.5 billion. (see Prepaid Tuition Plans in Chapter 8)

Innovative State Programs

No two states have the same programs. Here are some you should ask about. Your questions might lead you to little-known opportunities.

Reciprocal Arrangements I

Reciprocal arrangements between states often permit students living near a state's border to study in the adjoining state at discounted tuition rates. Sometimes this means students actually pay less by going out-of-state. Unfortunately, this kind of "trade imbalance" when combined with ever tightening state budgets are causing some states (especially those that take in more students than they send away) to rethink the finances of reciprocity and scale back on their agreements.

Reciprocal Arrangements II

Study out-of-state at reduced rates when your major is not offered in state. Such arrangements are coordinated by multi-state consortia:

- *The Western Interstate Commission for Higher Education* covers Alaska, Arizona, California, Colorado, Hawaii, Idaho, Montana, Nevada, New Mexico, North Dakota, Oregon, South Dakota, Utah, Washington and Wyoming. For program information, contact WICHE, PO Box 9752, Boulder, CO 80301, http://www.wiche.edu/.

- *The Southern Regional Education Board* covers Alabama, Arkansas, Florida, Georgia, Kentucky, Louisiana, Maryland, Mississippi, North Carolina, Oklahoma, South Carolina, Tennessee, Texas, Virginia, and West Virginia. For program information, contact SREB, 592 10th Street, NW, Atlanta, GA 30318, http://www.sreb.org.
- *The New England Regional Student Program* covers Connecticut, Maine, Massachusetts, New Hampshire, Rhode Island, and Vermont. For program information, contact the New England Board of Education, 45 Temple Place, Boston, MA 02111, http://www.nebhe.org/.
- *The Midwest Student Exchange Program* covers Kansas, Michigan, Minnesota, Missouri, and Nebraska. For program information, contact these states' higher education agencies, or http://www.umn.edu/mhec/.

Reciprocal Arrangements III

WICHE offers a second program in which undergraduates pay reduced tuition at any participating school in the region. The reduced rate equals resident tuition plus 50%; a large savings over non-resident rates. Graduate and professional students may study outside their home state and pay in-state tuition in certain fields of study.

Tuition Equalization

These programs reduce the difference in tuition costs between in-state public and private colleges. Examples: Alabama, Arizona, Florida, Georgia, Indiana, Kansas, Kentucky, New Mexico, North Carolina, Ohio, South Carolina, Texas, Virginia and Wisconsin. These states make grants worth well over $100 million, although the states which face insufficient funds for public schools might start rethinking giving tax money to private schools.

Private School Grant Programs

Forty-three percent all need-based state grant aid goes to students attending in-state private institutions.

Free Scholarship Searches

Several states offer their residents free (or low cost) scholarship searches. Examples: Arkansas, Florida, Illinois, Maine, Michigan, and Rhode Island.

Discounts for Senior Citizens

Most of our states give tuition discounts to seniors. Some states waive tuition entirely. See Chapter 23 for more information.

Dual Enrollment

Nearly forty states allow high school students to take real college courses and count them toward high school graduation. State officials say this allows high school juniors and seniors to get a more rigorous education and earn a year or two of college credit at the same time.

Brain Drain

Nebraska is making an all-out effort to keep bright students from leaving the state for more "cosmopolitan and less topographically challenged places." Nebraska businesses are providing scholarships, internships, and the promise of future jobs. The state government is offering merit scholarships to students who promise to earn their degrees in a high-demand field, and remain a Cornhusker for at least three years after graduation. Alabama, Alaska, Connecticut, Indiana, Mississippi, Oklahoma and South Carolina are also doing more to keep their high-ability students in state.

Western Governors University

The governors of Alaska, Arizona, Colorado, Idaho, Guam, Hawaii, Idaho, Montana, Nebraska, New Mexico, North Dakota, Oregon, Utah, Washington, and Wyoming are pooling their resources to create a virtual university with professors from throughout the region. They don't intend for this to replace the traditional college experience, but to serve the needs of nontraditional students. For more information, visit http://www.wgu.edu.

Community College Partnerships

Many states encourage partnerships between two- and four-year colleges to help make the transition seamless. Sometimes students are promised admission to the four-year school. Sometimes they are guaranteed that their course credits will transfer. Sometimes they're offered additional aid opportunities. And sometimes they just get guidance on course selection.

Community Service Programs

States were way ahead of the community service bandwagon. All fifty have ties to AmeriCorps, while others also fund their own projects. To find your State Commission on National Service and receive a list of funded programs, contact AmeriCorps, 202/606-5000, 1201 New York Ave. NW, Washington, DC 20525, http://www.cns.gov/.

State Standouts

There's lots of action on the state level—some of which will result in important new programs (and some which will fizzle).

Arizona. To encourage "geography bound" students to pursue four-year degrees, Arizona is experimenting with a plan that would give students money to use at under-utilized private colleges that are nearer to their homes than any of the state's public schools. This alternative is cheaper than building new public university facilities, and will help the state deal with its expected enrollment boom.

Arkansas, Indiana and Louisiana: In Arkansas, they're called Academic Challenge Scholarships. In Indiana, they're called Twenty-First Century Scholars. They have similar themes: States guarantee to pay in-state tuition for low-income students who make certain commitments. For example, they must maintain a minimum GPA in college prep courses. The theory behind this performance-based tuition waiver is that some students drop out because they perceive HS as a dead end. But, if you promise them a college education (assuming they stay out of trouble and meet admission standards), you'll see a huge increase in educational achievement.

Georgia: Helping Outstanding Pupils Educationally (HOPE) ensures that every Georgia HS grad can receive free tuition at one of Georgia's public colleges or universities, or up to $3,000 for a private, in-state school. To qualify, students on a college prep track must have a 3.0 GPA in sixteen core-curriculum courses (4 math, 3 science, 3 social studies, 4 English, 2 foreign languages). Students working toward a vocational/technical diploma must earn a 3.2 GPA in thirteen core-curriculum subjects (3 math, 3 science, 3 social studies, 4 English). Students must also maintain a 3.0 GPA while in college to continue receiving money. So far, 235,000+ students have benefited from HOPE, which is funded by the Lottery for Education. In Georgia, call 800/546-HOPE, http://www.hope.gsfc.org/. Connecticut, Florida, Illinois, Louisiana, Maryland, Mississippi, Missouri, New Mexico and Virginia are considering their own statewide merit programs.

Kentucky. Commonwealth Merit Scholarships allow high school students to earn college scholarships based on their year-end GPA. Annual awards range from $125 to $500 with $125 going to those with GPAs of 2.5 and $500 to those with a perfect 4.0. Students who maintain an A average for all four years would receive $2,000.

Louisiana. START Smart (Student Tuition Assistance and Revenue Trust) is an innovative approach to rewarding early savings for college. Participants save at their own pace and their money is professionally managed by the State Treasurer. The state then adds an annual incentive ranging from 4% to 14% of the amount deposited during the calendar year. For lower income depositors, those with AGIs under $15,000, that match would be at 14%. For higher income depositors, those with AGIs between $75,000 and $100,000, that match would be at 4%.

Maine. Education Network of Maine televises courses throughout the state at nearly 80 regional centers and high school sites. Students can request library materials via their computers, and speak with professors via toll free numbers.

Maine. Maine residents attending out-of-state schools, and out-of-state students attending Maine schools can take out a "Super Loan" at 1% below the current Stafford rate.

Massachusetts: UPlan is a hybrid of many other states' college savings plans. Both residents and nonresidents may invest in Massachusetts bonds and redeem them later for a guaranteed percentage of tuition at any of over 80 participating (public and private) Massachusetts colleges. Assume for example the parent buys a $5,000 bond. If tuition this year at State U. is $5,000 and tuition at Private U. is $20,000, that bond will be worth 100% of tuition at State U. or 25% at Private U. regardless of the cost of these two schools when the student eventually enrolls. Massachusetts has promised participating colleges they will be paid a rate equal to the bond's original value plus interest equal to 2% over inflation, compounded annually. The beauty of this plan is not only the peace of mind it gives investors that their savings will keep pace with tuition increases, but also the incentive it gives colleges to keep tuition increases at or below inflation plus 2%. Because Massachusetts invests the money in state-issued bonds, income from the bonds is exempt from state taxes, even if the money is not used for tuition. Investors who decide not to use the money for tuition receive a return equal to their original principal compounded by a rate equal to inflation.

For more information on UPlan, contact the Massachusetts Educational Financing Authority, 800/449-MEFA, http://www.mefa.org.

Texas, Montana, North Carolina, Florida, Maryland and Utah: These states are cracking down on the number of credits you may take at subsidized, in-state rates. Why? Too many students are taking too many extra courses and spending too many years in college. These states are fed up, and think they've found a way to get students through college more quickly, and save everyone a bit of money. Texas goes one better—state residents who graduate within three credit hours of their degree requirements earn a $1,000 rebate. In other words, if you need 120 credit hours to graduate, and you finish with 123 credit hours or less, you're a winner. Maryland imposes a four-year limit on state-aid and links awards to grade point averages. Recipients must maintain a "C" average.

Virginia and Texas: Special incentive grants to induce students of one racial group to attend a state public university in which another racial group makes up a significant proportion of the student body.

Directory of State Agencies

Many state agencies sport virtual addresses where you'll find student aid information, school links, research data, news releases, even staff bios. Link up at http://www.ed.gov/offices/OPE/agencies.html.

Alabama
334-281-1998
AL Commission on Higher Ed.
3465 Norman Ridge Rd
Montgomery, AL 36105

Alaska
907-465-2967
Comm. on Postsecondary Ed.
3030 Vintage Blvd.
Juneau, AK 99801

Arizona
602-229-2531
Comm. for Postsecondary Ed.
2020 N. Central Avenue, #275
Phoenix, AZ 85004

Arkansas
501-324-9300
Dept. of Higher Education
114 E. Capitol St.
Little Rock, AR 72201

California
916-526-7590
Student Aid Commission
PO Box 419026
Rancho Cordova, CA 95741

Colorado
303-866-2723
Comm. on Higher Ed.
1300 Broadway, 2nd Floor
Denver, CO 80203

Connecticut
860-947-1855
Department of Higher Ed.
61 Woodland Street
Hartford, CT 06105

Delaware
302-577-3240
Higher Ed. Commission
820 N. French Street
Wilmington, DE 19801

District of Columbia
202-727-3685
Postsecondary Ed. Office
2100 ML King Jr. Ave., SE #401
Washington, DC 20020

Florida
904-487-0649
Student Fin. Assistance
325 W. Gaines Street
Tallahassee, FL 32399

Georgia
770-414-3018
Student Finance Authority
2082 E. Exchange Pl., #245
Tucker, GA 30084

Hawaii
808-956-8213
Postsecondary Ed Comm.
Bachman Hall, Room 202
2444 Dole Street
Honolulu, HI 96822

Idaho
208-334-2270
State Board of Education
PO Box 83720
Boise, ID 83720

Illinois
847-948-8500
Student Assistance Comm.
1755 Lake Cook Road
Deerfield, IL 60015

Indiana
317-232-2350
Student Assistance Comm.
150 West Market St., 5th fl
Indianapolis, IN 46204

Iowa
515-281-3501
Iowa College Aid Commission
914 Grand Avenue, #201
Des Moines, IA 50309

Kansas
785-296-3517
Board of Regents,
700 SW Harrison, #1410
Topeka, KS 66603

Kentucky
502-696-7200
Higher Ed. Assistance Auth.
1050 US 127 South #102
Frankfort, KY 40601-4323

Louisiana
504-922-1011, 800/259-5626
Student Fin. Assistance Comm.
PO Box 91202
Baton Rouge, LA 70821-9202

Maine
207-287-2183
Finance Authority of Maine
PO Box 949
Augusta, ME 04330

Maryland
410-974-5370
MD Higher Ed. Commission
16 Francis Street
Annapolis, MD 21401

Massachusetts
617-727-9420
Higher Ed. Coord. Council
330 Stuart Street
Boston, MA 02116

Michigan
517-373-3394
Higher Ed Assistance Auth.
PO Box 30462
Lansing, MI 48909

Minnesota
612-296-3974
Higher Ed. Services Office
550 Cedar Street, #400
St. Paul, MN 55101

Mississippi
601-982-6663
Financial Assistance Board
3825 Ridgewood Road
Jackson, MS 39211-6453

Missouri
574-751-3940
Student Assistance Resources Services
3515 Amazonas Drive
Jefferson City, MO 65102

Montana
406-444-6594
MT University System
2500 Broadway
Helena, MT 59620

Nebraska
402-471-6506
Postsecondary Ed. Comm.
PO Box 95005
Lincoln, NE 68509

Nevada
702-687-5915
State Department of Ed
400 W. King St.,
Carson City, NV 89710

New Hampshire
603-271-2555
Postsecondary Ed. Comm.
2 Industrial Park Drive
Concord, NH 03301-8512

New Jersey
609-588-3268, 800/792-8670
Office of St. Fin. Assistance
4 Quakerbridge Plaza, CN 540
Trenton, NJ 08625

New Mexico
505-827-7383
Comm. on Higher Ed.
1068 Cerrillos Road
Santa Fe, NM 87501

New York
518-474-5642
Higher Ed. Services Comm.
One Commerce Plaza
Albany, NY 12255

North Carolina
919-549-8614
State Ed. Assistance Authority
PO Box 2688
Chapel Hill, NC 27515

North Dakota
701-224-2271
Student Financial Asst. Prgm.
600 East Boulevard Ave.
Bismark, ND 58505

Ohio
614-466-7420, 800/837-6752
OH Student Aid Commission
PO Box 182452
Columbus, OH 43218-2452

Oklahoma
405-858-4300
State Regents for Higher Ed
PO Box 3000
Oklahoma City, OK 73101

Oregon
541-687-7400
State Scholarship Comm.
1500 Valley River Dr., #100
Eugene, OR 97401

Pennsylvania
717-257-2800, 800/692-7435
Higher Ed Assistance Agency
1200 North 7th Street
Harrisburg, PA 17102

Rhode Island
401-736-1100, 800/922-9855
Higher Ed. Assistance Authority
560 Jefferson Boulevard
Warwick, RI 02886

South Carolina
803-737-1200
Higher Ed. Tuition Grants Comm..
1310 Lady Street, #811
Columbia, SC 29201

South Dakota
605-773-3134
Office of the Secretary
Dept. of Education
700 Governors Drive
Pierre, SD 57501-2291

Tennessee
615-741-3605, 800/342-1663
TN Student Assistance Corp.
404 James Robertson Pkwy
Parkway Towers, Suite 1900
Nashville, TN 37243-0820

Texas
512-483-6340, 800/242-3062
Higher Ed. Coord. Board
Box 12788, Capitol Station
Austin, TX 78711

Utah
801-321-7205
Utah State Board of Regents
335 W.N. Temple
3 Triad, # 550
Salt Lake City, UT 84180

Vermont
802-655-9602, 800/642-3177
Student Assistance Corp.
Champlain Mill, Box 2000
Winooski, VT 05404

Virginia
804-225-3146
Council of Higher Education
101 North 14th Street
Richmond, VA 23219

Washington
360-753-7800
Higher Ed. Coord. Board
917 Lake Ridge Way, SW
Olympia, WA 98504

West Virginia
304-588-2691
State Dept. of Education
1900 Washington St., #358
Charleston, WV 25305

Wisconsin
608-266-2354
Higher Ed. Aids Board
PO Box 7885
Madison, WI 53707

Wyoming
307-777-6265
State Dept. of Education
2300 Capitol Ave., 2nd fl.
Cheyenne, WY 82002

Guam
Univ. of Guan
303 University Drive
Mangilao, Guam 96923

Northern Mariana Islands
PO Box 1250
Saipan, Northern Mariana Islands
670-234-5498

Puerto Rico
PO Box 23305, UPR Station
Rio Piedras, PR 00931

Virgin Islands
PO Box 11900
St. Thomas, VI 00801

CHAPTER 12

LETTING THE BOSS PAY FOR IT

OK. You are willing to pick up a little maturity along with your education. You are willing to invest some extra time into earning a baccalaureate. And you want to start your professional career without the staggering burden of student debt. What can you do? You can investigate two major alternative methods of financing an education: (1) Letting the boss pay for it or (2) letting the military pay for it. Chapters 12 and 13 cover both of these "employee" tuition plans—those found in corporate offices and those sponsored by the US Military.

Company Tuition Aid

Once upon a time you could go to work for a company that had a tuition reimbursement plan, take college courses on your own time, and let the employer foot the bill. Then the IRS decided this was too good a deal. It ruled that courses had to be job-related to qualify as a benefit. Courses not job-related, but paid for by the employer, had to be declared as taxable income. That ruling pulled the rug out from what had promised to become a major alternative program for young people. The reason: Jobs at the bottom are often so narrowly defined that few courses required for a degree could pass the "job-related test." Why would a shipping clerk need a course in American History? While hurting people at the entry level, the law had little impact on the educational pursuits of the higher-ups. A manager might justify a literature course to improve her writing skills and a sales manager could qualify for an Anthropology program to better understand the cultural factors that influence buying.

The Tax-Reform Act of 1986 brought back the exclusion of non job-related tuition benefits (Section 127 for anyone who cares to read the 1.3 million word tax code), but limited the exclusion to $5,250 per year. The Taxpayer Relief Act of 1997 extended the exclusion for another three years, but limited it to undergraduate students. (This doesn't mean companies will stop paying tuition for their grad student employees, just that these employees will owe some money on the gift; all in all, still a pretty sweet benefit).

Reimbursement for job-related courses continues to be deductible for grad students as well as undergraduates.

If your employer reimburses you for tuition, he or she may do so with strings attached. For example, you may have to stay with your generous firm for a set number of years after you graduate, or maintain a certain grade point average while in school. These requirements are only fair—after all, employers help employees with their education for the good of the company, not just for the good of the employee. Ford is one company that realizes this; it pays 100% of any course approved by a boss.

Cooperative Education

Co-op Education combines formal studies with an off-campus job related to your major. The money you earn will, in most cases, cover college costs. In some schools, practically the entire student body participates in cooperative education. Examples: Northeastern University (MA), and GMI Engineering & Management Institute (MI). There are three common methods for rotating between school and work:

- **The alternating method.** Under this method, you are a full-time student for a semester, then you work for a semester, with the cycle repeating itself until you graduate—usually in five years.
- **The parallel method.** Here you attend classes part time and work between 15 and 25 hours a week. You may be a student in the morning and a worker in the afternoon, or vice versa. This method, too, may require five years for degree completion.
- **Extended day method.** The student works full-time and attends school in the evening.

Some cooperative education statistics: 900 participating colleges, 50,000 participating employers, and 200,000 enrolled students who earn $1.3 billion each year. Employers like co-op, considering it, in the Wall Street Journal's words, "a source of realistic, work-oriented, future full-time employees."

What's New in Federal Cooperative Education?

Uncle Sam has consolidated his various work/school programs into a two-part Student Educational Employment Program (SEEP):

The Student Temporary Employment Program gives students the flexibility to earn a salary while continuing their studies. The work may be during the summer or school year and need not be related to the their field of study.

The Student Career Experience Program gives students work experience directly related to their field of study. Students alternate formal periods of work and study and may be eligible for permanent employment after graduation.

Cooperative Education Resources

1. *The Advantages of Cooperative Education* and *Co-op/Career* brochure from the National Commission for Cooperative Education. The first brochure describes the benefits of co-op for students, employers and colleges. The other highlights career benefits from participation in co-op. NCCE, 360 Huntington Avenue, 384CP, Boston, MA 02115; Also, *Cooperative Education Undergraduate Program Roster.* A list of colleges offering co-op, arranged alphabetically by state.
2. *Directory of College Cooperative Education Programs* from Oryx Press and the Commission for Cooperative Education (address above).
3. *Earn and Learn: An Introduction to Cooperative Education* links you up with federal programs—you'll find an overview of federal co-op, the sponsoring agencies, and the participating colleges (inside back cover).
4. *Your Home State.* Most states have work-study or co-op programs. If your counselor doesn't have the address for your state's Co-op Education Center, get the information from your state agency (Chapter 11).
5. *The Cooperative Education Association* is developing a web site with links to a variety of co-op resources, http://www.ceaimc.org/.
6. *The Cooperative Education Network* web site has extensive descriptions of co-op programs, including employer and employee expectations, as well as links to programs at nearly 100 member schools (http://www.co-op.uc.edu/home).
7. *Your College.* Nearly 900 colleges have cooperative education programs. If the financial aid office doesn't have the information you need, ask if there's a separate co-op office on campus.

Internships

It can be hard to draw a clear line line between cooperative education and internships. Here are two general distinctions:

- Co-op participants alternate between formal studies and work throughout their college career, while internships often last only one semester or one summer break.
- Co-op participants always get a paycheck; interns may or may not. In fact, the more "desirable" the internship, the less the pay.

CHAPTER 13

PUTTING ON THE UNIFORM

Don't overlook the military! You can pick up tuition dollars before you enter the service, while in uniform and after being discharged. There are programs for active duty personnel and programs for Reservists. And there are programs for officers and programs for enlisted people.

Military tuition benefits are dispensed with no reference to financial need. You qualify for them whether you are rich or poor. But they are not free. The military will want something in return. At a minimum you'll have to get a haircut, salute superior officers and give a few years of your time. The U.S. Armed Forces have collaborated on a web site that links you up with lots of options, and answers your questions (oh-so-objectively), about whether the military is for you, http://myfuture.com (or 800/893-LEAD).

This chapter covers benefits to consider before you enter the service, while you're in the service, and after you get out of the service.

Before Entering Service

Military Academies

The academies are extremely competitive. Good grades, extracurricular activities, leadership and athletic excellence are in demand. So are superb health and solid SAT scores. You should have 600+ on the math portion and combined scores of 1200 or more. Contact the academies during your junior year of high school. Most appointments are made by U.S. Representatives and Senators. Tell your elected officials about your interest. Make sure they open a file on you in their offices. Keep feeding that file with your achievements. Also add recommendations. Make sure you obtain recommendations from people who are deemed important by the elected officials.

- **Army:** Admissions Office, US Military Academy, 606 Thayer Road, West Point, NY 10996, 800/822-USMA, http://www.usma.edu
- **Air Force:** Director of Cadet Admissions, US Air Force Academy, Colorado Springs, CO 80840, 800/443-9266, http://www.usafa.af.mil

- **Navy:** Candidate Guidance, US Naval Academy, Leahy Hall, Annapolis, MD 21402, 800/638-9156, http://www.nadn.navy.mil
- **Merchant Marines:** Admissions, US Merchant Marine Academy, Steamboat Road, Kings Point, NY 11024, http://www.usmma.edu
- **Coast Guard:** Admissions, US Coast Guard Academy, 15 Mohegan Avenue, New London, CT 06320, http://www.dot.gov/dotinfo/uscg

ROTC Scholarships

The military has one-, two- and four-year ROTC scholarships which pay for tuition and fees. You will also receive $450 annually for books and up to $1,500 in spending money. Some years the services place caps on their top awards. For example, the Army currently pays up to $16,000 per year.

A 1250 SAT (28 ACT) will enhance your chances for an ROTC scholarship. So will a varsity letter and membership in the National Honor Society. Nearly all scholarship winners are in the top 25% of their HS class; Three-quarters are class officers, and over 55% are captains of varsity athletic teams. Application should be made by November 1 of your senior year (the Army has an early application option with a July 15 deadline). There will probably be an interview. Before the interview, brush up on current events. Also, be prepared to give your reasons for seeking a military career. An interest in the physical sciences, engineering or nursing will help.

ROTC is not offered at all colleges. The services will provide you with a list. You may use your award at any college on that list assuming you are able to secure admission (something you must do on your own).

For more information on general recruiting and ROTC:

- **Army,** 800/USA-ROTC, http://www.goarmy.com, www.armyrotc.com
- **Air Force,** 800/423-USAF, http://www.airforce.com
- **Navy,** 800/USA-NAVY, http://www.navyjobs.com
- **Marines,** 800/MARINES, http://www.usmc.mil/wwwmcrc/mcrc.htm

The Regular ROTC Program

This is not a scholarship program. Students join the program in their freshman year, at colleges that offer ROTC. For two years they march and salute for free. In their junior and senior years, participants do get paid: $100 per month.

ROTC-Coop Education Combination

The Army reserves cooperative education positions for some ROTC cadets in nearby Army installations. These positions, which provide added earnings, will also lead to federal employment after the participant has served on active duty.

One-Shot Programs

On occasion, the Navy and the Air Force need highly specialized technical people and will use financial aid as a recruiting tool. For instance, the Air Force has a "College Senior Engineer Program" for students in electrical, nuclear, astronautical and aeronautical engineering. Students can sign up during their junior year. In their senior year, they will receive $1740 or $900 per month. After graduation, they are called to active duty, attend Officer Training School and serve as a commissioned officer.

Military Medical Programs

See Chapter 20

In-Service Educational Benefits

Commissioned Officer

Each year, the services select hundreds of officers to attend graduate schools. The chosen officers receive full pay and allowances and have all their educational expenses met while pursuing their master's degree or doctorate.

Off-Duty Programs

All services have arrangements with civilian colleges and encourage off-duty course work, with the services paying up to 75% of the tuition costs (amount varies with rank and length of service). Through credit transfers and arrangements with accrediting institutions, such off-duty courses can be accumulated to gain credit for associate, baccalaureate or even master's degrees. For more information on this and the 1300 schools participating in the Army's Concurrent Admissions Program (ConAP) contact Servicemembers Opportunity Colleges, National Headquarters, One Dupont Circle, Suite 680, Washington DC 20036.

Reserve Duty Programs

Through the National Guard and Army Reserves, you can receive approximately $7,316 in (tax-free) education benefits under the Montgomery GI Bill. That combined with good, part-time pay as a reservist can total $25,100 over six years. Furthermore, you can earn cash bonuses—for example up to $2,000 for enlistment in the reserves or completing advanced training in the National Guard.

Loan Repayment Options

The Army Reserve, National Guard, and the Regular Army also offer repayment on federal student loans (e.g., Stafford and Perkins). In the Army

Reserve and National Guard, you may have up to $10,000 forgiven at the rate of 15% or $1,500 per year, whichever is greater. As an incentive for enlistment in selected skills, the Army will double those amounts to $20,000 in total loans, forgiven at the rate of 15% or $3,000 per year, whichever is greater.

In the Regular Army you may have up to $65,000 forgiven at the rate of 33 1/3% or $1,500 per year, whichever is greater.

After Service Benefits

The Montgomery GI Bill

This is a contributory system. While on active duty, the soldier, sailor, or airman allocates $100 per month (to a maximum of $1,200) to an educational fund. At the end of a two-year enlistment, the Veteran's Administration contributes $12,865; at the end of a three- or four-year enlistment the VA contributes $15,835. After you leave the military, your money will be paid directly to you in monthly installments for each month you're enrolled in college. For example, if you enlisted for four years and qualified for $17,035 ($15,835 + $1,200), you would receive around $473 per month for 36 months to help you pay your educational costs. If your school year has nine months, this income stream should cover your full four years. You have ten years to use your education fund from the date of your discharge. Note: This benefit increases each year with the inflation rate.

For students who score 50 or higher on the Armed Forces Qualification Text (AFQT), the Army sweetens the pot with bonuses for enlisting in critical "Military Occupation Specialties" (MOS). This could add up to $12,435 for a two-year enlistment, $14,765 for a three-year enlistment, or $22,765 for a four-year enlistment bringing your total fund to $26,500, $33,000 or $40,000 respectively. The Army calls this bonus "The Army College Fund." Call 800/USA-ARMY for more information.

The Coast Guard and Marine Corps have similar college funds, which top out at $30,000 in tuition support, when combined with the GI Bill.

Dependents Education Benefits

Wives and children of veterans who died or were totally disabled as the result of service qualify for Veterans Administration educational benefits. These benefits are also extended to dependents of former Prisoners of War and soldiers classified as MIA—Missing in Action.

State Educational Benefits

Most states have aid programs for Veterans and their dependents. See

Chapter 11 and write to your state's Office of Veteran Affairs (addresses in *Need A Lift*).

Benefits for Military Dependents

Army

1. Army Emergency Relief. Scholarships for unmarried children of active duty, retired, or deceased soldiers. For scholarships, apply by March 1 to Army Emergency Relief, 200 Stovall Street, Alexandria, VA 22332.
2. Summary of Educational Benefits. DA Pamphlet 352-2, Headquarters, Department of the Army, TAPC-PDE, Washington, DC 20314.

Air Force

Air Force Aid Society. General Henry H. Arnold Education Grant program for surviving spouses and dependent sons and daughters of active duty, retired or deceased Air Force as well as spouses of active duty members (stationed stateside only) attending undergraduate college. Veterans and reservists are not eligible. Approximately 5,000 grants per year. $1,500 for freshmen; $1,000 for all other undergrads. Air Force Aid Society, Education Assistance, 1745 Jefferson Davis Highway, Suite 202, Arlington, VA 22202-3410, 800/429-9475. By mid-March.

Navy/Marines

Dependent's Scholarship Program for U.S. Navy, Marine Corps, and Coast Guard Dependents. More than 75 Navy-oriented organizations currently sponsor scholarships or offer aid for study beyond the high school level. Dependent sons and daughters of Navy, Marine Corps, Coast Guard, and former members are eligible for these scholarships or aid. Information may be obtained from *Need A Lift?* (see below)

Benefits for the Families of Former Military

Former military families tend to congregate in organizations after leaving the service. Nearly every military association sponsors student aid programs to the children of its members. For a comprehensive list, obtain *Need a Lift?* published annually by The American Legion, Emblem Sales, PO Box 1050, Indianapolis, IN 46206, $3.00, prepaid. Here are a few examples:

AMVETS Memorial Scholarship

15 awards of $4,000 each (spread over 4 years). Applicants must be AMVETS members, or the child or grandchild of an AMVET member (living or deceased) and have exhausted all government financial aid. Must

also demonstrate need and academic achievement and be a US citizen. Must maintain a 3.0 GPA. Applications available between January 1 and February 15 (due by April 15). Send SASE to AMVETS National Headquarters, attn. Scholarships, PO Box 1347, Lanham, MD 20706, 301/459-9600.

Reserve Officer Association

Henry J. Reilly Memorial Scholarships. 110 (merit) awards for dependents of Association members; 35 for graduate students, 75 for undergrads. Deadlines vary from April 1 to April 30. For additional criteria and application request, send SASE to Scholarship Fund, ROA, One Constitution Avenue, NE, Washington, DC 20002.

Retired Officers Scholarship Program

Interest-free loan program for undergraduate students who are dependent children of active, reserve and retired uniformed service personnel. Maximum loan: $15,000 ($3,000 per year) spread over five years. Repayment begins three to four months after leaving college. Recipients of this loan are automatically considered for several TROA-sponsored grant programs. Request application by December 30 from Scholarship Committee, TROA, 201 N. Washington St., Alexandria, VA 22314, http://www.troa.org.

A Possible Strategy

Go on active duty for three or four years. While on active duty, take off-duty courses (for which the military will pay up to 75% of the tuition costs) and make sure the courses add up to an associate degree. At the same time participate in the Montgomery GI Bill. When you are ready for discharge, you will have credit for two years of college and a tuition kitty of over $17,000 (more if you were in the infantry) to help you pay for the last two years of college. By the time you get your degree, you will be one or two years older than your non-saluting contemporaries. That minor disadvantage will be offset by greater maturity and self-confidence. Plus, you'll probably be free of debt.

CHAPTER 14

PRIVATE SOURCES WITH FEW STRINGS

Coca-Cola Scholars Foundation, Inc.

151 scholarships per year, 51 for $5000/year, renewable for 4 years. 100 for $1000/year, renewable for 4 years. Applications available only through high school guidance office. Applicants must be high school seniors. Application must be postmarked on or before October 31. Course of study in any discipline. Merit-based scholarship emphasizing leadership. Write to Coca-Cola Scholars Foundation, PO Box 442, Atlanta, GA 30301-0442, 1-800/306-COKE, http://www.coca-cola.com/scholars.

Elks National Foundation

Nearly 500 awards, over $2 million awarded. HS senior, Scholarship, leadership, and financial need. Application from local Elk Lodge, http://www.elks.org/enf.

Hattie M. Strong Foundation

Interest-free loans for last year of college. Up to $3,000 per year. Repayment based on monthly earnings. Applications available between 1 Jan. and 31 March. Hattie M. Strong Foundation, 1620 Eye St., NW, Suite 700, Washington, DC 20006.

Hitachi Foundation

The Yoshiyama Award recognizes outstanding community service and is accompanied by a gift of $5,000 disbursed over two years with no restrictions. Nominees need not be college-bound. By April 1 to Yoshiyama Award, PO Box 19247, Washington, DC 20036. (202) 457-0588.

Pickett & Hatcher Educational Fund, Inc.

Low interest (6%) loan to undergrads in fields of study *other than* law, medicine, or the ministry. Up to $22,000 total (over 4 years). Loan recipients must be legal residents of and attend four-year colleges in Alabama, Florida, Georgia, Kentucky, Mississippi, North Carolina, South Carolina, Tennessee or Virginia. Based on scholastic ability, character, financial need.

Pickett & Hatcher Educational Fund, P.O. Box 8169, Columbus, GA 31908, http://www.pickettandhatcher.org.

Product-Sponsored Scholarship Contests

Keep your eyes open. Companies often put their contest notices in with the Sunday newspaper ads (alongside their product coupons).

Tylenol

500 awards ranging from $250 to $2,500. Leadership, academic achievement is important. Check for applications in your local drugstore, or call 800/676-8437, November deadline.

USA Today

Twenty awards worth $2,500 each. Leadership, academic achievement is important. USA Today, 1000 Wilson Blvd., 10th floor, Arlington, VA 22229.

Walmart

Thousands of awards, $1000 each. Ask your HS counselor for an application.

CHAPTER 15

MONEY IN YOUR COMMUNITY

Nearly every community offers scholarship help to its young citizens. The grants can vary in size from one hundred dollars to several thousand. Community awards are usually circumscribed in their geographic coverage and you must learn about them yourself. There is no central registry. Read your local newspaper carefully, especially the page devoted to club and community affairs. Visit your Chamber of Commerce. It might keep track of local business and corporate scholarships. Also visit the American Legion Post. The legionnaires take a special interest in helping people with their education. And finally, ask your high school counselor!

This chapter gives you some examples.

Your Community

Look for scholarship bulletins from civic associations, businesses, PTA chapters, social and professional clubs, fraternal organizations, patriotic and veterans organizations. Some communities do very well by their students. For example, journalist Carl Rowan founded "Project Excellence," a program that gives scholarships to some of the Washington DC area's brightest African-American students. Each year Mr. Rowan raises nearly $4 million and awards 100+ scholarships (ranging from $4,000 to $60,000). In addition to private donors in your community, you should look toward larger local foundations. There are nearly 400 community funds nationwide which award nearly $100 million to education projects annually.

Your High School

Many high schools have established information clearinghouses to work in conjunction with the guidance office. Students (and their parents) may attend workshops on college financing; they receive individual assistance on filing aid applications; they have access to current financial aid literature; and in some instances, they can tap into computerized scholarship databases. ALL FOR FREE! Some schools have even created foundations to provide "last dollar scholarships" for students with exceptional financial need. Examples: The Scholarship Fund of Alexandria (VA), I Know I Can Columbus (OH), and California Community Foundation, Los Angeles.

"I Have A Dream"

Over a decade ago, the very-wealthy Eugene Lang promised college scholarships (and extra counseling) to an entire 6th grade class at his former elementary school in East Harlem. In 1986, he created the "I Have A Dream" foundation to help other people start similar projects. Reviews have been mixed. Many sponsors have had great success getting at-risk students through high school and into college. Others have found that money alone isn't enough to compensate for missing parents, missing discipline, missing expectations and missing hope. They've also learned it takes many volunteers to keep Dreamers on track. Today, about 10,000 students benefit from over 140 "I Have A Dream" projects in 41 cities across the country. Unfortunately, needy students can't apply directly for this assistance; they can only hope someone will adopt their class (and at a minimum investment of $300,000/class, benefactors are hard to find). For more information, write the foundation at 330 7th Avenue, 20th floor, New York, NY 10001.

Corporate Generosity

It's still too early to judge the effectiveness of "I Have a Dream," but corporate America is jumping on the bandwagon...witness "The Pepsi Challenge" in which the soft-drink company provided scholarship money for "at-risk" students at selected high schools in Detroit and Dallas who met certain GPA and attendance requirements. Similarly, *The Washington Post* gives students at Eastern High School in Washington DC $500 for college for each semester they get all A's and B's. More than 100 Post staffers serve as mentors and more than 30 colleges and universities offer matching grants. For more information on establishing student incentive programs like The Eastern High School 500 Club, please call (202) 334-6834.

Dollars for Scholars®

Dollars for Scholars is a national network of 765 community-based, volunteer-operated scholarship foundations affiliated with the *Citizen's Scholarship Foundation of America* (CSFA). Dollars for Scholars chapters provide financial assistance, academic support programs, and community support for students seeking postsecondary education. Last year, chapters awarded $10.5 million to 18,000 students. CSFA provides nonprofit status, guidelines and materials for chapter operations. All funds are distributed by a local awards committee to students of the community. Ask your counselor if your community has a Dollars for Scholars chapter. If not, and you'd like to start one, contact: Dollars for Scholars, PO Box 297, St. Peter, MN 56082, 800/248-8080.

Community Service Scholarships

If you have demonstrated a solid commitment to serving your community, you may be able to turn your good deeds into college scholarship money. For more information on both of these programs, contact your guidance counselor, or your principal.

National Service Scholars Program

The Corporation for National Service (see below) provides $500 matching scholarships to students who have received at least $500 from their school district, or a local community or civic organization, and who have performed at least one year of volunteer service.

Prudential Spirit of Community Awards

These $1,000 awards (plus an expense-paid trip to Washington) go to two students in each state who have demonstrated "exemplary, self-initiated community service." Schools may nominate one honoree for every 1,500 students, so tell your counselor of your good work.

Community Service Programs

The Corporation for National Service wants to continue funding for about 25,000 AmeriCorps positions (distributed across 450 different projects nationwide) but even if Congressional critics succeed in eliminating this highly and widely praised public service program (see Chapter 10), there will still be opportunities via your home state or a local agency. These 80 state and local organizations spend over $131 million annually on conservation and youth-service corps and enable 30,000 additional volunteers to be rewarded for work on education, environmental and public safety programs.

While each community is free to run its own program, there are several common threads. In general, corps members work in teams of 5-10 people from a wide variety of backgrounds (this racial, ethnic, and economic diversity is at the heart of most programs—everyone benefits from the experiences and perspectives of their fellow participants). In exchange for service, they receive a living allowance (ranging from $100 to $170 per week) and a bonus upon completion of their service commitment. Bonuses range up to $5000 per year of full-time service to a maximum of $10,000. Some programs don't require you to use the bonus for education expenses; others give smaller bonuses to the non-college bound. In general, the higher the stipend, the lower the education bonus. Also, in most programs, workers wear easily identifiable uniforms (such as fashionable red t-shirts).

To learn more about your state's community service programs, request a list of State Commission Contacts from the Corporation for National Service (see resources, below). Here are some sample programs:

City Year

City Year unites young adults, ages 17 - 24, for a year of full-time community service, development and civic engagement. Founded in Boston in 1988, the program now has over 900 corps members in sites across the country, including Chicago, Cleveland, Philadelphia, San Jose, San Antonio, and Seattle. While City Year's primary focus is on improving the lives of children, corps members also renovate housing and beautify urban spaces. Workers earn a weekly stipend, and a $5,000 education bonus at the end of 10-months. Workers receive college and career counseling, meet regularly with community and business leaders, and get the chance to earn their GEDs (if they have not yet graduated from high school). Contact: City Year, 285 Columbus Avenue, Boston, MA 02116, http://www.city-year.org.

Delta Service Corps

The Delta Service Corps places workers age 17+ in existing community organizations across some of the poorest regions of our country (142 counties in Arkansas, Louisiana and Mississippi). Corps members receive a $4,725 education voucher for each of two years of full-time service. For more information, visit http://www.eatel.net/~deltacorp/. In Arkansas, call 501/735-4373; in Louisiana, call 800/DSC-4719; and in Mississippi, call 601/846-4457.

Public Allies

Ten-month apprenticeship program designed and run by young people for young people who want to help solve some of our nation's most pressing social problems. Currently, more than 100 "Allies" between the ages of 18 and 30 receive a stipend ($15,000 plus health and education benefits) while working on projects in public safety, education, human needs and the environment. Highly competitive with as many as 35 applicants per position. Public Allies, 1015 18th Street NW, #200, Washington, DC 20036.

Teach For America

Recent college grads spend two years teaching in under-resourced public schools nationwide. 3000 people compete for 500 opportunities. http://www.teachforamerica.org, PO Box 5114, New York, NY 10185.

YouthBuild USA

Rehab abandoned housing, or build new housing for homeless, disabled and low-income individuals. Contact: YouthBuild USA, 58 Day Street, Somerville, MA 02144.

Resources

1. *Corporation for National Service.* Ask for the AmeriCorps brochure, a list of State Commission Contacts and a description of funded programs. 1201 New York Avenue, NW, Washington DC, 20525, 800/94-ACORPS. You can also read program descriptions, get contact information and link to many up-and-running organizations from http://www.cns.gov.
2. *National Association of Service and Conservation Corps.* More than 100 youth corps operate in 38 states and the District of Columbia. Most operate year-round, and allow participants to improve life-skills (budgeting, parenting, personal health) earn GEDs, and prepare for future employment. The NASCC publishes a directory of these youth service and conservation corps, 666 11th Street NW, Suite 500, Washington DC 20001, 202/737-6272, http://www.nascc.org.
3. *The AmeriCorps National Resource Center* contains frequently-updated links to community-service sites, including links to state commissions and funded AmeriCorps projects, http://www.etr-associates.org/NSRC/othersites.html.
4. *Americorps Alums.* If you're not sure whether a year of public service is for you, contact an AmeriCorps alum, http://www.americorpsalums.org.
5. *Who Cares.* If you're still not sure, read this quarterly journal devoted to community service and social activism. You'll find project profiles, lists of resources, issue discussions, as well as articles by some of our countries most interesting writers. The magazine is a true find, even if you decide that climbing the corporate ladder is more to your taste than climbing the rickety wooden one, with a bucket of paint in your hand. For a trial subscription, call 800/628-1692, http://www.whocares.org.

CHAPTER 16

ARE YOUR PARENTS ELIGIBLE?

You may be eligible for considerable financial assistance courtesy of your parents' employers or membership affiliations. Locating these opportunities requires a systematic approach and considerable parental cooperation.

This chapter reviews some questions to ask, and provides samples of the kind of information you will uncover. Remember, these are only a few of the many opportunities.

Where Do Your Parents Work?

Parents should ask their company's benefits manager about education-related employee perks—loans, scholarships and savings plans.

Loans

A growing number of large companies help make it easier for employee children to participate in the Stafford Loan program. The companies put up a reserve against loan defaults, then hire firms like United Student Aid Funds to administer the program and find banks to act as lenders. Ford, General Electric, Texaco, and Time, are among the 150 that provide this service. To find out if your company has such a plan, ask the employee benefits coordinator or call United Student Aid Funds, 800/LOAN-USA.

RJR Nabisco goes one better and pays the guarantee fee and subsidizes the interest rate for PLUS loan borrowers.

Scholarships

Many companies sponsor scholarships for employee children as part of their fringe benefit programs.

Merit scholarships. Approximately 2,500 renewable, need-based awards (ranging from $500 to $4,000) sponsored by over 400 corporations for employee children who are Merit Program Finalists (Chapter 18).

General scholarships for employee children. Most of these scholarships range in value from $1,000 to $2,500. The Citizen's Scholarship Fund of America manages scholarship programs for about 630 companies, distributing in excess of 30,000 scholarships each year worth about $47.8 million.

Collegiate-based Scholarships. Many colleges offer scholarship money to children of ministers and other clergy (also, to children of alumni).

Savings Plans

Ask your company's employee benefits coordinator about any special savings programs. More and more employers support and encourage their employees' efforts to save for college. Here are some examples:

Contributory Accounts. These work much like retirement accounts with companies matching their employee's contributions. RJR Nabisco, for example, matches employee contributions of up to $4,000 per child.

Educational Savings Plans. Using payroll deductions, employees stash money into a company-managed educational fund. These may be matched, or not, depending on the generosity of the employer. NIKE, for example, matches employee deposits at a ratio of 25 cents for each $1 to a maximum of $1,000.

Free Advice

Some companies don't provide you any extra money, but they will include free or discounted college advice as part of your benefits package. And sometimes good advice is worth more than a $500 employer match.

Military Service

If either of your parents served in the US Armed Forces, get a copy of *Need A Lift?* $3.00 from The American Legion, Attn: Emblem Sales, PO Box 1050, Indianapolis, IN 46206. Also re-read Chapter 13.

Are Your Parents Members of...

A Trade Group or Association?

Employees of member firms may be eligible. Examples: *National Continental Association of Resolute Employers*; *National Office Products Association*; *National Association of Tobacco Distributors*. Addresses in Gale's *Encyclopedia of Associations.*

You might also search the web. The American Society of Association Executives (http://www.asaenet.org) provides links to about 2000 association sites.

A Patriotic/Civic/Fraternal Association?

Among many organizations making awards to members and members' children: *Knights of Columbus; United Daughters of the Confederacy*; Even the *Society for the Preservation of Barber Shop Quartets* has sixteen scholarships.

Again, you'll find addresses in Gale's *Encyclopedia of Associations,* or at http://www.asaenet.org.

A Union?

Examples: AFSCME, American Federation of Teachers, Fire Fighters, Food and Commercial Workers, Teamsters, Letter Carriers, Postal Workers, Garment Workers, Hospital & Health Care Employees, Seafarers, Machinists, Mine Workers, Transport Workers, etc.

For a list of over $4 million in scholarships, request the *AFL-CIO Scholarships Guide: A Source for Union-Sponsored Scholarships, Awards, and Student Financial Aid.* Single copies are free to union members. All others should send $3.00 to AFL-CIO Publications and Materials Office, 815 16th Street, NW, Rm. 209, Washington, DC 20006.

CHAPTER 17

MONEY FROM YOUR AFFILIATIONS

Your background, employment record, religion, and nationality as well as your membership in clubs and associations may be the key to financial opportunity. Here, as in the previous chapter, you will have to develop a systematic search strategy.

The Affiliation Matrix

The questions below will help you build your own affiliation matrix:

Question. Could any of my past jobs lead to a financial aid award? (Rule out baby-sitting for grouchy Mrs. Grumpelstein). **Answer.** Check with the personnel office of your present or former employers.

Question. What about my future career ? Any hope for a scholarship if I become an engineer? **Answer.** See Chapters 20 and 21 for some ideas. Also, search the Web (starting at the American Society of Association Executives site, http://www.asaenet.org) and Gale's *Encyclopedia of Associations* (in the reference room of your public library) for addresses of professional associations that match your interests.

Question. How about my clubs? **Answer.** Check with chapter/club president or faculty adviser.

Question. What about my religious affiliation? Does my denomination sponsor aid awards? **Answer.** See your minister, priest, or rabbi or write to the national organizations sponsored by the denomination. Search the web or Gale's *Encyclopedia of Associations.*

Question. How about my ancestry or my nationality? **Answer.** Write to the organizations serving your ancestry or your nationality. Search the web or Gale's *Encyclopedia of Associations.*

What will you find? You can strike pay dirt or you can strike out. But even if you find nothing, there is a reward. You will develop good research skills and learn to use your computer for something other than e-mail, chatrooms and games (even better, you become reacquainted with the library which had greatly missed your patronage.)

Examples: Jobs You Have Held

Caddie

Evans Scholars Foundation. About 225 golf caddies receive renewable full-tuition scholarships each year. Students must be of outstanding personal character, require financial assistance, be in the top 25% of their HS class and have caddied for at least 2 years at a WGA member club. By Nov. 1. Scholarship Committee, Western Golf Association/Evans Scholar Foundation, 1 Briar Road, Golf, IL 60029, 847/724-4600.

Fast Food Worker

McDonalds and Burger King both have demonstrated serious commitments to higher education. For example, McDonald's is creating the nation's largest apprenticeship program (4,000 students in 15 states) while Burger King provides scholarships through endowments made to selected colleges and universities.

Newspaper Carrier

Thomas Ewing Education Grants for former *Washington Post* carriers; 33 awards ranging from $1000-$2000. Other papers have similar awards.

Examples: Clubs

Boy Scouts

Directory of Scholarships and Loan Funds lists programs open to scouts and explorers. SASE to Learning for Life, Boy Scouts of America, 1325 Walnut Hill Ln., Irving, TX 75015.

Girl Scouts

Girl Scout Gold Award Scholarships, $500-$3,000. For a list of sponsoring schools, write Membership and Programs, Girls Scouts of the USA, 420 Fifth Avenue, New York, NY 10018.

Boys & Girls Club

Youth of the Year Competition, five $2,000 awards for regional winners with an additional $8,000 for the national winner. For more information, contact your local Boys & Girls Club.

Distributive Education Club of America (DECA)

Must be member of high school DECA chapter, have financial need and an interest in marketing or distribution. Information from chapter advisor.

4-H Clubs & Future Homemakers of America (FHA)

Scholarships for current or former 4-H members who have won state honors. 250 awards ranging from $750 to $1,500. Contact State 4-H Leader or County 4-H Agent, or National 4-H Council, 7100 Connecticut Avenue, Chevy Chase, MD 20815.

Examples: Ancestry and Nationality

National Society Daughters of the American Revolution

Various scholarships programs for children of DAR members. SASE for an application packet from Office of the Committees, NSDAR, 1776 D Street, NW, Washington DC 20006-5392. By Feb. 15.

Descendants of Signers of Declaration of Independence

Must be able to prove direct lineal descent to a signer of the Declaration of Independence and be a member of the Descendants of the Signers. Requests not naming an ancestor signer will not receive a reply. Annual grants total $10,000 to $11,000, averaging $1,500. Before Jan. 15. Send SASE to Mr. Richard Stromberg, DSDI Scholarship Committee, 609 Irwin Avenue, Deale, MD 20751.

Italian

UNICO National, 72 Burroughs Place, Bloomfield, NJ 07003. $1,000 each year for four years. Applicant must reside in community with UNICO chapter. By April 15.

Japanese

Japanese American Citizens League, 1765 Sutter Street, San Francisco, CA 94115. Entering freshmen, undergraduate, graduate. Performing arts, Creative arts, Law. For more information, send SASE. Apply by March 1, http://www.jacl.org.

Polish

Grants Office, The Kosciuszko Foundation, 15 East 65th Street, New York, NY 10021-6595. Polish Studies, music, voice, and others. Mainly specialized, graduate and postgrad study awards. Domestic deadline Jan. 15. Exchange program deadline Nov. 15. Summer Session in Poland (March 15 deadline).

Membership Organizations

Chinese-American Foundation, Danish Brotherhood of America, Lithuanian Alliance, Polish Falcons, Daughters of Penelope, Order of AHEPA, Sons of Norway, Sons of Poland, many others. Addresses of all these organizations may be found in Gale's *Encyclopedia of Associations.* An increasing number may also be found on the Infobahn.

Examples: Denomination

Catholic

Knights of Columbus, Pro Deo and Pro Patria scholarships. Sixty two awards of $1,500 based on academic excellence. Applicant or applicant's father must be member of the Columbian Squires or Knights of Columbus. Must be used at a Catholic college. Apply by March 1. Sponsors other scholarships, as well. Director of Scholarship Aid, Knights of Columbus, PO Box 1670, New Haven, CT 06507, 203-772-2130 x224.

Christian Scientist

Loan progra, from $3,500-$4,000 per academic year. Interest is 3% below prime. Repayment starts six months after graduation. Loans are interest-free to Christian Scientist nurses if they achieve Journal listing. The Albert Baker Fund, 5 Third St., Suite 717, San Francisco, CA 94103. By August 1.

Jewish

Up to $7,500/year for 2 years for graduate students preparing for careers in Jewish Community Center work. Write Scholarship Coordinator, JCC Association, 15 East 26th Street, New York, NY 10010. By Feb. 1.

Lutheran

Aid Association for Lutherans

Two competitive programs for AAL members only: (1) All College Scholarship program offers 1,000 renewable and nonrenewable awards each year, value range: $1,000-$2,500. (2) Vocational-Technical School Scholarship program, 100 renewable awards each year to graduating high school seniors. Value range is $500/year, for a maximum of 2 years. AAL advises members of all additional program details.

One college-based program: AAL members who plan to enroll at participating Lutheran school may receive a Lutheran Campus Scholarship ranging from $200 to $1,000/year. Awards made by schools.

Lutheran Brotherhood

Approximately 800 Scholarships (value to $2,000). Must be member of Lutheran Brotherhood. By Jan. 31 to Scholarship & Loan Coordinator, Lutheran Brotherhood, 625 4th Avenue South, Minneapolis, MN 55415. By January 15.

Also, approximately 500 awards (from $800 to $1,500) to Lutheran students who attend Lutheran colleges. Selections made by schools. Awardees do not have to be members of Lutheran Brotherhood.

Presbyterian

Scholarships from $100 to $2,000. Undergraduate and graduate. Also grants, loans, and special minority awards. Manager, Financial Aid for Studies, Presbyterian Church in the USA, 100 Witherspoon St., Louisville, KY 40202-1396.

United Methodist

Loans and scholarships for US citizens who have been active, full members of the United Methodist Church for at least one year prior to submitting application. More information from your church.

CHAPTER 18

MONEY FOR BRAINS AND TALENT

The SAT has become a national industry. The money spent designing tests, administering tests, scoring tests, taking tests, teaching test skills, coaching test takers, disseminating test results, selling the names and scores of test takers to eager college recruiters, interpreting scores, analyzing scores, publicizing scores, and writing about the test, pro and con, places the SAT somewhat behind the automobile industry but far ahead of the horseradish trade as a contributor to our gross national product.

Then, a few years ago, when the Scholastic Aptitude Test adopted a slightly new name—The Scholastic Assessment Test—and a slightly new format, the nationwide panic among little Fermat wanabees (and their parents), caused test prep enrollments to double, and our GNP to soar!

Despite the prevailing attitude, this testmania still has no rational underpinnings. It is a modern addendum to the classic treatise "Popular Delusions and the Madness of Crowd." For the SAT is not an intelligence measure. It is not an aptitude measure. Despite its name change, it doesn't really assess anything. It is not a predictor of academic success. And getting high scores isn't always important for gaining college admission. It's only verifiable characteristics are: (1) test scores correspond quite closely to family income—the higher the income, the higher the scores; and (2) it thrives on criticism. The more it is attacked and exposed, the more it gains in universality and acceptance.

But don't let this outburst scare you away. High test scores have a direct impact on your family budget. They can cost you money or they can make money for you.

High Test Scores Can Cost You Money...

Cost you money? How? Suppose you live in a school district which emphasizes test teaching. That emphasis will raise scores. And higher scores cause property values to soar because parents from everywhere now want to move to your district so the smarts rub off on junior. Your $50,000 home with a swampy basement, shaky foundation, and indigenous population of overweight termites is suddenly worth $100,000, a nice increase that adds $2,800 to your family contribution. Frankly, we think enterprising real estate firms should underwrite SAT prep courses. It could be their smartest investment.

...Or Make You Money

Now that we have learned how the SAT can cost you money, let's see how it can make you money. Here is what good scores can do:

1. Qualify you for a National Merit or Regent Scholarship.
2. Push you over the eligibility cutoff for collegiate academic scholarships.
3. Give you bargaining power when negotiating the content of an aid package. Your higher scores make you more valuable to the school because they help raise the average for the entire entering class.

The hard way to raise SAT scores is to find an error in the test and appeal it. An easier way is to take a good SAT prep course—but take it for the practical reasons listed above and not for any mythological reasons (like, "test prep makes you smarter"). If a $700 investment in a SAT prep course yields a $5,000 no-need scholarship, renewable each year for four years, you have done far better with your money than the shrewdest Wall Street stockbroker.

SAT Prep Courses

Good news. Despite anything the College Board says, SAT coaching will improve your scores. Students who already have a strong vocabulary, who read with perception and think logically, will benefit from taking practice tests. Students who are a little shaky in these areas, will benefit from learning good SAT test-taking skills. Two national organizations are Kaplan (800/KAP-TEST, http://www.Kaplan.com) and The Princeton Review (800/2-REVIEW, http://www.review.com). Their "teaching" styles are very different and they have no great love for each other, but they both have great track records for raising scores. Call the above numbers for the nearest test center.

Currently, most students taking test prep courses come from wealthier school districts (and families), thus furthering the correlation between high test scores and high income. Fortunately, cost is no longer a barrier to solid coaching, and you have no excuse not to work on pumping up your scores. First, both Kaplan and Princeton Review have free on-line help as well as reduced-cost programs and scholarships for low-income students. Second, more and more high schools are feeling pressured to produce students who score well on tests and are sponsoring their own (free) test prep classes. Third, if you're willing to spend a little money, local test prep services usually get good results and are fairly inexpensive. Fourth, you can try Stanford Testing Program's free on-line test prep course at http://www.testprep.com. And finally, if you're really disciplined, several publishers produce test prep books and CD Roms for "self-study."

At the very least, you should buy (or borrow) a copy of "10 Real SATs" from the College Board. It's important that you practice for the test using authentic test questions. If you've been prepping on-line, it's also important that you take at least one practice exam in a setting that simulates real test conditions—complete with timer, paper and pencil.

Where Are the Rewards for the Bright?

The A's & B's of Academic Scholarships (inside back cover) describes 100,000 academic awards offered at 1200 colleges; awards that range from $200 to $25,000 per year. Most of these awards are not based on need.

Do You Have Brains, Leadership, Talent?

Many scholarship opportunities are reserved for students with extraordinary abilities. There are two main ways to link up with these awards: via competitions and through recommendations of teachers, coaches, and bandmasters.

In following this route, make certain the honor you're applying for isn't going to cost you a fortune. Many companies would love to make a profit off your achievement. They buy mailing lists of good students (e.g., those with B+ averages or better) and try to sell them everything from $50 books featuring (surprise) their very own biography and photo, to $750 trips to Washington to hobnob with the political elite.

Art and Photography

The Scholastic Art Awards. Over $350,000 in cash, scholarships, other. Grades 7-12. By November 1, The Scholastic Art & Writing Awards, 555 Broadway, New York, NY 10012.

Arts (Dance, Music, Theater, Visual Arts, Writing)

Up to $3 million in scholarships, also, nomination to the White House Commission on Presidential Scholars in the Arts, and identification of talented students to colleges which may lead to additional awards. HS seniors or those who are 17 or 18 years old by 1 Dec. of the year they apply. $25 fee for early June 1 deadline; $35 fee (may be waived in hardship cases) for late, Oct. 1 deadline. Nat'l Foundation for Advancement in the Arts/Arts Recognition & Talent Search, 800 Brickell Ave., #500, Miami, FL 33131. 305/377-1148, 800/970-ARTS.

Brains

1. *National Merit Scholarship Program.* Participants take the PSAT/NMSQT (in the fall of their Junior year of HS). Semifinalists are contacted by the Merit program through their HS and finalists compete for 2,400 one-time Merit Scholarships and about 5,200 other Merit Scholarships, most of which are renewable with stipend amounts that vary from $250 to $2,000+ per year for four undergraduate years. For more information, obtain *PSAT/NMSQT Student Bulletin* from your high school guidance counselor or the National Merit Scholarship Corporation, 1560 Sherman Ave., #200, Evanston, IL 60201.
2. *National Honor Society.* 250 $1,000 scholarships for National Honor Society members. Nominations through HS chapter. Late Jan. deadline.
3. *Mensa Scholarships.* Awards to $1,000. Based on essay contest. For an application, send SASE to Scholarship Chairman, American Mensa Education and Research Foundation, 3437 W. 7th Street, #264, Fort Worth, TX 76107, January 31. If you have doubts about whether you're Mensa material, try "The Mensa Workout" at http://www.mensa.org.

Citizenship

Youth Citizenship Awards, HS juniors and seniors. Entries judged on basis of an application. (2) $1,250 awards given in each of 29 Soroptimist regions and (1) $2,000 finalist award. Deadline December 15. Contact your local Soroptimist Club or send SASE to Soroptimist International of the Americas, Two Penn Center Plaza, #1000, Philadelphia, PA 19102.

Drama

Thespian Society. Members-only scholarships through HS chapter.

Geography

The National Geography Bee is sponsored by the National Geographic Society. Top prizes (to fourth- through eighth-grade participants) are three college scholarships worth $25,000, $10,000 and $5,000. (Five million contestants per year.)

General

Advisory List of Contests and Activities. An approved list of nearly 85 contests—spelling bees, math bees, history bees, geography bees, etc. Be forewarned, however, in going for the honey, do it because you enjoy the competition and not because of the prize money. In some cases, millions of students compete for a handful of awards. $8.00 from the Nat'l Assoc. of Secondary School Principals. 1904 Association Dr., Reston, VA 20191, http://www.nassp.org/camain.htm.

Internet Technology

The Cutting Edge Scholars Program recognizes new ideas in Internet technology. Students must submit a written description of an original Internet project. $150,000 program sponsored by MCI and the College Board. For more information, visit http://www.mci.com/cuttingedge.

Inventors

BF Goodrich Collegiate Inventors Program. National competition that recognizes innovative discoveries and research by college students. Three awards of $7,500 and three awards of $3,000. For more information, contact BFG-CIP, c/o Inventure Place, 221 S. Broadway Street, Akron, OH, 44308, http://www.invent.org/bfg/bfghome.html.

Leadership & Brains

1. *Wendy's High School Heisman Award.* Recognizes scholarship, citizenship and athletic ability. Schools may each nominate two students (one male, one female). 1020 state finalists, 102 state winners, and 12 national finalists (who are flown to New York City for the collegiate Heisman Awards ceremony). Administered by Nat'l Association of Secondary School Principals. Program announcement placed in high schools each spring. September deadline.
2. *Principal's Leadership Award (PLA).* 150 $1,000 scholarships. Applications sent to HS principal in October. December deadline. Seniors only. Program is administered by Nat'l Association of Secondary School Principals.
3. *U. S. Senate Youth Program.* 104 $2,000 scholarships to elected student officers plus week long trip to Washington DC. Selections by state. Deadlines vary by state but are usually late Sept.- mid Oct. Contact your HS principal or the William Randolph Hearst Foundation, 90 New Montgomery St., #1212, San Francisco, CA 94105. (800) 841-7048.
4. *Truman Scholars.* $30,000 max. spread over 4 years. 80 awards. You must be nominated by your college in your junior year. Awards are for senior year plus up to 3 years of grad school. Solid class standing. Outstanding potential for leadership in government and public service. Harry S. Truman Scholarship Foundation, 712 Jackson Place, NW, Washington, DC 20006, http://www.truman.gov.

Math, Engineering and Natural Sciences

Barry M. Goldwater Scholarship. Undergraduate scholarships to outstanding college sophomores and juniors who plan to pursue careers in math, engineering or the natural sciences. Tuition, fees, books, room and board, up to $7,000/year for one or two years. One scholarship to a resident of each state. Additional scholars-at-large (285 scholarships were awarded last year). Applicants are selected and nominated by their college. By January 15. Contact your campus faculty representative.

Math, Science and Computer Science

Radio Shack/Tandy Scholars. 100 awards of $1,000 each. Final selection based on GPA, SAT/ACT scores, excellence in math, science or computer science, and service to the community. Nominated by HS. For more information, write Radio Shack/Tandy Scholars, TCU Box 298990, Fort Worth, TX 76129.

Music

Competitions and Awards Chart listing hundreds of competitive award opportunities ranging from $400 to $10,000. Include $1.00 for the chart and postage. Mail to: National Federation of Music Clubs Headquarters, 1336 N. Delaware St., Indianapolis, IN 46202.

Oratory & Essays

Large awards. Lots of competition. The American Legion, Optimist International and Civitan all sponsor contests (example: about 25,000 students compete for a top prize of $18,000 in the American Legion's Oratorical Contest).

Poetry

The National Library of Poetry awards $48,000 per year to over 250 poets in the North American Open Poetry Contest. Send one original poem (any subject, any style, no more than 20 lines) to the National Library of Poetry, 1 Poetry Plaza, #1945, Owings Mills, MD 21117, http://www.poetry.com. By July 31.

Political Science

First Nationwide Network Scholarship Program. 32 awards of $1,000 each to college juniors majoring in political science, history, or government. Established to honor John F. Kennedy. Essay and application required. Call First Nationwide Network program manager at 507-931-1682 for more information.

Presidential Scholars

Presidential Scholars. No application. Approximately 120 students selected from high scorers on the SAT and ACT. Also 20 students picked for achievement in the arts, as identified by the Arts Recognition & Talent Search (see above). A four-day visit to Washington. A handshake from the President. And $1,000 from the Dodge Foundation.

Science

Intel Science Talent Search. HS seniors must submit a report on a research project in science, math or engineering, along with SAT/ACT scores, transcript and application. $360,000 in scholarships, ranging from $50,000 to $4,000. Deadline is late November. For applications contact Science Service, Science Education Programs, 1719 N Street, NW, Washington, DC 20036. (202) 785-2255, http://www.sciserv.org.

Spelling

National Spelling Bee sponsored by Scripps Howard Newspapers Eight million students compete for $50 - $5,000 awards. Ask your teachers for more information.

Sports and Brains

ESPN awards 8 $2,500 scholarships to high school seniors based on academic achievement, sports participation, and community service. 860/585-2000 x3999.

Writing

1. *The Scholastic Writing Awards.* Over $350,000 in cash, scholarships, other. Grades 7-12. The Scholastic Art & Writing Awards, 555 Broadway, New York, NY 10012, by 1 Nov.
2. *Youth Writing Contest.* High School juniors or seniors. (1) $8,000; (1) $7,000; (1) $5,000; and (5) $1,000 scholarships. Write and submit a first person, 1200 word story about a memorable or moving experience you have had. Deadline November 30. GuidePosts, 16 E 34th St., New York, NY 10016, http://www.guideposts.org
3. *National Federation of Press Women*, $500 non-renewable scholarships for female members of their school newspaper staff. For an application, send SASE to National Federation of Press Women, 1163 320th Avenue, Charlotte, IA 52731. By May 1.

CHAPTER 19

MONEY FOR ATHLETES

Athletic scholarships are not limited to those with prowess in the big sports—football, baseball, basketball, hockey, soccer, tennis, and track. There is scholarship money for sailing, gymnastics, lacrosse, bowling, archery, fencing, rowing, synchronized swimming, skiing and volleyball.

All-star athletes don't need this book. They need an (unofficial) agent who can sort through all the offers, enticements, contracts and gifts that come their way. They might need a mechanic, too, to advise them on the relative merits of a Porsche vs. a Mercedes.

This chapter is for the better-than-average athlete with varsity potential in major and minor sports. What's available for this athlete? Here is the situation in a nutshell: There is considerable financial aid at most colleges for students who are good, but not necessarily great, athletes. This aid is either "reserved" for athletes (through designated scholarships) or awarded on a preferential basis as part of the aid packaging process.

The key to receiving this kind of aid is your determination to market your own talents. You must contact the appropriate college coaches and get them to shepherd your admission and financial aid requests through the bureaucracy of the admission and financial aid offices. All college coaches, if convinced of your potential contribution, will take an active role in facilitating your requests. Some schools even have admission representatives whose main responsibility is to coordinate referrals from the athletic department.

On Your Mark, Get Set, Go!

Here is a step-by-step outline to follow in marketing your athletic talents:

1. Start early. Discuss with your counselor the range of colleges for which you are academically qualified. In selecting schools, keep in mind that approximately 20% of all colleges will reconsider their admission standards to "land" an athlete.
2. Talk to your coach about the quality of athletic programs for which you might qualify. Don't sell yourself short. Colleges need backup players as well as starters.

3. Narrow your college selection list to a manageable size, taking into consideration the quality of athletic and academic programs and your "fit" with them. In other words, you *don't* want to be a four-year benchwarmer; you *do* want to be challenged by the school's academic program (but not over- or underwhelmed).
4. Research the name of the coach in your sport at each college on your list. Best source: your high school athletic director's copy of *The National Directory of College Athletics* (there are separate editions for men and women). You should probably do a follow up call to the athletic department to verify this name, and make certain the coach is still at the school and coaching your sport.
5. Draft a personal letter to each coach. This letter should include a profile of your academic interests and achievements. The letter's main part, however, should be a thorough and detailed discussion of your athletic accomplishments and be supported by statistics, clippings, letters earned, records, and honors. Include mention of any camps or clinics you've attended, and if appropriate, a videotape of yourself in action. (Keep it to 10 minutes, look enthusiastic, start with skills, move on to "game" highlights and make certain you're easily identifiable.) If your real value to the team is as a leader and motivator rather than a top scorer, make that clear. (Have you won any awards for sportsmanship?) Lastly, indicate you will need financial aid.
6. If your approach elicits interest, ask your high school coach to follow up with a letter of recommendation or a phone call. You should also send the college a schedule of your games in case recruiters are nearby.
7. Now you must decide where to apply. Few coaches will take an interest in you unless your initial letter is followed by a formal application. And remember, as with any other application, apply as early as possible.
8. After applying, remain in touch with the college coaches. Inquire about the status of your application and request for financial aid. If possible, visit the college and sell yourself as a person and as an athlete. Get to know the coach, and make certain his or her coaching philosophy is compatible with your style!

Gender Equity: Slowly But Surely

"No person in the United States shall, on the basis of sex, be excluded from participation in, be denied the benefits of, or be subjected to discrimination under any education program or activity receiving federal financial assistance."

That's the text of Title IX of the Education Act of 1972. Although the law has been in effect for over 25 years, its implementation received a major boost in the spring of 1997 when the Supreme Court refused to hear a challenge from Brown University. Any school that receives federal money, which means virtually every school in the country, must now move promptly to get on the right side of Title IX.

Title IX Crash Course

In 1979, the Education Department's Office of Civil Rights established a three-prong test to determine whether athletic programs satisfied Title IX.

- Schools must have roughly the same proportion of female athletes as female undergraduates. (Women now make up 53% of the enrollment of Division I schools but only 37% of the varsity athletes.) ...or...
- Schools must demonstrate a continuing history of expanding athletics opportunities for women. ...or...
- Schools must fully accommodate the interests and abilities of female students.

Colleges are dealing with Title IX in a number of ways: adding women's sports programs, dropping men's sports programs (wrestling, gymnastics and swimming have been the hardest hit), adding women's athletic scholarships, limiting the number of non-scholarship athletes on team rosters—all to help even out the numbers game.

Why is it so important that women get a fair shake in college sports? It goes beyond fun and games. Statistically, women who play sports are more successful than women who don't. They have higher graduation rates, lower teenage pregnancy rates, and a better chance of avoiding abusive relationships.

Academic Eligibility

All students who want to practice and play their sport at a Division I or II school during their freshman year must have their eligibility certified by a central clearinghouse. Essentially, the NCAA wants to make certain all student-athletes are exactly that, and has instituted minimum academic requirements for athletes.

Students who plan to compete at a Division II school must have a GPA of at least 2.0 in a core curriculum of 13 academic courses; a combination of English, math, social science, natural or physical science, foreign language, computer science, philosophy, etc. Furthermore, they must have a combined SAT score (after re-centering) of 820 or an ACT composite score of 68.

Students who plan to compete at a Division I school have it a little tougher. They must also successfully complete a core curriculum of 13 academic courses; a slightly different combination of English, math, social science, natural or physical science, foreign language, computer science, philosophy, etc. Furthermore, they must meet the NCAA's sliding scale of acceptable GPA/SAT/ACT scores. If you squeak in with an 820 SAT (or 68 ACT), you must have a 2.5 GPA in your core curriculum to qualify. If your SATs (or ACTs) are higher than 820, you can get away with a slightly lower GPA (but never lower than a 2.0). For example, if your SATs are 920, your GPA must be at least 2.25.

Currently, if you don't meet this criteria, you cannot play your sport during your first year, however, the NCAA will modify the core course requirement for LD students to include some special-education classes. This loosening of the rules may pave the way for adjustments to all the academic requirements, especially the test-score requirements, as they are having an adverse-impact on participation rates of low-income and minority students.

The Initial-Eligibility Clearinghouse

If a school is interested in recruiting you, it will request a copy of your eligibility status from the centralized Initial-Eligibility Clearinghouse. To register for the Clearinghouse, ask your counselor for a copy of the NCAA brochure *Making Sure You Are Eligible to Participate in College Sports,* then complete the accompanying student release form and send one copy of it (along with a check for $18) to the Clearinghouse. Give the other two copies of the form to your counselor; one to put in your HS files, the other to send to the Clearinghouse, along with a copy of your HS transcript (listing core courses). Students who qualify for a fee waiver for the SAT/ ACT may also receive a fee waiver for the Clearinghouse.

If you have attended more than one high school, each of your schools will need to send your official transcript to the Clearinghouse.

Your counselors can obtain all these registration materials (which are free) by calling the Clearinghouse at (319) 337-1492. Note: Eligibility certification has no bearing on your admission to a particular Division I or II institution.

Graduation Rates

Don't let headlines scare you. Most of the abuses you read about are restricted to big name (Division I) men's football and basketball programs. The fact is, most student-athletes have a higher graduation rate than other students and fare better economically in the job market.

Recruiting Violations

The NCAA publishes a 512-page book full of rules and regulations. Violating one of these rules or regulations can quickly turn you into an "ineligible" athlete. For a brief overview of recruiting guidelines, ask your counselor for a copy of the NCAA *Guide for the College-Bound Student-Athlete.* While this pamphlet is by no means complete, it does touch on the major issues, and warn you about what kinds of behavior can cause trouble.

When should you start worrying about these do's and don'ts? As soon as you become a "Prospective Student Athlete" (which happens when you start ninth-grade), although there's no need to become obsessive until you are a "Recruited Prospective Student Athlete." This occurs the moment a college coach (or representative of the school's "athletic interests") contacts you or a family member about participating in athletics at that college. "Contact" means providing you (or a family member) with an official visit, calling you more than once, or visiting you anywhere other than the college campus.

Commercial Scouting Services and Agents

Colleges often pay services to help them find top notch athletes. These services go around the country evaluating talent and selling this data to colleges, usually in the form of ratings booklets. Scouting services might also sell videotapes of HS games. You, however, are not likely to have any contact with these services. Why? In an effort to stem the growing perception that college sports are little more than feeders for professional teams, the NCAA keeps tightening the rules regarding recruiting and limiting the type of contact a coach may have with prospects.

As for agents, be careful. You can jeopardize your college eligibility by speaking to an unauthorized rep, by speaking to an authorized rep outside the approved contact period, or by agreeing to professional representation while still in HS or college (even if "the deal" doesn't become effective until after you finish college).

The Pros and Cons of Exposure Services

Exposure services, or placement services, represent the student in the search for athletic scholarships. These services can cost from $500-$800 and generally just follow the eight steps outlined previously. In other words, some people feel they're a waste of money since you can easily "sell" yourself and save the services' fee. Also, some college coaches say they're skeptical of organizations that claim they can do more for a student than his or her high school coach (after all, your coach is the person who should be most familiar with your abilities). Furthermore, you shouldn't base your choice of college on its athletic opportunities alone!

On the flip side, some exposure services are good and many students and schools are pleased with their results. From the students' perspective, it's an easy way to get their athletic profile sent to as many as 800 colleges. Students can then just sit back and wait for nibbles. From the school's perspective, since the athletes pay the fee, the school is getting perfectly good, free information on hundreds of potential student-athletes. These services are most useful for students who participate in "minor sports" (regardless of the school) or who are interested in smaller, less athletically prominent schools (regardless of the sport).

If you decide to use a placement service, make certain you choose a reputable one. Here are two suggestions: (1) Ask your high school coach about services that specialize in your sport and (2) Go with one of the biggies:

- College Prospects of America (12682 College Prospects Drive, Logan, OH, 43138, 740/385-6624, http://www.cpoa.com) or
- College Bound Student-Athletes (N19, W6717 Commerce Court, Cedarburg, WI 53012, 800/382-6817, http://www.cbsa.com).

These organizations have agents (salesmen?) scattered across all fifty states and serve thousands of students each year. In doing so, they recognize the need to match a student's level of athletic and academic ability with appropriate colleges and say they reject students without real athletic potential. Why? Because overselling students would cause them to lose credibility with the colleges and in a word-of-mouth type of business, you can't put a price tag on credibility.

Again, most students can do as well on their own, however, if you have questions about placement services, call the NCAA. The NCAA can't make endorsements, but it can steer you clear of shady businesses. If you use a service, be careful about how it determines your fee. The NCAA prohibits them from receiving money based on the value of your scholarship.

Locating Scholarships in Your Sport

Check your guidance office for Peterson's *Sports Scholarships and Athletic Programs* ($21.95). It lists colleges that offer sports scholarships. Women should also get *The Women's Collegiate Sports Scholarship Guide* $3.00 from the Women's Sports Foundation, Eisenhower Park, East Meadow, NY, 11554, 800/227-3988.

Sports Careers

The NCAA awards more than $1 million to student-athletes who are pursuing an athletics-related career or post-graduate program. Four programs are for postgraduates; one is for undergraduates. Request information from the NCAA, 6201 College Blvd, Overland Park, KS 66211.

Preferential Packaging vs. Athletic Scholarships

Preferential aid packaging can be a better deal than an athletic scholarship. If you have a personality conflict with the coach or run into a physical problem that keeps you from competing, you can lose your scholarship. The financial aid package, once it is wrapped up, will hold for a year.

References for Further Reading

1. The NCAA publishes stiff rules on recruiting. Learn them! Get *The NCAA Guide for the College-Bound Student* from NCAA Publishing, 6201 College Boulevard, Overland Park, KS 66211-2422. You can usually get a single copy by calling 800/638-3731. If not, ask your coach to order a set; they're inexpensive. You can also read it on-line at the NCAA's Web site, http://www.ncaa.org.
2. For more comprehensive information, ask your counselor (or coach) to get a series of NCAA guides. *The NCAA Guide to Financial Aid* describes the types of financial aid available to student-athletes and the limits on individual and institutional aid. *The NCAA Guide to Recruiting* describes permissible activities for colleges to use to attract student-athletes. *The NCAA Guide to Eligibility* assists students and counselors in understanding eligibility regulations and compliance requirements. These books are updated annually, cost only $5 each and are available from the NCAA (address above).
3. For more information on NAIA schools, contact the National Association of Intercollegiate Athletics, 6120 South Yale Ave., #1450, Tulsa, OK 74136.
4. For more information on competing at the junior college level, write to the National Junior College Athletic Association, PO Box 7305, Colorado Springs, CO 80933, http://www.njcaa.org.

CHAPTER 20

MONEY FOR HEALTH CAREERS

As a budding nurse or doctor or therapist, don't limit your reading to this chapter, or you will never blossom into a nurse or doctor or therapist. For instance, you can benefit from all the major federal student aid programs (Chapter 10). And you can get money from your home state (Chapter 11) if you enter a medical field in which it believes it has a shortage.

Federal Support for the Health Professions

Uncle Sam pours great amounts of money—almost a half billion dollars per year—into the training of health professionals. The assistance programs fall into two broad categories: Individual-based programs which fund students, and school-based programs which fund schools (which in-turn parcel out some of their money to students).

Individual-Based Programs

Individual-based programs are fairly easy to locate. You apply directly to Uncle Sam or through the school you plan to attend. One bit of advice: You will gain an advantage over fellow applicants if you indicate a willingness to practice in a shortage area. Don't worry about what a shortage area is. Its definition and location will change several times between the time you apply and the time you graduate. What's important to know is that "shortage areas" are a big thing at the Department of Health & Human Services. It has "primary medical care shortage areas," "dental manpower shortage areas," "rural dental shortage areas," "vision care shortage areas," "podiatry shortage areas," "pharmacy shortage areas," "psychiatric shortage areas," even "veterinary care shortage areas."

For more information on Uncle's health care programs, visit the Department of Health and Human Services on-line at http://www.dhhs.gov or the Bureau of Primary Health Care at http://www.bphc.hrsa.dhhs.gov.

Health Education Assistance Loans. Program has been discontinued, but as you will see under "Private Programs," there is no shortage of loan money for doctors- and dentists-to-be! For more information, current HEAL holders can write: HEAL, Room 8-37, 5600 Fishers Lane, Rockville, MD 20857, 301/443-1540.

Health Professions Student Loan. Tuition plus $2,500/year. 5% interest begins to accrue 12 months after completion of training. Must show financial need and practice in primary care. Apply through school.

National Health Service Corps Loan Repayment Program. In exchange for providing primary care in federally-designated health profession shortage areas, the program will pay up to $25,000 each year for a minimum 2-year commitment; additional one-year extensions may be awarded at qualifying sites for a maximum of $35,000 per year. Program is open to licensed or certified primary care physicians, nurse practitioners, nurse midwives, dentists, dental hygienists, clinical psychologists, clinical social workers, psychiatric nurse specialists and marriage and family therapists. The NHSC also gives money to nearly 30 states to help fund their loan repayment programs. NHSC Loan Repayment Program, 2070 Chain Bridge Road, McLean, VA 22182, 800/221-9393.

National Health Service Corps Scholarship Program. The NHSC will pay tuition, fees, books and supplies, plus a monthly stipend for up to four years. For each year of support, award recipients owe one year of full-time clinical practice in high-priority health professions shortage areas. Minimum 2 year obligation. For more information, write: NHSC, Scholarship Program, 2070 Chain Bridge Road, McLean, VA 22182, 800/221-9393.

Exceptional Financial Need Scholarships. All tuition plus stipend. Good for one year only. At year's end, participants have priority for a NHSC Scholarship. Must practice in general dentistry or primary care medicine for five years after residency. Apply through school.

Nursing Student Loan Program. Long-term, low interest loan to full- and half-time nursing students. Apply through school.

Commissioned Officer Student Training & Extern Program (COSTEP) Work Program. For graduate awards, students must have completed minimum of 1 yr. graduate work in medical, dental, veterinary school. For undergraduate awards, students must have completed 2 yrs in a dietary, nursing, pharmacy, therapy, sanitary science, medical records, engineering, physician's assistant, or computer science field. For other health-related areas, students must be enrolled in master's or doctoral program. Student must return to studies following completion of the COSTEP assignment. Serve as an extern in medical facilities of the Public Health Service during school breaks of 31-120 days duration. Get ensign's pay during work phases.

For more information: COSTEP, Room 4A-07, Parklawn Bldg., 5600 Fishers Lane, Rockville, MD 20857.(800) 279-1605.

Rehabilitation Training. Monthly trainee stipends. When inquiring, refer to Program 84.129. (Rehab Counseling, Physical and Occupational Therapy, Prosthetics-Orthotics, Speech Language-Pathology, Audiology, Rehab Services to the Blind and Deaf). Department of Education, Rehabilitation Services Administration, 800 Independence Avenue, SW, Washington, DC 20202-2649.

School-Based Programs

School-based programs are something else. Here, the available dollars go directly to schools, and usually become part of the faculty payroll (Reason: Medical faculties are so high-priced, without federal aid to help pay their salaries, schools would have to foot the bill alone. To do this, they would have to raise tuition so high, no student could afford to enroll). Your challenge is to look for funded schools and negotiate with the Dean for some of the spoils. Or at least to take advantage of any extra student aid dollars. When writing to the addresses below, be sure to ask for a current list of funded schools—and be persistent (yet polite) in your request. The program officers usually won't understand why you need this information.

Nursing Students. Several separate programs. Professional Nurse Traineeships. Advanced Nursing, Nurse Practitioners, Nurse Educators, Nurse Midwives, Nurse Anesthetist, Public Health Nurses, and other nursing specialties. Partial tuition and stipends. Contact your financial aid office for more information. Department of Health and Human Services, Division of Nursing, Room 9-36 Parklawn Bldg., 5600 Fishers Lane, Rockville, MD 20857.

Mental Health Research (biomedical and behavioral). National Research Service awards for individual fellows. Funded through participating schools. Pre-doctoral stipend, $10,000. Post-doctoral stipend, $19,000 to $32,300 depending on years of experience. Grants Management Branch—National Institute of Mental Health, 5600 Fishers Lane, Rm. 7C-15, Rockville, MD 20857.

Military Medical and Nursing Programs

Armed Forces Health Professional Programs

Health Professions Scholarships for medical, dental, veterinary, optometry, nurse anesthesia and clinical/counseling psychology students. Provides full tuition, fees and $913 monthly stipend (adjusted each July). Service obligation.

Financial Assistance Program. Specialized (residency) training for graduate physicians, endodontists, periodontists, orthodontists and oral surgeons. Annual $19,333 grant plus $913 monthly stipend (adjusted each July). Service obligation.

Each branch of the service has its own point of contact:

- **Army:** HQ, USAREC, Health Services Div., 1307 Third Avenue, Ft. Knox, KY 40121, 502-626-0367.
- **Navy:** Medical Command, Naval School of Health Sciences, OM16, 8901 Wisconsin Ave., Bethesda, MD 20889, 301/319-4118.
- **Air Force:** Dir. of Health Professionals, HQ, USAF, Recruiting Service, Randolph AFB, TX 76150, 800/531-5980.

ROTC Nurse Program (Army, Navy, Air Force)

Students at approved nursing schools affiliated with an Army, Navy, or Air Force ROTC unit. 2, 3, 4 year scholarships; tuition, textbooks, and fees, plus a monthly stipend (e.g., $180/month in the Air Force; $150/month in the Army and Navy). Service obligation.

- **Army,** Army ROTC, ATCC-N, Ft. Monroe, VA 23651, 800/USA-ROTC.
- **Navy,** Commander, Navy Recruiting Command, (Code 314), 801 N. Randolph Street. Arlington, VA 22203, 800/USA-NAVY.
- **Air Force,** HQ AFROTC, Scholarship Actions Section, 551 East Maxwell Blvd., Maxwell AFB, AL 36112.

AF ROTC Pre-Health Professions Program

Pre-medicine. Attend a school offering AF ROTC. 2 and 3 year scholarships. Tuition, textbooks, fees, plus $180/month. Service obligation. HQ AFROTC Scholarship Actions Section, 551 East Maxwell Blvd, Maxwell AFB, AL 36112-6106.

Army-Specific Programs

For more information on the following programs, contact Headquarters, US Army Recruiting Command, Health Services Division, 1307 Third Avenue, Fort Knox, KY 40121, 502/626-0373, 800/USA-ARMY, http://www.goarmy.com.

1. *Specialized Training Assistance Program.* Monthly stipend for critically-needed specialties in the Army Reserve (specialties are identified every two years). $913/month with two years of payback for every year or partial year you receive the stipend.

2. *Health Professional Loan Repayment.* Army will repay designated educational loans for officers serving in critically-needed specialties in the Army Reserve (specialties are identified every two years). Up to $3,000 per year to a maximum of $20,000.
3. *Bonus Program.* Annual bonus to health care professionals in selected specialties (specialties are identified every two years) who accept a commission in the AMEDD with a subsequent assignment in the US Army Select Reserve. Bonuses vary from $3,000 to $10,000 per year for up to 3 years, depending on the specialty.
4. *Active-Duty Health Professional Loan Repayment.* Education loan repayment to qualified health professionals for active duty service. $22,000 per year for a maximum of four years. The service requirement equals one year for each year of loan repayment received, with a minimum of 3 years of active service.

F. Edward Hebert School of Medicine

This tuition-free institution's main emphasis is on training medical officers for the Army, Navy and Air Force. While enrolled, students serve on active duty as Reserve commissioned officers in grade O-1 with full pay and allowances for the grade. Both civilian and uniformed services personnel are eligible for admission. Minimum seven year service obligation, exclusive of internship, residency or other service obligations. 165 students each year (63-Army, 51-Navy, 51-Air Force). Request catalogue, from F. Edward Hebert School of Medicine, Admissions Office, 4301 Jones Bridge Rd., Bethesda, MD 20814; 800/772-1743, http://www.usuhs.mil.

Private Programs

Dental

Dental Access Loan. Up to $195,000, with 20 years to repay. Interest rate equals the 91-day T-bill plus 2.75%, 6% guarantee fee, 1.5% (or higher) supplemental fee prior to repayment. Also, loans to help you during your residency. The Access Group, 800/282-1550, on-line application, http://www.accessgrp.org.

Dental Assistant

American Dental Assistants Assoc., student scholarship, $500/$5,000. By Jan. 31. Juliette A. Southard/Oral-B Laboratories Scholarship Program, ADAA, 203 North LaSalle St., #1320, Chicago, IL 60601, 312/541-1550.

Dental Hygienist

ADHA. Numerous AA, BA, MA, Ph.D. awards to enrolled dental hygiene students. To $1,500. Also, 25 $1,000 scholarships sponsored by Proctor and Gamble. ADHA Institute for Oral Health, 444 N. Michigan, #3400, Chicago, IL 60611. By May 1.

Dental Lab Technology

ADA Assistance Fund, Up to 25 scholarships per year. Maximum annual award is $2,500. Apply by June 15. ADA Assistance Fund, 211 E. Chicago Avenue, Chicago, IL 60611, http://www.ada.org

Medicine

Howard Hughes Medical Institute, Research Training Fellowships consist of a $15,000 stipend plus a $5,500 research allowance and a $5,500 institutional allowance. These fellowships enable 60 medical students to do full-time research for one year (renewable for an additional year). Additional grant programs as well. For more information and a fact sheet, write Howard Hughes Medical Institute, 4000 Jones Bridge Road, Chevy Chase, MD 20815-6789, or http://www.hhmi.org/fellowships/.

Medicine

Medical Access Loan. Up to $195,000 with 20 years to repay. Interest rate equals the 91-day T-bill plus 2.5%, 6% guarantee fee, 1.5% (or higher) supplemental fee prior to repayment. Also, loans to help out during your residency. The Access Group, 800/282-1550, on-line application, http://www.accessgrp.org.

Medical and Biological Sciences

Howard Hughes Medical Institute. College seniors or first-year grad students. Leads to doctoral degrees in biological/medical sciences. 80 awards/year, consisting of $15,000 stipend plus $15,000 cost-of-education allowance to the fellowship institution. Renewable for up to five years. National Research Council, 2101 Constitution Avenue, Washington, DC 20418, http://fellowships.nas.edu.

Medicine and Dental

MEDCASH Loan. Up to $88,000 with 20 years to repay. Interest rate equals the 91-day T-bill plus 2.5% (increasing to 2.85% during repayment). 5% guarantee fee. MOHELA, PO Box 6997, Chesterfield, MO 63006, 800/666-4352. Other non-federal loan sources for health professionals: Chiroloans and Doc-Op (800/252-2041), MedCAP (800/633-2270), MEDFUNDS (800/665-1016), DEAL and MedAchiever (800/225-6783).

Medicine, Nursing and Therapy (Occupational and Physical)

DAR Scholarship Committee. Scholarships for students sponsored by their local DAR chapters. Amounts range from $500 to $4,000. Applications from DAR Scholarship Committee, 1776 D Street, NW, Washington, DC 20006-5392. Ask for complete listing of awards.

Nursing

National League for Nursing. Information on scholarships, loans, grants, fellowships, awards. Send $16.95 (postpaid) for the book *Scholarships and Loans for Nursing Education 1997/98*. Prepayment must accompany order. NLN, 350 Hudson St., New York, NY 10014, http://www.nln.org.

Nursing (Advanced)

Nurses' Educational Funds, Inc., Scholarship for registered nurses, members of a national, professional nursing association, for advanced degrees. $2,500-$10,000. Full-time student at master's level, full-time or part-time at doctoral level. GRE or MAT scores required. Application kits are available after August 1 for $10, Nurses' Educational Funds, Inc., 555 W. 57th St., 13th Floor, New York, NY 10019. By Feb. 1.

Physician Assistant

American Academy of Physician Assistants, 40-50 awards ranging from $2,000 to $5,000 for student APA members. By 1 Feb. Also, for a brochure listing financial assistance sources, write American Academy of Physician Assistants, 950 N. Washington Street, Alexandria, VA 22314-1552.

Surgical Technology

Association of Surgical Technologists, One $500 award and several $250 awards. For students currently enrolled in CAAHEP-accredited surgical technology programs. Association of Surgical Technologists, 7108-C S. Alton Way, #100, Englewood, CO 80112, http://www.ast.org. By March 1.

Therapy

AMBUCS, Physical, Occupational, Music, Hearing Audiology, Speech Language Pathology and Recreational Therapy. 500 awards per year, $500-$6,000 juniors, seniors and graduate student scholarships. National AMBUCS Scholarships for Therapists, P.O. Box 5127, High Point, NC 27262. 910/869-2166. Deadline is April 15.

Therapy (Respiratory)

American Respiratory Care Foundation, various scholarships, $500-$3,500. 11030 Ables Ln., Dallas, TX 75229, www.aarc.org. By June 30.

CHAPTER 21

MONEY FOR OTHER CAREER INTERESTS

The best way to capitalize on your career interest is through cooperative education (Chapter 12). The next best way is to enroll in a school with a strong reputation in your career field (e.g., Agriculture—*Iowa State*; Hotel Management—*Cornell*). Strong departments usually attract scholarship funds. These funds, however, do not start flowing until you declare your major.

The third—and hardest method—is to look for portable scholarships that will fund your major at any accredited school. The following list is illustrative, rather than complete. To dig for additional awards, contact organizations that provide career information in your field of interest—you'll find them listed in *Need a Lift?* from the American Legion. Also, look for professional associations which serve these careers—you'll find them listed in Gale's *Encyclopedia of Associations* at your public library. You can also search the web. Over 2000 associations have sites linked to the American Society of Association Executives, http://www.asaenet.org.

When writing, always enclose a self-addressed, stamped business-size envelope (SASE).

Accounting

1. *National Society of Public Accountants.* 22 $500-$1,000 awards; one $2,000 award. Undergraduates only. B+ GPA. By Mar. 10. Must be a US or Canadian citizen attending an accredited US school. Nat'l Society of Public Accountants Scholarship Foundation, 1010 N. Fairfax St., Alexandria, VA 22314.
2. *Robert Kaufman Memorial Scholarships.* Up to 20 awards, from $250 to $5000. Undergrads who plan to pursue accounting can get more information from the Independent Accountants International Education Fund, 9200 S. Dadeland Blvd., Suite 510, Miami, FL 33156. By March 1. All information, including the application, may be found at http://www.accountants.org.

Architecture

American Institute of Architects offers undergrad and graduate scholarships. Obtain applications through an accredited school. From $500-$2,500. By Feb. 1. Also, post- professional awards from $1,000-$2,500. By Feb. 15th. Applications from AIA, Scholarship Programs, 1735 New York Ave., NW, Washington, DC 20006, http://www.aiaonline.org.

Art & Architecture

Cooper Union (New York City). Extremely competitive admissions. All admitted students receive a full scholarship for the duration of their study.

Education

Phi Delta Kappa. Fifty at $1,000, one at $2,000, one at $4,000 and one at $5,000. International grants to HS seniors planning on a teaching career. Scholarship Grants, Phi Delta Kappa, PO Box 789, Bloomington, IN 47402. Request application in October, due by January 31.

Engineering

General Motors, 400 full tuition scholarships at participating colleges for students pursuing careers in engineering. For more information and a list of schools, write General Motors, Placement and College Relations, 3044 West Grand, Detroit, MI 48202.

Engineering (Civil/Construction)

AGC Education & Research Foundation. 90-100 renewable undergrad awards of $1,500/yr. 2-4 graduate awards of up to $7,500. Director of Programs, AGC Education & Research Foundation, 1957 E St., NW, Washington, DC 20006. 202/393-2040, http://www.agc.org, by Nov. 1.

Engineering (Materials)

ASM. 34 $500 scholarships, 3 $2,000 scholarships. Undergraduates majoring in materials science and engineering (metallurgy, ceramics, ceramics engineering, polymers, polymer engineering, composites, composite engineering). Citizen of US, Canada, or Mexico. ASM, Scholarship Program, Materials Park, OH 44073. By June 15.

Engineering (Mining)

Society for Mining, Metallurgy, and Exploration. 100+ scholarships up to $2,000. Inquire through your college.

Enology & Viticulture

American Society for Enology and Viticulture. Several awards to graduate students and undergrads majoring in enology or other science basic to the wine and grape industry. Applicants must be at least a Junior and meet minimum GPA requirements. By 1 Mar. American Society for Enology and Viticulture, PO Box 1855, Davis, CA 95617.

Entomology

ESA. Several undergrad scholarships, $1,500. Major in biology, entomology, zoology, or related science at recognized school in U. S., Canada, Mexico. Min. of 30 semester hrs. accumulated with at least one course in entomology. Send SASE to Undergraduate Scholarship Application, ESA, 9301 Annapolis Road, Lanham, MD 20706. By May 31.

Family and Consumer Sciences

AAFCS. National and International fellowships. $3,000-$5,000. For more information, write AAFCS, 1555 King St., Alexandria, VA 22314, 703/706-4600, after 1 September.

Federal Employees

The Federal Employee Education and Assistance Fund awards 300+ scholarships ranging from $300 to $1,750 to civilian federal employees and their dependent family members. Apply by May 31 to FEEA Fund Scholarship Award, 8441 W. Bowles Ave., #200, Littleton, CO 80123.

Food (Management)

Internat'l Food Service Executives. Local branches offer $500-$1,000 grants totalling $90,000/ year. Internat'l Food Service Executives, 1100 S. State Road 7, #103, Margate, FL 33368. For application, send SASE or download from http://ifsea.org/ifsea, by Feb 1.

Food (Management, Dietetics, Culinary Arts, etc.)

*National Restaurant Assoc.*100+ undergrad awards. 3.0 GPA. $1,000-$5,000. The Educational Foundation of the National Restaurant Assoc., 250 South Wacker Drive, #1400, Chicago, IL 60606, http://www.restaurant.org, 312/715-6760. By Mar. 1.

Food (Science and Technology)

Institute of Food Technologists. 133 undergrad and grad scholarships. $1,000-$5,000. By Feb. 1 for juniors, seniors and graduate students, by Feb. 15 for freshmen, and March 1 for sophomores. Scholarship Dept., Institute of Food Technologists, 221 N. LaSalle St., #300, Chicago, IL 60601, http://www.ift.org.

Foreign Study

The Rotary Foundation offers three types of awards: Academic-Year Ambassadorial Scholarships of up to $23,000 for one year of study in another country (undergrad, graduate or vocational study), Multi-Year Ambassadorial Scholarships of up to $11,000 per year for two or three years, and Cultural Ambassadorial Scholarships for intensive language study (3 to 6 months). Apply through local Rotary Club. For an application, contact your local club or write: The Rotary Foundation, One Rotary Center, 1560 Sherman Ave., Evanston, IL, 60201, http://www.rotary.org.

Geology

Geological Soc. of America. Last year, $349,000 in grants to 218 students doing masters/doctoral thesis research at universities in U.S., Canada, Mexico, Central America. Members and nonmembers eligible. Contact Research Grants Administrator, Geological Soc. of America, PO Box 9140, Boulder, CO 80301, http://www.geosociety.org. By Feb. 1.

Geophysics

SEG Foundation. Need and ability. 60-100 awards. Average: $1,200. Studentsworking toward career in Geophysics. Scholarship Committee, SEG Foundation, PO Box 702740, Tulsa, OK 74170. By March 1.

Graphic Arts

National Scholarship Trust Fund. Over 300 scholarships from $500-$1,000. NSTF, 200 Deer Run Rd., Sewickley, PA 15143, http://www.NSTF.com. HS seniors by March 1, college students by April 1.

History

Daughters of the American Revolution. $2,000/year. Renewable. HS senior. Top third of class. Major in American History. All students are judged on the basis of academic excellence, commitment to the field of study and financial need. All applications must be sponsored by the local DAR Chapter. Send applications to the DAR Scholarship Committee State Chair by 1 Feb. One winner from each state is submitted to the National Chair. For more information, send SASE to: NSDAR, Office of the Committees, Scholarships, 1776 D St., NW, Washington, DC 20006.

Horticulture

1. *Bedding Plants Foundation.* $500-$2,000 undergrad and $1,000-$2,000 graduate scholarships. Renewable. By April 1. Bedding Plants Foundation, PO Box 27241, Lansing, MI 48909. (517) 694-8537, http://www.grafix-net.com/BPFI.
2. *American Orchid Society.* Grants for orchid research in areas such as biological research, conservation, ecology. $500-$12,000. Up to 3 years working on orchid-related dissertation projects that lead to the Ph.D.

Must be enrolled full-time in an accredited doctoral program. Application by Jan. 1 or Aug. 1. American Orchid Society, 6000 South Olive Ave., West Palm Beach, FL 33405.

International Education

1. *Foreign Language and Area Studies* (FLAS) program to stimulate foreign language fluency and develop a pool of international experts. About 600 academic year awards ($10,000 stipend, plus $10,000 institutional payment in lieu of tuition and fees) and 350 summer fellowships ($2,400 stipend, plus $3,600 institutional payment in lieu of tuition and fees). Students apply through funded institutions. For more information and a school list write: International Education and Graduate Program Service, Advanced Training and Research Team, FLAS Fellowships, US Department of Education, Washington, DC 20202.
2. *National Security Education Program.* Federal scholarships for foreign languages and international affairs. Nearly 500 scholarships for undergrads and graduate students (800/498-9360).
3. *International Education Finance Corporation.* Loans to international students studying in the US, or to US students studying abroad. IEFC, 424 Adams Street, Milton, MA 02186, 617/696-7840, http://www.IEFC.com.

Journalism

The Journalist's Road to Success: A Career and Scholarship Guide lists several million in print journalism scholarships. 150 pages. Has minority section. Dow Jones Newspaper Fund, Inc., PO Box 300, Princeton, NJ 08543-0300. $3.00/copy prepaid, 800/DOW-FUND, http://www.dowjones.com/newsfund.

Librarianship

Financial Assistance for Library and Information Studies lists scholarships available for Technical Assistants and Librarians. New edition each November. Include $4.00. Committee on Education, American Library Association, 50 E. Huron St., Chicago, IL 60611, http://www.ala.org, 312/280-4282.

Merchant Marine

Maritime Academies. $750/quarter subsistence allowance for students at CA, ME, MA, NY, TX, and Great Lakes Maritime Academies. Service obligation. Academies Program Officer, Maritime Administration, 400 Seventh St., SW, Washington, DC 20590.

Naval Architecture

Webb Institute. Ship design. All tuition paid. Top students. High SAT. Crescent Beach Rd., Glen Cove, NY 11542-1398.

Public Service

Public Employees Roundtable scholarships. Undergrad and graduate level. 3.5 GPA, $500 and $1,000 awards for students who plan to pursue careers in government service at local, state or federal level. Send SASE to PER, PO Box 44801, Washington, DC 20026-4801, or (202) 401-4344, http://www.patriot.net/users/permail. Applications by mid-May.

Real Estate Appraisers

Appraisal Inst. Education Trust, 50 scholarships. $3,000 for grad. students, $2,000 for undergrads. Appraisal Inst. Education Trust, 875 N. Michigan, #2400. Chicago, IL 60611. By Mar. 15.

Science and Engineering

Bell & Howell Scholarships. Electronics, engineering computer science, technology, business. Scores, transcript. sixty $11,000 scholarships ($2,750/yr. for 4 years). Bell & Howell Education Group, Inc., B & H Science & Engineering Scholarship, 1 Tower Lane. Suite 1000, Villa Park, IL 60181.

Travel Agents

American Society of Travel Agents Scholarship Fund. Travel, tourism and hospitality majors, undergrad and graduate level, 2.5 GPA, 24 scholarships, $500-$3,000. ASTA Scholarship Foundation, 1101 King St., Alexandria, VA 22314. By July 28.

CHAPTER 22

MONEY FOR MINORITIES AND WOMEN

Most financial aid is based on need—not race, and not gender—which means many of you have an edge in the competition for aid. Why? Because, statistically, the income of minorities is lower than that of their majority peers, and because women earn less than men who hold equal positions.

Also, as part of their effort to retain more students, many schools give minorities and women more favorable aid packages (e.g., more grants than loans). The General Accounting Office (GAO) has shown that grant money has a strong effect on low-income student persistence; that an additional $1,000 in grant funds means a 14% decrease in dropout rates while a $1,000 increase in loan aid means a 3% increase in dropout rates. (The GAO defines low income as around $21,000.)

Resource List

What these numbers say is that for once you have a leg up. You are a stride ahead. So take advantage of that lead, and then, only after you have navigated the traditional, need-based route with savvy, should you look for the icing, found in this chapter, or from the following scholarship sources:

1. *Higher Education Opportunities for Minorities and Women,* free from the Dept. of Education, Higher Education Programs, 400 Maryland Avenue, SW, Portals C-80, Washington DC 20202.
2. Books from Reference Service Press, 5000 Windplay Drive, #4, El Dorado Hills, CA 95762:
   - *Directory of Financial Aids for Women* ($45),
   - *Financial Aid for African-Americans* ($37.50),
   - *Financial Aid for Asian-Americans* ($32.50),
   - *Financial Aid for Hispanic-Americans* ($35)
   - *Financial Aid for Native-Americans* ($37.50).

Before you decide to purchase these guides, look for them in your guidance office or public library. For a complete catalogue, call 916/939-9620, http://www.rspfunding.com.

Federal Assistance for Minorities

All Minorities

Graduate Fellowship Program. Graduate study in science, mathematics, engineering. Master's level and doctorate. Up to three years of support. $14,400 per year. By early Nov. Write: NSF Graduate Research Fellowship Program, Oak Ridge Associated Universities, PO Box 3010, Oak Ridge, TN 37831. By early September.

Minority Access to Research Careers. Biomedical science. Funded through schools with substantial minority student bodies. Undergrad through graduate level. For school list, write MARC Program, Nat'l Institute of General Medical Sciences, National Institutes of Health, 45 Center Drive, MSC 6200, Bethesda, MD 20892.

Minority Participation in Graduate Education Programs. $6 million program to encourage minority students to pursue graduate education. Funded through 73 colleges. For school list: Office of Higher Education Program Services, Dept. of Education, 400 Maryland Ave., SW, Washington DC, 20202

Office of Minority Health Resource Center. A central resource for minorities interested in the health professions. The Resource Center does not offer scholarships, but its trained information specialists will be glad to help you search its database of funding opportunities—via the web, http://www.omhrc.gov or telephone, 800/444-6472.

Native Americans

Native American Fellowship Program. Need-based program for eligible Indian students in undergrad programs in business, engineering, natural resources, Graduate programs in education, law, medicine, psychology, natural resources, business, engineering, clinical psychology. All tuition and stipends. Apply through your tribe or area office of Indian Education Programs. For more information, or to request a list of additional resources, call the Postsecondary Education Branch of the Bureau of Indian Affairs at 202/208-4871. By Jan. 1.

Indian Health Service Scholarships. Health fields include pharmacy and nursing. Two programs: (1) Preparatory Scholarship Program. Two years. (2) Health Professions Scholarship Program. Both restricted to American Indians and Alaskan natives. Tuition plus stipend. Also, a loan repayment program and extern (student) employment program. Apply to Indian Health Service, Twinbrook Plaza, Suite 100, 12300 Twinbrook Parkway, Rockville, MD 20857. By May 1.

Native American Scholarship Fund. MESBEC (math, engineering, science, business, education, computers) is for high-achieving Native American students in any of these fields, or in the humanities, social science, or fine arts. NALE (Native American Leadership in Education) program is for Native American paraprofessionals who plan to complete their degrees, obtain credentials as teachers, counselors or administrators, and who plan to teach in Indian schools. Students in both programs must have high GPAs and test scores. Recruiter, 8200 Mountain Road NE #203, Albuquerque, NM 87110. (505) 262-2351.

Private Assistance for Minorities

All Minorities

Accounting. Undergrad and graduate for enrolled students. Approximately 400 merit and need-based awards. Individual grants up to $5,000. Apply by July 1. Manager, Minority Recruitment, American Institute of Certified Public Accountants, 1211 Avenue of the Americas, New York, By 10036-8775.

Architecture. 20 awards, $500-$2,500. Renewable. Nomination by HS counselor, school, professional architect. Nomination deadline is Dec 1. Open to HS seniors and college freshmen. Nomination forms from AIA, Scholarship Program, 1735 New York Avenue, NW, Washington, DC 20006.

Dental Hygienists. For at least the second year of dental hygiene curriculum. To $1,500. Also $1,000 for student accepted into entry level dental hygiene program in certain areas. American Dental Hygienists Assoc., Institute for Oral Health, Suite 3400, 444 N. Michigan, Chicago, IL 60611. By May 1.

Dentistry. 20 scholarships of $1,000 for first year in dental school. By May 1 to American Dental Association, 211 E. Chicago Ave., Chicago, IL 60611, http://www.ada.org.

Engineering. $2 million plus awarded through schools. Schools select. Obtain scholarship guide and list of funded schools from National Action Council of Minorities in Engineering, 3 West 35th Street, New York, 10001-2281.

Engineering. Tuition, fees, stipend of $6,000/year. US citizen. Must carry full academic load towards a master's degree in engineering and intern for a member employer during summer. Also, $12,000 stipends for students enrolled in Ph.D. programs. National Consortium for Graduate Degrees for Minorities in Engineering and Science, Inc.,

Executive Director, GEM Fellowships, Box 537, Notre Dame, IN 46556. 219-631-7771. By Dec. 1.

General Studies. Minority members of the United Methodist Church (for at least one year). $100-$1,000. Contact your church for more information.

General Studies. Minority Leadership Program, $2,000 and $5,000 awards. Washington Center for Internships and Academic Semesters, 1101 14th Street NW, #500, Washington, DC 20005.

General Studies. 1. Student Opportunity Scholarships for Communicant members of the Presbyterian Church, $100-$1,400. By April 1. 2. Native American Education Grant Program for Indians, Aleuts, and Eskimos pursuing postsecondary education. $200-$1,500. By June 1. Mgr., Financial Aid for Studies, Presbyterian Church, 100 Witherspoon St., Louisville, KY 40202-1396.

General Studies. Ford Foundation Fellowships. 50 3-year predoctoral fellowships (of $14,000), 29 1-year dissertation fellowships (of $18,000), and 25 1-year postdoctoral fellowships (of $25,000). For program announcement, write, The Fellowship Office, National Research Council, 2101 Constitution Ave., Washington, DC 20418, http://fellowships.nas.edu.

Geosciences. 80+ scholarships. Undergrad/grad. Undergrad up to $10,000/yr. Graduate to $4,000/yr. AGI-MPP, American Geological Institute, 4220 King St., Alexandria, VA 22302-1507. By Feb. 1.

Graduate Studies. The Committee on Institutional Cooperation (CIC) offers funding opportunities to students interested in attending one of its fifteen member institutions (primarily large, midwesterm research universities). *CIC FreeApp* allows women and minorities to apply for graduate admission to three CIC universities and pay no application fees. *CIC GE Fellowships* go to students beginning graduate programs in the sciences and engineering. For more information, write CIC Predoctoral Clearinghouse Office, 302 East John, #1705, Champaign, IL 61820, 800/457-4420, http://www.cic.net/cic/.

Legal Training for the Disadvantaged. Pre-law summer institute. For more information, write: Council on Legal Education Opportunity (CLEO), ABA, 740 15th St. NW, 7th fl., Washington, DC 20005.

Sciences, Engineering. Tuition plus stipend. Up to five years support leading to Ph.D. CIC Pre-doctoral Fellowships, Clearinghouse Office, 302 East John, #1705, Champaign, IL 61820, 800/457-4420, http://www.cic.net/cic/. By Jan.1.

African American

General Studies. National Achievement Scholarship Program. African-American students request entry to the competition when they take the PSAT/NMSQT (in their junior year of HS). Finalists compete for 440 nonrenewable $2,000 scholarships, and about 360 other awards, most of which are renewable (and worth $250-$2,000 per year). For more information, obtain the PSAT/NMSQT Student Bulletin from your HS counselor or write the National Merit Scholarship Corp., 1560 Sherman Avenue, Suite 200, Evanston, IL 60201.

Law. Awards for public interest law. Preferred consideration for need and under 35 years of age. Earl Warren Legal Training Program, 99 Hudson St., Suite 1600, New York, By 10013. By April 1.

Latino

Communications. Scholarships to exceptional Latino students pursuing a graduate degree in journalism, communications, or media and who have a commitment to pursue a career in these fields. Applicants must meet financial and academic criteria. Write: MALDEF, 634 S. Spring St., 11th Floor, Los Angeles, CA 90014. By June 30.

Engineering. General Motors/LULAC Scholarship. 30 $2,000 awards to engineering majors with at least a 3.25 GPA. SASE to LULAC Educational Service Centers, 1133 20th Street, NW #750, Washington, DC 20036. By July 1.

Engineering and Business. General Electric sponsors engineering and business awards for college sophomores via LULAC, Educational Service Centers, 1133 20th Street, NW #750, Washington, DC 20036.

General Studies. LULAC National Scholarship Fund. Request scholarship applications from the LULAC council in your community. For list of participating councils, send a SASE to LULAC National Educational Service Centers, 1133 20th Street, NW #750, Washington, DC 20036. Enrolled students only.

General Studies. Undergraduate and graduate students. SASE to National Hispanic Scholarship Fund, Selection Committee, One Sansome Street, #100, San Francisco, CA 94104. Between August 15 and October 1, http://www.nhsf.org

General Studies. National Hispanic Recognition Program identifies outstanding Hispanic students and furnishes their names to colleges to encourage recruitment and financial support. To be eligible, students must take the PSAT/NMSQT by the fall of their Junior year, identify themselves as being of Hispanic descent, and indicate they'd like to participate in the program. No monetary awards, but may lead to collegiate awards. Ask your counselor for more information, or write: The College Board, National Hispanic Scholar Recognition Program, 1717 Massachusetts Ave., NW, #401, Washington, DC 20036.

Law. Scholarships to outstanding Latino law students who have demonstrated commitment to serve the Latino community upon graduation. Applicants must meet financial and academic criteria. MALDEF, 634 S. Spring St., 11th Floor, Los Angeles, CA 90014. By June 30.

Native American

Graduate Study. Master's, doctorate and professional level assistance to students who are at least 1/4 American Indian or enrolled members of federally-recognized tribes. Write: American Indian Graduate Center, 4520 Montgomery Blvd., NE, #1-B, Albuquerque, NM 87109. 505/881-4584. By May 1. Current funding shortage. $25 application fee is used for additional AIGC fellowships, http://www.aigc.org.

Private Assistance for Women

Tip: If you have small children who require care while you attend class, be sure to let the college know. The aid administrator will increase your expense budget to reflect child care expenses, thus you qualify for more aid.

Aerospace Science or Engineering

Amelia Earhart Fellowship Awards, 35 $6,000 grants for graduate students. Women only. Zonta International Foundation, 557 W. Randolph St., Chicago, IL 60661, 312/930-5848. By Nov. 1.

Athletics

Women's Sports Foundation. Complete listing of colleges and universities offering athletic scholarships. Guide is available for $3.00 from Women's Sports Foundation, Eisenhower Park, East Meadow, New York, 11554.

Engineering

1. *Society of Women Engineers,* 120 Wall St., 11th floor, New York, NY 10005. 80 scholarships, from $1,000 to $5,000.
2. *BPW Loan Fund* for Women in Engineering Studies. $5,000 per year, 7% interest. By April 15. Send SASE with 2 first class stamps to BPW Foundation, 2012 Massachusetts Avenue, NW, Washington, DC 20036.

General

Junior Miss. $5 million annually in local, state, and national awards. Apply early in junior year of high school. Contestants are evaluated in areas of scholastic achievement (20%), fitness (15%), presence and composure (15%), creative and performing arts (25%), and judges interviews (25%). America's Junior Miss, Dept. DMO, PO Box 2786, Mobile, AL 36652, http://www.ajm.org. Awards count as taxable income.

General

American Association of University Women. Nearly 300 fellowships. Application by Nov. 15 for dissertation/postdoc. By Feb. 1 for research and project grants. AAUW Educational Foundation Fellowships and Grants, PO Box 4030, Iowa City, IA 52243, (319) 337-1716, http://www.aauw.org.

General

Executive Women International. Six awards, $2,000- $10,000 from Exec. Women International, 515 South, 700 East, #2E, Salt Lake City, UT 84102.

General

Kappa Kappa Gamma awards are available only to members of KKG. For complete information, send SASE (with 55 cents) to KKG Foundation, PO Box 38, Columbus, OH 43216. Please note your chapter membership on your request. Also, graduate students should state whether they are full- or part-time. Application deadline, February 1.

Golf

1. *Gloria Fecht Memorial Scholarship Fund.* Academic scholarships of $1,000-$3,000 per year for qualified student golfers from Southern California. No specific level of golfing skill required. Must have 3.0 GPA and demonstrated need. By March 1. Gloria Fecht Memorial Scholarship Fund, 402 W. Arrow Hwy., Suite 10, San Dimas, CA 91773.
2. *Women's Western Golf Foundation.* Renewable $2,000 awards for undergraduate room, board, tuition, fees. Involvement in golf is required, skill not a criterion. Selected on basis of academic achievement, financial need, excellence of character. Contact Mrs. Richard Willis, 393 Ramsay Rd., Deerfield, IL 60015. Request application by March 1.

Older Women

Four programs (500-$2,000), each has its own eligibility requirements. BPW Career Advancement, Avon Foundation Scholarship for Women in Business Studies, New York Life Scholarship for Women in the Health Professions. Wyeth-Ayerst Scholarship for Women in Graduate Medical and Health Business Programs. Apply between January and April 15. For information and application, send SASE with 2 first class stamps to Scholarships, BPW Foundation, 2012 Massachusetts Ave., NW, Washington, DC 20036, 202/296-9118.

CHAPTER 23

SPECIAL SITUATIONS: NON-TRADITIONAL STUDENTS

Physically-Disabled

Physically-disabled students frequently incur special expenses while attending college. Make sure these expenses are reflected in your student budget. This, in turn, will increase your need and you'll qualify for more aid. Your best source of information on special student aid is the Office of Vocational Rehabilitation, or the Office of Special Education Programs in your home state's education department. For additional information:

1. *HEATH Resource Center,* One Dupont Circle, NW, Suite 800, Washington, DC 20036-1193. 800/544-3284 or (202) 939-9320. You may also learn more about HEATH through the American Council on Education web site, http://www.acenet.edu. HEATH is the national clearinghouse on postsecondary education for individuals with disabilities, so be specific about your situation to make certain you receive the correct materials. As a start, request their publications entitled *Financial Aid for Students with Disabilities* and *Make the Most of Your Opportunities.*
2. *National Information Center for Children and Youth with Disabilities.* Another information clearinghouse. Copies of their publications are available on their Web site, http://www.nichcy.org, or you can contact them at PO Box 1492, Washington DC, 20013, 800/695-0285.
3. *Financial Aid for the Disabled and Their Families,* Reference Service Press, 1100 Industrial Road, #9, San Carlos, CA 94070. Check your library or guidance office, first. The book costs around $40 and lists about 900 aid sources available to people with disabilities, including a list of state sources of benefits.

Here are some national programs that provide good work and assistance:

The Alexander Graham Bell Association for the Deaf, 3417 Volta Place, NW, Washington, DC 20007, sponsors an annual scholarship awards program for auditory-oral profoundly or severely deaf college students. $250 to $1,000. Request application ASAP and submit no later than 90 days after receipt.

American Council of the Blind offers 25 scholarships ($500 to $4,000). Must be legally blind in both eyes. Contact Scholarship Administrator, ACB, 1155 15th St. NW, Suite 720, Washington, DC 20005. 202-467-5081. By March 1.

National Association of the Deaf. William C. Stokoe Scholarship for deaf students pursuing part-or full-time graduate studies in field related to Sign Language or the Deaf Community. $1,000. Contact Stokoe Scholarship Secretary, National Assoc. of the Deaf, 814 Thayer Ave., Silver Spring, MD 20910. By March 15.

Recording for the Blind & Dyslexic. Learning Through Listening Awards to HS seniors with specific learning disabilities who plan to continue their education. Three awards, $6,000 each; three awards $2,000 each. Must have B average or better and be registered with Recording for the Blind and Dyslexic for at least one year. By 21 Feb. Public Affairs Dept., Recording for the Blind and Dyslexic, 20 Roszel Rd., Princeton, NJ 08540, http://www.rfbd.org.

Sertoma International. Scholarship program for students pursuing four-year college degrees. $1,000 awards. Applicants must have documented hearing loss and be a full-time entering or continuing student. SASE to Scholarships, Sertoma International, 1912 East Meyer Blvd., Kansas City, MO 64132, http://www.sertoma.org.

Part-Timers

Most financial aid is reserved for students who attend college at least half-time. But take heart. Uncle's definition of "half-time" is more generous than most schools' so apply for federal student aid even if you aren't sure of your status. Also, under current law, colleges must set aside some of their SEOG and Work-study fund for part-timers. And thanks to the new Lifetime Learning Credit, you are eligible for a tax credit. Finally, Key Education Resources will be happy to lend a hand (and some money) with a Key Career Loan (800/KEY-LEND, http://www.keybank.com/educate.htm).

Our Suggestion: Take another course, and boost your status to half-time.

Are You 50, 60 or Older?

If you plan to study at least half-time, most financial aid is awarded on the basis of need and not age. Hence, you can freely compete with those who are just out of high school and anybody else for all available aid.

If you plan to take just a few courses, many schools will let you attend for free or on a space available basis. Check with your local college.

Similarly, many states reduce tuition for older citizens. Some waive tuition entirely. Eligibility varies from state to state, but generally, students must be state residents age 60+ and attend state schools. Sometimes the discount is given to students only on a space available basis. These states have some sort of program: Alabama, Arkansas, Colorado, Delaware, Georgia, Guam, Hawaii, Illinois, Indiana, Iowa, Kentucky, Louisiana, Maine, Massachusetts, Minnesota, Mississippi, Montana, Nebraska, New Hampshire, New Mexico, North Carolina, Rhode Island, South Carolina, Tennessee, Texas, Vermont, Virginia, Washington, Wisconsin, and Wyoming. Write your state higher education agency (addresses in Chapter 11).

Other information sources (not scholarship sources) for older students:

1. The American Association for Retired Persons' *Back-to-School Money Book: A Financial Aid Guide For Midlife and Older Women Seeking Education and Training,* single copies are free from AARP Fulfillment, 601 E Street, NW, Washington DC 20049 (request publication number D15400).
2. AARP's *Directory of Learning Opportunities for Older Persons.* This book is for older students who want to continue their education, but don't need college credit or a college degree. Single copies free. Request publication number D13973 from AARP Fulfillment, address above, or http://www.AARP.org.
3. Adult Learning Services, The College Board, 45 Columbus Ave., New York, NY 10023.

Are You Only 25? 30?

Over 44% of all college students are 25 or older. Your best bet for financial aid (assuming you aren't a multimillionaire) is that you will be filing your FAFSA as an independent student, thus only your own income and assets are assessed in calculating expected family contribution.

CHAPTER 24

A FEW WORDS ABOUT GRADUATE SCHOOL

Graduate student aid falls into three main categories: Fellowships, assistantships and loans. Neither fellowships nor assistantships need to be repaid, however both usually require some sort of service (e.g., conducting research, working with faculty or teaching undergraduates). Most students rely on a combination of these three aid sources, however, Doctoral candidates are most likely to receive fellowships and assistantships, Master's students are most likely to receive a balance of assistantships and loans, and professional students are most likely to receive loans.

Further analysis of graduate student aid shows that of non-doctoral students, those in law, medicine and business have the largest loans. Those in engineering and the natural sciences receive the largest assistantships, and those in the natural sciences, medicine and the social sciences receive the largest fellowships.

Similarly, of Doctoral students, those in medicine have the largest loans, those in engineering and the natural sciences receive the largest assistantships, and those in the natural sciences and the humanities receive the largest fellowships.

Tax Considerations

Tuition discounts (or tuition payments) received in exchange for services is considered taxable income. The University of Wisconsin (as reported by Jane Bryant Quinn) sums up graduate aid quite nicely: Stipends for teaching assistantships are taxable because the work helps the school without being central to a student's studies. Stipends for research assistants are tax free because the research, while of interest to the student and the teacher, isn't necessary to the school. Fellowships are clean—no work, no tax.

70% of All Graduate Aid

To learn where 70% of all graduate aid is, re-read the first part of this book. The lessons in Chapters 2 through 10 are as applicable to graduate students as they are to undergrads.

Second, review Chapter 10 and become familiar with federal sources of aid: Stafford Loans, Perkins Loans and Work-Study. (Graduate students are not eligible for Pell Grants or SEOGs.) If your future is in a medical field, add Chapter 20 to your reading.

And, if all else fails, investigate the commercial loans listed in Chapter 7.

3% of All Graduate Aid

For 3% of all graduate aid, check with your home state. Last year, Alabama, Alaska, Arizona, Arkansas, California, Colorado, Delaware, DC, Florida, Georgia, Idaho, Iowa, Kansas, Kentucky, Maine, Maryland, Michigan, Minnesota, Mississippi, Nevada, New Hampshire, New Jersey, New Mexico, New York, North Carolina, Ohio, Oklahoma, Oregon, Pennsylvania, Rhode Island, Tennessee, Texas, Utah, Vermont, Virginia, Washington, West Virginia, and Wisconsin offered $22.43 million in need-based aid, $29.8 million in non need-based aid, and another $36 million in loans and loan forgiveness to teachers and health professionals.

Also, many of these opportunities are sharply restricted in terms of major field of study (e.g., medicine, law, dentistry) or population group which benefits (e.g., minority). Furthermore students must usually enroll at an in-state school.

10% of All Graduate Aid

About 10% of all graduate aid is dispersed throughout this book. For instance, if you get a commission in the military and are willing to extend your period of service, you may qualify for graduate training. Employer-paid tuition and cooperative education (Chapter 12) are also rich in graduate opportunities. And you'll find more in Chapters 21 and 22.

12% of All Graduate Aid

For 12% of all graduate aid you must talk to your department chair. Here is how these people can help you:

- With departmental fellowships and grants. These are the most prestigious forms of aid and require very little from you in return.
- With graduate assistantships. Consider this an apprenticeship. While you have to work (quite a bit) for your money, the experience will look wonderful on your Curriculum Vitae (the academic version of a resume).
- With internships and summer jobs. With any luck, you may even find work you can turn into your thesis or dissertation.

- With employment funded by a grant. In most instances, the professor gets the grant, but will need grad students to help count chromosomes, wash test tubes, show slides, or lead discussion groups.

In graduate school, the committee that decides on admission also decides on these departmental awards. To better your chances for both, get to know the faculty. After you apply for admission, make appointments to meet professors in your area of interest. If it's relevant, send them a copy of your undergraduate thesis (or a research paper). Visit their classrooms. Observe their teaching styles. Be humble. And remember, unless you're applying to professional schools (law, medicine, business, engineering), your most important consideration should be to find a professor with whom you want to work. The reputation of the university can be secondary to the reputation of individual departments. And top name professors attract the largest grants, no matter where they are teaching.

You might also consider going to work for a university. Many schools discount tuition for full-time employees, and while it may take you a few extra years to get through the program, you won't have a huge debt burden when you're through.

And check the placement office. Where do graduates work? If you're going to leave school with large loans, you should know more about your job prospects.

1% of All Graduate Aid

Private foundations may award funds for projects in your area of interest. These you have to discover yourself. The best bet starting points: two publications put out by the Foundation Center (http://fdncenter.org/grantmaker/priv.html) and one by the Oryx Press.

We don't recommend you buy these references. They are expensive. But do locate them on-line, or in the reference room of your library and spend some time looking through them.

1. The Foundation Center's current *Foundation Directory*.
2. The Foundation Center's current *Foundation Grants to Individuals*.
3. The Oryx Press' current *Directory of Grants in the Humanities*.

4% of All Graduate Aid

All Disciplines

You're a graduate student. You should be good at research. So spend some time surfing government resources. Even as Uncle shrinks his budget, hundreds of little grant programs remain. The White House site will link you to every federal agency and commission (http://www.whitehouse.gov/WH/Independent_Agencies/html/independent_links.html), as well as every cabinet department (http://www.whitehouse.gov/WH/Cabinet/html/cabinet_links.html).

You should also click through the 200+ programs funded by the Department of Education. There's an index of programs (by title and category) at http://www.ed.gov/pubs/GuideEDPgm/indx.html.

Communicative Disorders

Sertoma. For students pursuing master's degrees in audiology or speech pathology from institutions in the US, Canada or Mexico. 30 awards of $2,500 per year. For more information, send SASE to Sertoma World Headquarters, Communicative Disorders Scholarship, 1912 East Meyer Blvd., Kansas City, MO 64132, http://www.sertoma.org.

Engineering and Science

The Fellowship Office of the National Research Council administers a variety of predoctoral and dissertation fellowships. For program brochures, write The National Research Council, Office of Scientific and Engineering Personnel, Fellowship Programs, 2101 Constitution Ave., Washington, DC 20418, http://fellowships.nas.edu.

Engineering and Science

Nat'l Defense Science and Engineering Graduate Fellowship Program sponsored by the Dept. of Defense. Three year fellowships leading to graduate degree in science or engineering. Full tuition plus $18,500 stipend. No service obligation. NDSEG Fellowship Program, 200 Park Drive #211, Research Triangle Park, NC 27709, Attn: Dr. George Outterson, http://www.battelle.org/ndseg/. By mid-January.

Engineering and Science

Hughes Aircraft Company. Fellowships. College seniors for graduate study. US citizenship required. GPA must be 3.0/4.0. Most on a work-study basis. Spend summer vacation working at Hughes Aircraft Co. Tuition, fees, stipend, travel and relocation expenses, salary for summer and other periods of full-time work. Hughes Aircraft Company, PO Box 80028, Bldg. C1/B168, Los Angeles, CA 90080-0028. (310) 568-6711.

Humanities

Mellon Fellowships. Eighty awards (one-year only) for students entering a program leading to a Ph.D. in preparation for careers of teaching and scholarship in the humanities. Tuition, fees, plus $14,500 stipend. Request application by December, 1998. Include your full name, mailing address, city and state, telephone number, location on Feb. 26, 27 and 28, 1999, undergraduate institution, undergraduate major, year of graduation, intended discipline in graduate school, e-mail address (if available) and whether you want to receive an application via Internet, e-mail or regular mail. Send all this to: Mellon Fellowships, Woodrow Wilson National Fellowship Foundation, CN 5329, Princeton, NJ 08543-5329, http://www.woodrow.org/mellon.

International Education and Business

Some student fellowships. 51 funded projects. For school list, write: International Education and Graduate Programs Service. US Department of Education, 500 Independence Ave., SW, Washington, DC 20202-5332.

International Exchange

Fulbright Fellowships. Possession of BA degree. Live and study abroad as a USIA Fulbright student. 800 students go to over 100 nations. Write USIA Fulbright Student Programs, 809 UN Plaza, New York, NY 10017. (212) 984-5330.

Languages and Teaching

FLAS. Graduate fellowships for foreign language and international studies. Funded through schools. Schools select students. Direct inquiries to university of choice. Or, write for school list: International Education and Graduate Programs Service, Advanced Training and Research Team, (FLAS), US Department of Education, Washington, DC 20202-5331.

Law

The Access Group and *Lawloans* both offer Bar Examination Loans of up to $8,000 to help students pay for living expenses and a bar review course. While the rates can be high, students who can't get a loan from their parents or an advance from their future employer often have no other choice. After all, what bank is going to lend money to a person with no income and $40,000 in law school debt? You can call the Access Group at 800/282-1550 or Lawloans at 800/366-5626.

Librarianship

Library and Human Resource Development Program. Funded through schools. For school list and copy of *Financial Assistance for Library and Information Studies*, write: Discretionary Library Programs Division, OERI, Dept. of Education, 555 New Jersey Avenue, NW, Washington, DC 20208.

Marine Sciences

John A. Knauss Marine Policy Federal Fellows Program for enrolled graduate/professional students. Request brochure from National Sea Grant College Program Office, Attn: Fellowship Director, 1315 East West Highway, Silver Spring, MD 20910.

Music

The Musicological Society offers 5 dissertation fellowships per year. Twelve-month stipend (nonrenewable) of $10,000. Application forms from AMS 50, Department of Music, Smith College, Northampton, MA 01063. By October 1.

National Needs Areas

National Needs. Stipends of $14,000 to enhance teaching and research in designated academic needs areas (examples—math, agricultural science, and foreign languages). These awards go to graduate students of superior ability who demonstrate financial need. $25 million is distributed through 84 different schools. Funding is tenuous. For school list, write Division of Higher Educational Incentive Programs, Office of Postsecondary Education, Department of Education, Rm. 3022, 400 Maryland Avenue SW, Washington, DC 20202-5339.

Professional Students

Assorted Loan Programs. Most financial aid for professional students takes the form of loans. Try not to overborrow. Law students are now graduating with an average debt of $40,000; medical students with $65,000. If your school (or state) does not offer loan forgiveness programs for students who enter low-paying, public service professions, your job choice may be influenced by the size of your monthly loan payments.

That said, the Access Group (800/282-1550, http://www.accessgrp.org) and Educaid (800/255-8374, http://www.educaid.com) will be happy to loan MBAs, law students and other grad students up to $120,000 - $130,000, with 20 years to repay. The interest rate equals the 91-day T-bill plus 2.9%, 3.0% or 3.4% (it varies with the program of study). 6% guarantee fee, 1.5% (or higher) supplemental fee prior to repayment. Chapter 20 listed oodles of loan sources for medical professionals.

Science, Social Science, Math, Engineering

Oak Ridge University. Graduate study in sciences, social sciences, mathematics and engineering. Three separate competitions: NSF Graduate Fellowships, Minority Graduate Fellowships and Women in Engineering and Computer Science Awards. Three years of support. Approximately $14,400 per year. 750 new fellows yearly. For more information (and a catalogue), write Oak Ridge Associated Universities, PO Box 3010, Oak Ridge, TN 37831). Deadline is early Nov.

Space-Related Science and Engineering

1. *NASA*. Summer programs and renewable graduate school awards of up to $22,000. For more information: Graduate Student Researchers Program, Education Division, NASA Headquarters, Mail Code ehb2, Washington, DC 20546, http://ehb2.gsfc.nasa.gov/gsrp.
2. *NASA*. Graduate and doctoral fellowships at affiliated schools. For more information: Space Grant College and Fellowship Program, University Programs Branch, NASA Headquarters, Mail Code FEH, Washington, DC, 20546.

Additional Resources

The National Association of Graduate and Professional Students has an active and extensive web site: http://www.nagps.org/NAGPS/nagps-hp.html.

CHAPTER 25

A TREASURE CHEST OF TIPS

We've always said, that in an ideal world, the sound of the budget axe one year would be replaced by the burble of flowing federal funds the next. This year, it finally happened, sort of. Students today must still cope with aid funding that doesn't keep pace with rising tuition costs. But this year's passage of the "Taxpayer Relief Act" amounts to a windfall for middle-income families with college-bound students.

Of course, to get all the money due you (from your college, from your state, and from your Uncle), the slogan is "know more about every aspect of financial aid or dig deeper." To save you the purchase of a new shovel, here is a summary of the skills you, as a student today, must master.

Selecting a College (I)

When picking a college, go beyond the normal search criteria, such as majors offered, academic reputation, and distance from home, and inquire about innovative tuition aid features. For example, matching scholarships, sibling scholarships, installment plans, middle income assistance programs, tuition remission for high grades, etc. **See Chapter 9.**

Selecting a College (II)

All factors being equal, pick colleges most likely to offer you a financial aid package rich in grants you don't have to repay. Such a package is a lot better than one made up of loans which will saddle you with a repayment burden for many years after graduation. Best bet: Any school in which your academic record places you in the upper 25% of the profile of the incoming freshman class. **See Chapters 7 and 9.**

Selecting a College (III)

Send applications to two colleges of equal merit. If you get accepted by both, you might be able to play one against the other in securing a more favorable package. **See Chapters 7 and 9.**

Try the External Degree Route

Win a sheepskin without ever leaving home or job. Such a diploma will cost less in money and time than if it had been earned through campus attendance. External degrees offer academic credit for documented learning and experience you have already acquired, and couples these with formal assessments. **See Chapter 7.**

Do Four Years Work in Three

You must attend summer school, but the compressed time will save you the "inflationary increase" of the fourth year. On a similar note, try to avoid taking extra years to get through college. Fewer and fewer students are graduating in four years...costing them a whole extra year's tuition. **See Chapter 7.**

Start at a Community College

Work hard. Get good grades. Transfer to a solid four-year institution. This way, you pick up a prestige diploma at half the cost. **See Chapter 7.**

Understand How Need Analysis Works

By knowing the formulas, the shrewd family can present its financial picture in such a way as to obtain a more favorable need analysis. This isn't unlike presenting one's financial picture to the IRS so as to qualify for the smallest possible tax liability. **See Chapters 6 and 7.**

Try Some "What If?" Calculations

But first, learn how need analysis works. A typical "what if": Is this a good time for mom or dad to finish their college work, along with son and daughter? Or will it be more advantageous, financially, for your parent to go back to work and help with expenses? You'll be surprised at the dollar figures generated by "what if" drills. **See Chapter 7.**

Don't Pass Up the Entitlement Programs

Billions in low-interest, subsidized federal student loans go unused each year simply because students think they are ineligible, don't bother to go through the paper work hassle, or just don't know about the program. **See Chapter 10.**

Cash Flow (I)

Search for a low-interest, private loan. Numerous states have set up loan authorities which float tax-exempt bonds to raise student loan money. And colleges themselves have received permission to issue such bonds. At the same time, private banks are becoming more innovative in sponsoring combination savings/lending plans. Keep an eye out for these developments. They can help middle-income families with the cash flow problem of paying for college. **See Chapters 6, 7, and 9.**

Cash Flow (II)

Go to college on the house. Many home owners have accumulated large amounts of equity in their houses and they want to put it to work. Your strategy: Releasing this equity either through a line of credit or through refinancing the first mortgage. **See Chapters 7 and 9.**

Improve Your Aid Package

The FAA will present you with an aid package that should, in theory, cover the difference between what college costs and what your family can contribute. If you feel the college really wants you, because you are a brain or an athlete or the child of an alum or you help it meet a geographic or minority quota, you should ask the FAA about improving the package. Your objective: To increase the grant component (money you don't have to repay) and reduce the loan component (money you must repay).
See Chapters 6, 7, and 9.

Try for an Academic Scholarship

Over 1200 colleges offer academic scholarships to students with a B average and SAT scores of 900 or more. Middle income folks take notice: Most of these scholarships are not based on financial need. If you are just outside the SAT eligibility range for one of these awards, take a good SAT preparation course. It may raise your scores enough to enter the winner's circle. **See Chapter 18.**

Go the Cooperative Education Route

Over 900 colleges offer co-op education programs. Alternate formal study with periods of career-related work. Earn up to $8,000 per year during the work phase. It may take an extra year to win the degree, but it will be easier on the pocketbook. **See Chapter 12.**

Athletic Student Aid

We aren't talking about the "Body by Nautilus, Mind by Mattel" tackle who can do 40 yards in 4 seconds. Husky U. will find that person. We're talking about students who are better than average in a variety of sports, ranging from tennis to golf to lacrosse. Many colleges seek people who might become varsity material. The rewards come in two forms: outright scholarships or "improved" financial aid packages. **See Chapter 19.**

Acceleration

Can you get credit for a semester or a year of college work? You can through the Advanced Placement Program or by enrolling in college courses in high school. When credits can cost as much as $400 each, receiving tuition credit for academic credit leaves money in the bank. **See Chapters 7.**

Be An Accurate, Early Bird

Be as accurate as possible in filling out financial aid forms. Submit them as early as you can. When resources are tight, it's first-come, first-served. Those who must resubmit their forms and those who are slow in applying come in at the end of the line. By then, all the money is gone. **See Chapters 6 and 7.**

Check the Military Offerings

For a hitch in the National Guard you can pick up a state benefit, a federal bonus, partial loan forgiveness, drill pay, sergeant stripes (if you also participate in ROTC), and in some cases, tuition remission at the state university. And these are not "either/or" opportunities. You can have most of them, or all of them. **See Chapter 13.**

Take Advantage of Teacher Mania

Individual colleges and most states all have loan forgiveness programs for prospective teachers. Go this route and your education will cost you very little. You teach Ohm's law for four years to pay off the obligation. You pick up a little maturity, a lot of patience. You contribute to the well-being of hundreds of scholars-to-be. And you're still young enough to begin a different career if teaching is not for you. **See Chapters 9 and 11.**

Sacrifice

You may have to give up a few luxuries: Cancelling your pet's Beverly Hills grooming sessions can save you $3,200 per dog per year; using a Volkswagen instead of your Lear jet can save you $540 per tank of gas.

APPENDIX 1: DEPENDENT STUDENTS (1999/2000 ACADEMIC YEAR)

Parent's Contribution from Income

1. Parents' Adjusted Gross Income .... $_____
2. Parents' Untaxed Social Security Benefits .... $_____
3. Parents' Aid to Families With Dependent Children Benefits .... $_____
4. Parents' Other Untaxed Income and Benefits. This may include child support received, earned income credit, workers compensation, disability payments, welfare benefits, tax-exempt interest income, housing, food and living allowances for military, clergy or others .... $_____
5. Deductible IRA, KEOGH, 403 (b) and 401(k) pymnts made by parents ... $_____
6. **Total Income.** Add Lines 1 through 5 .... $_____
7. US Income Taxes paid .... $_____
8. State Income Taxes paid .... $_____
9. Social Security Taxes paid .... $_____
10. Child Support paid by you for another child .... $_____
11. Hope Tax credit and/or Lifetime Learning credit .... $_____
12. Income Protection Allowance from Table A .... $_____
13. Employment Expense Allowance. If both parents work, enter 35% of the lower income or $2,800, whichever is less. If your family has a single head of household, enter 35% of that income or $2,800, whichever is less $_____
14. **Total Allowances.** Add Lines 7 through 13 .... $_____
15. **Parents' Available Income.** Line 6 minus Line 14 .... $_____

Parents Contribution from Assets[1]

16. Cash, savings and checking accounts .... $_____
17. Net Worth of real estate (excluding primary residence), investments, stocks, bonds, trust funds, commodities, precious metals .... $_____
18. Business and/or Commercial Farm Net Worth from Table B .... $_____
19. **Total Assets.** Add Lines 16 through 18 .... $_____
20. Asset Protection Allowance. From Table C .... $_____
21. Discretionary Net Worth. Line 19 minus Line 20 .... $_____
22. **CONTRIBUTION FROM ASSETS.** Multiply Line 21 by 12%. If negative, enter $0 .... $_____

Parental Contribution

23. Adjusted Available Income. Add Lines 15 and 22 .... $_____
24. **PARENT CONTRIBUTION.** From Table D. If negative, enter 0. .... $_____
25. Number in College Adjustment. Divide Line 24 by the number in college (at least half-time). Quotient is the contribution for each student[2] .... $_____

Student's Contribution from Income

26. Student's Adjusted Gross Income .... $_____
27. Untaxed Social Security Benefits .... $_____
28. Other Untaxed income and benefits. See Line 4. Also include any cash support paid on your behalf which was not reported elsewhere .... $_____
29. Deductible IRA payments made by student .... $_____
30. Total Income. Add lines 26 through 29 .... $_____
31. US Income Taxes paid .... $_____
32. State Income Taxes paid .... $_____
33. Social Security Taxes paid .... $_____
34. AmeriCorps awards, student financial aid that may have been included in Line 30, taxable earnings from Federal Work-Study or other need-based work programs .... $_____
35. Income Protection Allowance. Enter $2,200[2] .... $_____
36. Total Allowances. Add Lines 31 through 35 .... $_____
37. Students Available Income. Line 30 minus Line 36 .... $_____
38. **STUDENT'S CONTRIBUTION FROM INCOME** Multiply Line 37 by 50% .... $_____

Student's Contribution from Assets[1]

39. Add net worth of all of student's assets—cash, savings, trusts, business value, investments, real estate .... $_____
40. **STUDENT'S CONTRIBUTION FROM ASSETS** Take 35% of Line 39[2] .... $_____

Family Contribution

41. If one student is in college, add lines 24, 38, and 40. .... $_____
42. If two or more students are in college at the same time, add for each, Lines 25, 38, and 40. .... $_____

APPENDIX 2: INDEPENDENT STUDENTS WITH DEPENDENTS (1999/2000 ACADEMIC YEAR)

Contribution from Income (Student's and Spouse's)

1. Student's (and Spouse's) Adjusted Gross Income .... $_____
2. Student's (and Spouse's) Untaxed Social Security Benefits .... $_____
3. Student's (and Spouse's) Aid to Families With Dependent Children Benefits .... $_____
4. Student's (and Spouse's) Other Untaxed Income and Benefits. This may include child support received, workers' compensation, earned income credit, disability payments, welfare benefits, tax-exempt interest income, cash support from others, housing, food and living allowances for military, clergy or others .... $_____
5. Deductible IRA, KEOGH, 403 (b) and 401(k) payments made by student (and spouse) .... $_____
6. **Total Income.** Add Lines 1 through 5 .... $_____
7. US Income Taxes paid .... $_____
8. State Income Taxes paid .... $_____
9. Social Security Taxes paid .... $_____
10. Child Support paid by you for another child .... $_____
11. Hope Tax credit, Lifetime Learning credit, AmeriCorps awards, taxable earnings from Federal Work-Study (or other need-based work program) and other student financial aid that may have been included in Line 6. .... $_____
12. Income Protection Allowance from Table A .... $_____
13. Employment Expense Allowance. If both student and spouse work, enter 35% of the lower income or $2,800, whichever is less. If student qualifies as a single head of household, enter 35% of that income or $2,800, whichever is less .... $_____
14. **Total Allowances.** Add Lines 7 through 13 .... $_____
15. **Student's (and Spouse's) Available Income.** Line 6 minus Line 14...... $_____

Contribution from Assets (Student's and Spouse's)[3]

16. Cash, savings and checking accounts .... $_____
17. Net Worth of real estate (excluding primary residence), investments, stocks, bonds, trust funds, commodities, precious metals .... $_____
18. Business and/or Commercial Farm Net Worth from Table B .... $_____
19. **Total Assets.** Add Lines 16 through 18 .... $_____
20. Asset Protection Allowance. From Table E .... $_____
21. Discretionary Net Worth. Line 19 minus Line 20 .... $_____
22. **CONTRIBUTION FROM ASSETS.** Multiply Line 21 by 12%. .... $_____
23. Adjusted Available Income. Add Line 15 and Line 22. .... $_____
24. **TOTAL CONTRIBUTION.** From Table D. If negative, enter 0. .... $_____
25. Number in College Adjustment. Divide Line 24 by the number in college (at least half-time) at the same time. Quotient is the contribution for each student .... $_____

APPENDIX 3: INDEPENDENT STUDENTS WITHOUT DEPENDENTS (1999/2000 ACADEMIC YEAR)

Contribution from Income (Student's and Spouse's)

1. Student's (and Spouse's) Adjusted Gross Income .... $_____
2. Student's (and Spouse's) Untaxed Social Security Benefits .... $_____
3. Student's (and Spouse's) Earned Income Credit .... $_____
4. Student's (and Spouse's) Other Untaxed Income and Benefits. This may include workers' compensation, disability payments, cash support from others, tax-exempt interest income, welfare benefits, housing, food and living allowances for military, clergy or others .... $_____
5. Deductible IRA, KEOGH, 403 (b) and 401(k) payments made by student (and spouse) .... $_____
6. **Total Income.** Add Lines 1 through 5 .... $_____
7. US Income Taxes paid .... $_____
8. State Income Taxes paid .... $_____
9. Social Security Taxes paid .... $_____
10. Income Protection Allowance of $4,250 for single students or married students if both are enrolled in college at least half time; $7,250 for married students if only one is enrolled at least half-time[4] .... $_____
11. Child Support paid by you for another child .... $_____
11. Hope Tax credit, Lifetime Learning credit, AmeriCorps awards, taxable earnings from Federal Work-Study (or other need-based work program) and other student financial aid that may have been included in Line 6. .... $_____
13. Employment Expense Allowance. If the student is single, enter $0. If the student is married and both the student and spouse are working, enter 35% of the lower income or $2,800, whichever is less. Otherwise, enter $0 .... $_____
14. **Total Allowances.** Add Lines 7 through 13 .... $_____
15. **Available Income.** Line 6 minus Line 14 .... $_____
16. **Contribution from Income.** Take 50% of Line 15 .... $_____

Contribution from Assets (Student's and Spouse's)[3]

17. Cash, savings and checking accounts .... $_____
18. Net Worth of real estate (excluding primary residence), investments, stocks, bonds, trust funds, commodities, precious metals .... $_____
19. Business and/or Commercial Farm Net Worth from Table B .... $_____
20. **Total Assets.** Add lines 17 through 19 .... $_____
21. Asset Protection Allowance. From Table E .... $_____
22. Discretionary Net Worth. Line 20 minus Line 21 .... $_____
23. **CONTRIBUTION FROM ASSETS.** Multiply Line 22 by 35%. If negative, enter $0 .... $_____
24. **TOTAL CONTRIBUTION.** Add Line 16 and Line 23 .... $_____
25. Number in College Adjustment. Divide Line 24 by the number in college (at least half-time) at the same time. Quotient is the contribution for each student .... $_____

Table A—Income Protection Allowance

Family Members (Including Student)	Allowance
2	12,260
3	15,260
4	18,850
5	22,240
6	26,010
Each Additional	2,940

Note: *For each student over one in college, subtract $2,090 from the appropriate maintenance allowance.*

Table B—Adjustment of Business/Farm Net Worth

Net Worth of Business/Farm	Adjustment
To $85,000	40% of Net Worth
$85,001 to $260,000	$34,000, plus 50% of NW over $85,000
$260,001 to $435,000	$121,500, plus 60% of NW over 260,000
$435,001 or more	$226,500 plus 100% of NW over $435,000

Table C—Asset Protection Allowance, Dependent Student

Age of Older Parent	Two-Parent Family	One Parent Family
40-44	$39,400	$25,100
45-49	44,600	28,000
50-54	50,900	31,600
55-59	58,900	35,700
60-64	69,000	40,900
65 plus	75,900	44,400

Table D—Parent and Independent Student Contribution

Adjusted Available Income (AAI)	Parent Contribution
To minus $3,409	-$750 (negative figure)
Minus $3,409 to plus $11,000	22% of AAI
$11,001 to $13,700	$2,420 plus 25% of AAI over $11,000
$13,701 to $16,500	$3,095 plus 29% of AAI over $13,700
$16,501 to $19,300	$3,907 plus 34% of AAI over $16,500
$19,301 to $22,100	$4,859 plus 40% of AAI over $19,300
$22,101 or more	$5,979 plus 47% of AAI over $22,100

Table E—Asset Protection Allowance, Independent Student

Age	Single	Married
25 & Under	$ 0	$ 0
26	1,600	2,500
29	6,400	10,000
32	11,200	17,500
35	16,100	24,900
38	20,900	32,400
40	24,100	37,400
50	30,100	48,400
65	44,400	75,900

Notes to Appendices

[1] Contribution from student and parent assets will equal $0 if Parents' AGI (Line 1) is less than $50,000 and the family is eligible to file a 1040A, 1040 EZ, or no tax return at all (or, files a regular 1040 only because of the education tax credits). If you want to get a rough estimate of your EFC under the Institutional Methodology, ignore this $50,000 rule and include home equity in the value of your assets (Line 19).

[2] The House version of the reauthorization bill excludes parents from the number of family members enrolled in college. It also eliminates the unequal treatment of parent and student assets (it would lump them together as "family assets" and assess them like parental assets). Finally, it increases the income protection allowance to $3,000. The Senate version of the reauthorization bill contains none of these changes.

[3] Contribution from assets will equal $0 if Student (and Spouse) AGI (Line 1) is less than $50,000 and the student (and spouse) are eligible to file a 1040A or 1040EZ or no tax return at all (or, files a regular 1040 only because of the education tax credits). If you want to get a rough estimate of your EFC under the Institutional Methodology, ignore this $50,000 rule and include home equity in the value of your assets.

[4] The House version of the reauthorization bill increases the income protection allowances to $5,500 and $8,500. The Senate version sets them at $4,250 and $7,250.

If you're interested in the final outcome of Reauthorization, please contact us using the form on page 10.